Mount St. Helena
&
R.L. Stevenson State Park

a history and guide

Ken Stanton

by

Ken Stanton

Bonnie View Books

St. Helena, California

All pictures are by the author, with the exception of the
following contributions: California State Archives, 101;
California State Library, 23(tr,bl),81(l),111(t); Mike
Chegwyn, (courtesy San Quentin Prison) 81(r); Gene
Dekovic, 147,207,231,239; Val Fuentes, 39; Betty Patten
Johnson, 12; Robin Madgwick, 195; Arthur W.Orton, 163(tl);
Marie Rogers, 10,23(br),179(t); Napa County Recorder's
Office, 11; Sharpsteen Museum, 23(tl),52(all),53(t),64(tr,b);
Jack Smith,53(b).

Library of Congress Catalog Card Number: 93-79308
ISBN 0-9661209-0-6
Third Printing

dedicated to the memory of Steve Zanelli

acknowledgements

Researching and writing this book has been the most rewarding work experience of my life. Great effort and time (almost three years) has been spent endeavoring to make an accurate and interesting account. Nevertheless, in a book this size some mistakes are inevitable. Ten witnesses will give ten different accounts of the same incident. After a hundred years, fact and fiction are often indistinguishable. Thus, when a story or incident was not verifiable through other sources, I have tried to preface it with "according to" or "legend has it" for example.

Sometimes I wished for unlimited time to track down all the clues, leads, stories, myths and people associated with the mountain. New information was coming in right up to the time of publication. It made me realize how fluid a document a book really is. My interest in the mountain does not end with publication. If any of my readers have special knowledge about aspects of Mt. St. Helena they feel were not covered adequately, please feel free to write. I plan on adding to my research file indefinitely.

Without doubt the best part of the research period, but at first the most anxiety ridden, was doing interviews. To this sweet turn of expectations I owe a great debt to my interviewees who, one and all, were enthusiastic and supportive of the project and willing to answer my long lists of questions. I would like to personally thank Earle Wrieden, John Livermore, Norman Livermore, Betty Patten Johnson, Emmy Lou Sands, Professor Rolfe Ericsson, Whitey Sawyer, Val Fuentes, inimitable story teller Spud Hawkins and Park Ranger Bill Grummer, who filled four tape cassettes with core information.

Three of the chapters required proofreading by experts in their fields. Thanks go out to Dean Enderlin for the geology chapter, to Bill Grummer who sent the fauna chapter back with a humbling number of corrections, and to Joe Callizo for not only the flora chapter but also for a critical reading of the rest of the text as well. In addition, he named for me every single plant encountered on the five miles of trail to the north peak.

Many people I never met willingly talked to a stranger and provided valuable information: Bob Smith of Smith's Trout Farm, John Aldrich, Phil Burton, Vera Lewelling, Neal Banditini, Dana Cole and Don Martinelli of the Division of Forestry, Paul Thompson, Paul Hopkins, Lennie Howard, Dr. Ken Fox of the U.S. Geological Survey, Cindy Craig of the National Geodetic Survey, Greg Denevers at the Academy of Sciences Pepperwood Ranch, Steve Smith at Sonoma Forestry, Francis Ingalls, Bennie Troxel, Terry Wright, Bob Beattie, former head of geology at Napa College, Ruth Marra, Dan Patten, Mitch Holman, Ted Wooster from the Dept. of Fish and Game, John Werminsky, Richard A. Nelson from the San Quentin Museum Association, Judge Thomas Kongsgaard, Orville Magoon of Guenoc Winery, and Denzil Verardo.

Monte Kirven provided insight on the peregrine falcon's predicament and let me coil *both* 300 foot ropes out at the nesting site. K.K. Burtis convinced me to let Earl Couey read the section on the Wappo and thus saved me considerable error. Through his interest, Richard Dillon gave legitimacy to the project when early on I felt like a bit of an imposter. Professor Rich Della Valle took time out to tour the mountain on a freezing December day. Barbara Neelands gave some fine constructive criticism and support. Tom McFarling, Dr. Don Hemphill and Thomas M. Dye provided documents otherwise unobtainable. Pete Cooper accepted material for publication sight unseen.

I would like to thank the fine volunteer staff at the Sharpsteen Museum including Elaine Hudson, Betsy Kilburn, and Betty Cumpston for all their help, encouragement and support. The Sharpsteen has provided many historical photographs included here. Rolf Penn did the photo reproductions. Others who provided photos are Norma Wright and Wanda Wolf of the Lake County Historical Society, Rie Rogers, Val Fuentes, Mike Chegwyn and Jack Smith. Additional thanks to the professional staffs at the California State Archives and the California State Library, California Room for their help in providing important photos.

Marianne Taylor and Donna Howard always made me feel welcome at the Lake County Museum, where a wealth of information was available. Sandy Frey at the Lakeport Library showed me the

Henry Mauldin files. June Ingrahm at the Calistoga Library, Julie Fraser and all the staff at the St. Helena Library and the busy staff at the Napa Library endured many requests for information and more information. Important taped interviews were available at the Napa County Historical Society and Stevenson memorabilia at the Silverado Museum.

Others who helped the project along are Leonore Wilson, Anne Seagraves, Dr. Barry Brown, Duane Newcomb, Jim Hench, Yolande Beard, Hank Houck at UCB, the late Elaine Gilleran at the Wells Fargo History Museum, Sandy Stillwell, and Tony Cerar, whose memory is still sharp as a miner's pickaxe.

A special thanks must go to Mary Stokes, former director of Bothe Park, who had great enthusiasm for the project from the start and who gave me unlimited access to the park's historical file as well as the copy machine.

A better publisher than Gene Dekovic could not be found. He showed patience with a novice in the field and sacrificed time from his own projects to spend over a half a year on this one.

Finally, I'd like to thank my mother for giving me an early appreciation for literature and for Susan who knew about the dream before anyone else and never lost faith that I could do it.

～ ～ ～

In addition to all of the assistance and support cited above, grants have made it possible to provide additional information. Appendices, photographs and other visuals have been made possible through the interest and financial assistance of:

The Livermore Family
The Giles W. and Elise G. Mead Foundation
The Napa Valley Heritage Fund
Joseph Phelps

Contents

foreword

The first book on the Mountain was written by a poet who was a great traveler. I once took the occasion to analyze his tome for every reference in it to nature. My conclusion was that he was a great poet.

Now, a second book on the Mountain has been written; this one by a great hiker. Clearly, he writes from personal experience and knows his massive subject intimately. He eschewed poetry for the facts of history, both natural and cultural. My conclusion is that he is well on his way to becoming a great historian. His attention to sources of information and to the tenuous nature of the facts -- that is, the problematic nature of truth -- is evident throughout this volume.

For those who prefer poetry, I would recommend the work of the first author on the Mountain. But, for those who prefer the truth -- as best as we can understand it -- this book will surely provide for their satisfaction.

Joe Callizo, *biologist*

Classic oak and grassland habitat on Mt.St.Helena's southwest flank.

Landowners on mountain's west side, circa 1877

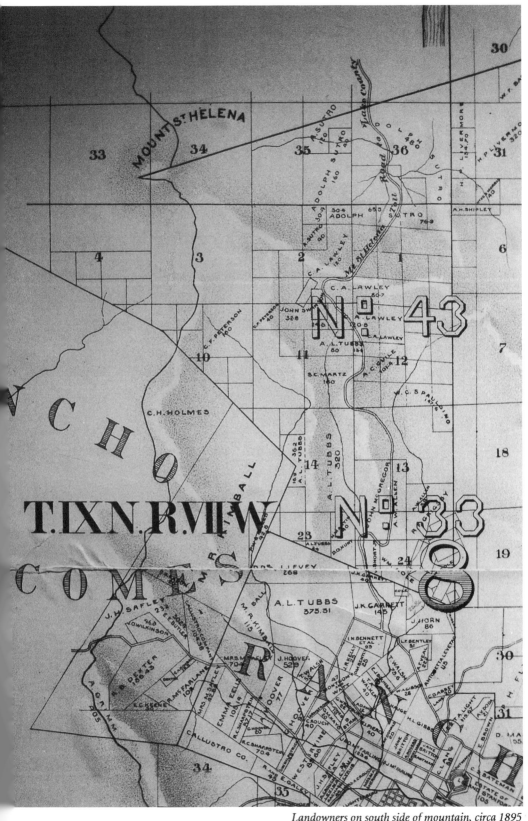

Landowners on south side of mountain, circa 1895

Passenger stage on the Old Lawley Toll Road between the Old Toll House and the Mountain Mill House.

Chapter 1

Historic Mount Saint Helena

"Great heights charm the eye, but the steps which lead to them do not." Goethe

" You cannot stay on the summit forever; you have to come down again... So why bother in the first place? Just this: What is above knows what is below, but what is below does not know what is above."

Rene Daumal - *from* Mount Analogue, A Novel of Symbolically Authentic Non-Euclidean Adventures in Mountain Climbing.

It is a mistake to think that European explorers, from Columbus on, found a virgin wilderness in the New World. The idea of a primeval and untouched land is a myth that has persisted right up to the present. The truth is that Native Americans had actively and successfully managed the land for diversity and abundance, for thousands of years. Ethnobiologists are only just now realizing how extensive was this involvement.

That erroneous image of native peoples as passive food collectors is also changing. The methods they used to encourage food production included burning, clearing, tilling, transplanting and seeding desirable species, irrigation, weeding, and 'pruning'. The park-like forests sans underbrush found by early European explorers were often those carefully managed by natives. The difference between their kind of agriculture and ours is one of generalization over specialization. The Indians actually created more diversity of plant and animal life, while present day methods trend to monoculture

13

and extinction.

The untrained, city-bound eyes of the first Europeans saw the environs of Mt. St. Helena as a blueprint wilderness. Ancient redwood forests grew in many shady creek bottoms, tall stands of pine and fir clothed the upper slopes and grizzlys without number roamed the mountain at will. Indigenous Americans, Wappo, did not inhabit the mountain, but had trails over its sides and to its summit. They burned the mountain in the fall to clear underbrush, leaving the larger trees unharmed. Thus wildlife had more mobility and forage, and the Indians had more game.

Into this dynamic balance stepped the white man. Disease, slavery, prostitution, and murder decimated the Indian in less than two generations. By 1880, most of the redwoods were gone to fences and barns, the grizzly was exterminated forever from the region, and miners' scratchings had pockmarked the mountain from one end to another. Logging, mining, roads, resorts, summer homes -- it was the greatest assault on Mt. St. Helena since its own violent volcanic origin five million years past. Yet today it is the least altered of the major Bay Area peaks, with as fine a biodiversity as any area in California. The peregrine falcon's comeback from the edge of extinction here is proof to that. Wildlife and plant life in great number and diversity live here today. How has the mountain managed to survive the depredations of man and the ravages of fire to maintain its wilderness links with the past? That is the question this chapter will seek to answer.

Anthropologists inform us that Native Americans have lived in the land we call California for perhaps 12,000 years. In all that vast length of time, longer than all of civilization's reign, the land lay essentially unchanged. The Native American's genius was the ability to give and take while maintaining a world balance. Like the bear and panther, they were a smoothly functioning part of a self-governing, self-regulating ecosystem. Without foreign intrusion, another 12,000 years may have passed with the same ease.

The Wappo were loosely divided into three main tribes, the Mishewal (northern), the Mutistul (central) and the Meyahk'ama (southern). Their land encompassed Napa Valley, Knight's Valley,

1 4

Geyserville and part of the Russian River, Cobb Mountain, Coyote, Chiles, and Pope valleys. It also included an islanded piece near Mt. Konocti called Leeleek. It was here some Wappo fled for sanctuary in the Mission days, rather than bow to religious coercion. The Spanish, in fact, gave them the name *guapo,* meaning brave, for their proud resistance to the Mission Fathers. The name was later anglicized to Wappo.

Mt. St. Helena was in the heart of Wappo territory. It was the physical and spiritual center of their domain. Earl Couey, an authority on the Wappo, informs me that their name for Mt. St. Helena was *kana' mota,* meaning 'human mountain.' Kana' mota was one of the most sacred mountains in northern California. In recent times, revered Wappo elder, Laura Fish Somersal, refused an offer to travel to the summit, out of respect for kana' mota.

By today's norms, human populations were small. Estimates range from 500 to 1,650 in Napa Valley, to 4,600 for the Wappo as a whole. The famous anthropologist, A. L. Kroeber, believed from linguistic clues that they were the oldest tribe in California. His research indicated competing tribes had whittled away what was once a much larger territory:

> "They were not conquerors from a distant land who came seeking new land, but a tenacious and stubborn remnant of a people holding on to the rough upland core of a once more widely spread domain of mellower lands."

The Wappo were mountaineers, masters of a rugged country. The mountains, though, were a place to hunt, gather food and materials, not to live. They preferred to locate their villages in the more hospitable valleys. Villages close to Mt. St. Helena were found in Knight's Valley, Coyote Valley, and Napa Valley. These were winter homes only. From spring to fall, the Wappo relocated frequently in response to fishing and hunting opportunities.

Within each village the sweat lodge served as the social and spiritual center of the community. It is the oldest educational institution in America. Here the men of the village would go for purification and for instruction twice a day. Stories of all kinds were told, intended for social and spiritual edification as well as entertainment. Some

15

of these stories have been preserved as told by an old Wappo elder, Jim Trippo, in a University of California publication, *American Archaeology and Ethnology*. One of these in particular, *The Adventures of Coyote* is so uninhibited and bawdy, it's hard to believe it comes from some stuffy old ethnology text. From the sweat lodge to the Saturday night poker game, some things don't change over the centuries. The story goes something like this:

Coyote is a God-man who plays a trick on his grandson Elk by pretending to be a deer caught in a snare. He reappears as himself just as Elk is about to skin the carcass. To get back at Coyote, Elk gives him bad advice on various gathering and hunting techniques, which the hapless Coyote follows to his dismay. To gather firewood he jumps on a limb from above, only to have it crash down on him so that he passes out. He commands pine nuts to fall on his face, until he is bloody and scratched. His snares burn up in a fire meant to drive game into them. His real demise, though, comes when he asks advice on how to get into a yellow jacket's nest.

Elk replies: "Well, I put it in the hole and then for a long time, I hold it there. All right, said Coyote. Then in the morning he went and found the yellow jackets nest and there he put his membrum virile in the nest. Now there he sat. It hurt but although the yellow jackets were eating it up and biting it all over, yet he held it there. After a long time he pulled it out. There on his body, right upon it the yellow- jackets had built their nests. A big nest, they had built. He could not pull it out. He pulled it up and it moved all around. When he pulled it out the whole world shook."

Coyote got out of that scrape but his troubles are far from over. "The next morning he went into their house and there were two girls, female rats, were sweating and there Coyote sweated with them. Then the old man there is showing his membrum virile. Then the two girls, one was saying to the other, 'Don't you believe it sister? It looks nice. He is showing it. Show it to us closer. Let's look. Here it is. Isn't it pretty? Now do you believe it, sister? Yes, isn't it pretty! Let's look at it more closely.' Then the old man showed it more closely, and the woman kicked Coyote's membrum virile and it broke right off and fell at the edge of the fire in the ashes. The old man picked it up, jumped out, and ran uphill. When he got where there was pine pitch he applied it to the place where his membrum virile had been pulled out, and his membrum virile he stuck back..."

The pine pitch proved ineffective when he got too near the fire that night, and the two girls decided Coyote must be dressed as a girl. In his sleep Blue Jay, fooled by the disguise, married Coyote, who later became pregnant. When he felt pain in his stomach, he ran uphill and hung himself in a tree. This signalled the end of Gods in human form on earth, the others like blue jay and turtle, despondent over Coyote's death, turned themselves into their namesakes.

There are other stories that tell of the creation of the world with striking resemblances to the Christian Eden and Flood myths. In it we see the mountain was holy ground, central to the Wappo Creation story. It goes something like this:

God man Coyote, and his grandson Chicken Hawk and their people lived at Lok'noma in harmony where there was always plenty of deer to snare. One day Chicken Hawk's wife tempts her brother-in-law to lie down with her. In retribution Chicken Hawk gouges out his brother's eye. His brother, Tsupenihdek takes his belongings and leaves home, followed by the woman.

On their journey north Tsupenihdek discovers the secret of the weather. He is still angry at his brother Chicken Hawk and makes it rain on Lok'noma for twenty days. All the people are drowned except Chicken Hawk, his two sisters and Coyote, who fly to the dry top of Mt. St. Helena. When the waters subside, Coyote reconstructs every habitation, and places a feather there for each dead person. Then he makes them live again.

Coyote goes to Moon because the people cannot talk. He is given a sack of words and the people talk. But the people cannot move, so he goes again to Moon, who gives him a sack of fleas. Then the people move. He returns for gifts of laughter and walking. Finally he brings bread and acorn mush and pinole for eating and the people are whole again. The whole village helps to build a new sweat lodge, whereupon the people throw the God man Coyote and his grandchildren out the window, symbolizing the new reign of the people on earth.

The Pioneers

White Americans, when they arrived, found either a 'howling waste-land' or parkland paradise, depending on their preconceived ideas. Those that stayed, found it to their liking. Early pioneers found Napa Valley a particularly rich part of California. John Cyrus was one of Napa's original settlers. His daughter, Elizabeth Cyrus Wright has preserved his first impressions:

> "It lay fresh from the hand of God, like a great unfenced park. The hillsides, unscarred by scratches of road grades, or square clearings for vineyards and orchards, wore their full dress of trees down to the floor of the valley. There were groups of noble oaks scattered across the valley lands, no cut down trees, no stumps, save those trees that had died honorably of old age. Flowers every where in the spring and berries in the fall to feed the bears and 'coons... On the floor of the valley the native grasses, clover, wild oats, and flowers grew shoulder high -- high enough to furnish not only food but a hiding place to the herds of deer and elk that ranged the open spaces...while the hills served as a residence for the large grizzly bears and panthers... and the smaller animals."

Napa provided a hunting and fishing extravaganza for pioneers in the 1840's. Ten grizzlies shot in a single expedition was reported, and it was not exceptional to see 50 or 60 in a day . Salmon choked the river in spring, while elk were seen in great numbers at the Napa River. One visitor counted 156 deer drinking at a single stream site. This wildlife Eden lasted on the valley floor at most two decades after George Yount arrived in 1836. After the Gold Rush of 1849, settlers occupied and tamed the valley floor and those animals that survived took refuge in the hills. Through the 1870's, grizzlies wallowed in shady river bottoms during summer months on Mt. St. Helena. Extinction came quickly. In 1880 Rufe Hanson, one of Robert Louis Stevenson's favorite 'Silverado Squatters', could still make a living as a deer hunter. But, by 1890, the woods were lamented as virtually empty of game.

Thrice Named Summit

Mt. St. Helena's nomenclature is as varied as the cultures that have lived at her base. The Wappo name, as we have seen was Kana'mota. The Spanish called it Serra de los Mallacomes. Briefly Devil's Mount was used in Gold Rush times. Later Helena Mountain was in use. The National Geodetic Survey, better known by its old name, U.S. Coast and Geodetic Survey, has it mapped even today as Mt. Helena. Even so, its present name seems generally accepted since the mid 1800's.

Whether legend or not, history has it that Mt. St. Helena was given the same name by three different persons, of different cultures, at different times over a twenty-one year period. The most remarkable thing about it, we are told, is that each nomenclator knew nothing of a previous designation. Each thought he was the first to bestow the label. In the spring of 1823 Father Jose Altimira, a Franciscan padre, searched the coastal valleys north of San Francisco for a suitable mission site. He eventually chose Sonoma, the last of the line. In his travels he crossed from Napa to Knight's Valley. Father Altimira may have been the first white to take notice of the prominent mountain to the east.

From the west the mountain is a long elevated ridge with four distinct high points. A European, the padre was reminded of a scene in an old abbey in Rheims, France, and exclaimed, "Behold Saint Helena on her bier! It is her effigy, even to the pall!" Others have described in great detail the figure of a recumbent woman covered by heavy cloth. The main peak is said to be her head, the second peak her breast, a third her hands folded on her waist, and the south peak her knees, slightly bent. One wonders on the quirks of history. Suppose Father Altimira had approached first from the north? From this angle, especially on the geysers road, the shape of a raptor with wings outstretched is obvious. Perhaps we would now know Mt. St. Helena as Eagle peak. Or from the south? In evening silhouette, the huge bulk of the south peak resembles the massive head of an elephant, facing west, with his trunk the left skyline, half sunk in the ground. Pachyderm Peak? The nearby town of St. Helena, named for the mountain, might not have been so pleased. The good padre, as it turned out, left us a more pious legacy. And another: the mustard that grows in the fields every spring came from seed scattered by Father Altimira to guide him on his return.

George Concepcion Yount, Napa Valley's first white settler, arrived in 1836 when General Vallejo granted him two square leagues near present day Yountville. He named it Rancho Caymus, after a sub-tribe of Wappo Indians living nearby. Several years earlier he is said to have first seen the valley of the Wappo from the top of Mt. St. Helena.

> "In such a place I should love to clear the land and make my home; in such a place I should love to live and die."

Whether he made this statement from the top, as legend has it, or elsewhere, may never be known. What is certain is that he had a five year head start on the Russians, who claimed first ascent in 1841. George Yount may well be the first white to have climbed Mt. St. Helena.

In 1839, Il'ia G. Voznesensky was commissioned by the Academy of Sciences in St. Petersburg to perform botanical and ethnographic work in Russian America. Significantly, the boat he sailed around Cape Horn in was called the *Helena.* In the spring of 1841 he set out from Fort Ross with Chernykh, an agronomist, on an expedition to the interior. Positive proof of their ascent was left in the form of a copper plate with this inscription in Russian letters:

> June, 1841
> I.G. Voznesensky and E.L. Chernykh
> Russians

A second story still circulates: the governor-general of the Russian colony, Alexander Rotcheff and his wife, the Princess Helena de Gargarin, also made the ascent. Joan Parry Dutton in *They Left Their Mark* points out this is extremely unlikely since their names do not appear on the copper plate. The story went that the Princess named the mountain in honor of the Empress of Russia. When it was discovered that the Empress in 1841 was Alexandra, not Helena, it was then attributed to the Empress of Rome. In *California Place Names,* Erwin Gudde, an author usually known for his sobriety, ridicules the

20

story with this observation:

> "The story became more romantic as the years passed: no less
> than Princess Helena de Gargarin, a 'niece of the Tsar', braved
> the chaparral and the rattlesnakes and christened the mountain
> in honor of her patron saint, Saint Helena, the mother of
> Constantine the Great (of Constantinople), while the Russian
> flag fluttered above in the breeze."

After that there was some speculation it was named for the Princess
herself. The most likely truth is that the Princess never set foot in the
interior and the mountain was named after Voznesensky and Chernykh returned. The Princess de Gargarin was a beautiful, cultured
woman around whom another story was told by General Mariano
Vallejo, Governor of the free Mexican state of California:

> "The beauty of this lady excited so ardent a passion in the heart
> of Prince Solano, chief of all the Indians about Sonoma, that he
> formed a plan to capture, by force or strategem, the object of
> his love; and he might very likely have succeeded had I not
> heard of his intention in time to prevent its execution."

By December of 1841 the Russians left America for good, having
found a buyer for Fort Ross and adjoining lands. He was John Sutter,
later of Gold Rush fame. Three years later, General Vallejo granted
another portion of the Russian land near Bodega Bay to yankee sea
captain, Stephen Smith. An abandoned ship, the *Saint Helena*, went
with the grant. Was it the same ship Voznesensky sailed to America ?
The story of the third naming of Mt. St. Helena diverges here. Some
say he christened the mountain from the sea, which is certainly possible since it is visible 50 miles out to sea. Some say it was from land.
In both cases it is agreed the captain was inspired to use his ship's
name. There it is: three separate namings, probably a good deal of
truth in all of them. But all independent? Not likely. It's too hard to
believe Smith knew nothing of the Russians ascent of the mountain
and the Russians knew nothing of Altimira's travels. The Russian
colony was in friendly and steady contact with the Spanish mission at
Sonoma for close to twenty years. Two outposts in the wilderness
would surely be eager to convey any and all information of this kind.
Without tangible evidence, nothing is certain, but it seems likely the

Russians honored the original Spanish christening. All the coincidences with the name, Helena, may have inspired some romantic wag to weave a tale for future generations to unravel.

There is a fascinating footnote to this story concerning the Russian plaque and the stone of tuff to which it was bolted. Twelve years after the first ascent, in 1853, it was discovered by Dr. T.A. Hylton, of Petaluma, and removed to a museum in San Francisco for safekeeping. There it lay until it was destroyed, like so many priceless treasures, in the 1906 earthquake and fire. It was after several years of research that historian, Honoria Tuomey, discovered where a copy of the plaque was kept. A pamphlet loaned her by long-time Mt. St. Helena resident, Daniel Patten, directed her to H.L. Weston of Petaluma, friend of the late Dr. Hylton. The doctor had made a paper rubbing of the Russian plate and entrusted it to Weston. On the back of the copy he had written, "fastened to a rock on the summit of Mt. St. Helena."

While preparations were made by Tuomey for a new commemorative marker to be made, she scoured the summit for the original rock. In her words:

> "To find just the identical boulder on a couple of square miles
> of rough surface might seem an impossible undertaking. But
> knowing that the Russians had held the ceremony on the north
> peak eliminated five-sixths of the difficulty. The highest point
> of the north peak is easy ground to travel, and small in extent.
> An age-old trail lies along its length, for the Indians used to go
> here to reconnoitre. Beside the trail I soon came upon a
> circular tufa block with crumbling little holes.
> Russ nails must have made them, for they made a regular
> octagonal sort of figure. Three smaller stones shaped to fit
> about one side of the round central stone were still in place."

In 1912, on the centennial of the Russian founding of Fort Ross, a new plaque made from a copy of the original was placed on the same block of volcanic rock the Russians had used. Scratched by vandals and almost hidden by the lookout tower, the plate and rock are, nevertheless, still there for all to see.

Journalist, Bayard Taylor

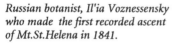

Replica of the original plaque placed by the Russians on the north peak in 1841.

Russian botanist, Il'ia Voznessensky who made the first recorded ascent of Mt.St.Helena in 1841.

Legendary stage-coach driver, Clark Foss.

The First Tourists

The Gold Rush of 1849 put California on the economic world map. Following the gold seekers, a new breed of traveller began arriving, not for business but for pleasure. Sightseers embarking at the port of San Francisco were advised not to miss three great marvels, the Big Trees, Yosemite, and the Geysers of Lake county. Due to the shorter travel time, the Geysers became the most popular of the three.

The man most responsible for the Geysers' popularity was a journalist for the New York Tribune, Bayard Taylor. In the summer of 1859, Taylor and his wife were in Petaluma, California on a lecture circuit. Stung by a desire to see the Geysers, he covered 125 miles in two days by horse and buggy, and still kept another appointment in the city of Napa. At this mad pace he managed to come up with some wonderful, early descriptions of Knight's Valley and Mt. St. Helena's west face. In it, he seems aware of Father Altimira's impressions 36 years before:

> "The pass opened into a circular valley (Knight's), behind which towered in the east, the stupendous bulk of Mt. St. Helene. This peak received its name from the Russian settlers, as a compliment to the Grand Duchess Helene. It is generally called St. Helena by the Americans - who, of all people, have least sense of the fitness of names. The mountain, 5,000 feet high, rises grandly above all the neighboring chains. As seen from this point, its outline strikingly resembles that of a recumbent female figure, hidden under a pall of purple velvet. It suggests to your mind Coreggio's Magdalen, and a statue of St. Cecilia in one of the churches of Rome. The Head is raised and propped on the folded arms; the line of the back swells into the full, softly rounded hip, and then sweeps away downward in the rich curve of the thigh. Only this Titaness is robed in imperial hues. The yellow mountains around are pale by contrast, and the forests of giant redwood seem but the bed of moss on which rests her purple drapery."

Only four months after Taylor's visit, the area saw an equally famous author on tour, Richard Henry Dana, best known for *Two Years Before the Mast*. Ten years after its publication, he visited the Geysers in a relentless December downpour. The storm darkened his inner impressions and obscured his outer views of the region. Though he rode past Mt. St. Helena, no mention is made. His positive comments are saved for the venerable George Yount, who showed him much needed hospitality.

The publication of Bayard Taylor's *Home and Abroad* in 1862, brought tourists by the hundreds. Cashing in on this influx was Clark Foss, whose home at the western base of Mt. St. Helena was called Fossville. He constructed a narrow, precipitous road to the Geysers and soon had a monopoly on the trade.

The 'Old Chieftain' as he became known, was a giant bull of a man, six foot six and 265 pounds. He was the best known driver of his generation, some say the most famous in the world. He ran the stage at breakneck speed the whole 26 miles. The wealthy and famous came more to ride behind the charismatic Foss than for the destination. And wealthy, one had to be; the charge for a round trip was a phenomenal $50.

The misnamed Geysers, more accurately called fumaroles, eventually waned in popularity. Perhaps the opening of Yellowstone National Park in 1870 with its Old Faithful geyser, showed the world what a geyser really was. Wild man Foss, so talented with horses, finally lost control of a stage around 1881. It plunged off the hill, injuring himself and seven others and killing a young lady. The chastened Foss toned down his style and soon handed the reins over to his less flamboyant son, Charlie. With the abdication of the Chieftain, quieter days returned to Knight's Valley.

Along Foss's Geysers Road, real estate moguls, F.E. Kellogg and W.A. Stuart, envisioned a town the size of Calistoga to be called Kellogg. By the mid-1870's, it was situated at the junction of Highway 128 and Franz Valley Road, nourished by the perennial waters of Rattlesnake Creek. Avenues were laid out, lots marked and offered for sale. Very little came of all this planning. Only a post office and store survived into the twentieth century. Dozens of hot spring resorts began springing up in Lake County at this time. Soon, emphasis turned away from this side of the mountain in favor of the east side, serviced by the well-maintained Lawley Toll Road. Together, these turns of events have helped to retain Knight's Valley as the delightful rural backwater it is today.

James Lick

An eccentric San Francisco millionaire, wishing to erect a monument in his name, came within a bumpy wagon ride of radically altering history on Mt. St. Helena. James Lick made his first fortune in South America as a skilled craftsman of fine pianos. His second was made by snapping up real estate in San Francisco when most of the city was still sand hills and tidal marshes. Three weeks after his last purchase in January, 1848, gold was discovered. San Francisco's population increased twenty fold in two years. Lick's 'water lots', so called because of inundation at high tide, quickly multiplied in value exponentially.

Spurned by a woman when young, Lick turned his back on the other sex and never married. In later life, without any heirs he cared for, Lick sought a way to leave a public legacy. His original idea was to erect huge statues of himself and his parents, visible miles out to sea. Then, pharoah-like, he planned a gigantic pyramid, larger than the Great Pyramid of Egypt, at the corner of 4th and Market streets in San Francisco.

Sensible friends talked him out of these ideas, and led him to an interest in observatories. One of these was George Davidson, head of the Pacific branch of the U.S. Coast and Geodetic Survey. All observatories at that time, were found in lowlands. Davidson was convinced that a mountain top would be a better place. James Lick was enthused about the idea, intitially promising a million dollars for the project.

Although now in poor health, he was sufficiently recovered from a stroke to personally make an inspection of Mt. St. Helena as a possible observatory site. Lick probably stayed at the Calistoga Hot Springs, while reconnoitering the mountain. On the way up the Old Lawley Road to the summit, the buggy hit a rough spot as he was lying prone on a mattress in back. The mattress was pitched out the back with Lick on top, hitting the ground with a jolt. He did not break his leg as some have said, but decided in his instantaneous and irreversible way that Mt. St. Helena had it out for him. He never returned to the mountain.

26

Soon after, he realized that Santa Clara County's Mt. Hamilton, in his own backyard, was a perfect observatory site. Lick died in 1876 before construction ever began, but the trustees of his estate carried out his wishes. In 1888, Lick Observatory became the first ever placed on a mountain summit, with the finest telescope in the world. Lick found his final resting place in the foundation under the pier that supports the 36 inch telescope. The fame that could have been Mt. St. Helena's went to Mt. Hamilton, along with the paved road, the traffic, the tourists and perhaps unwanted associated development. Once again fate decreed that the greater Mt. St. Helena area remain saved from 'progress'.

The Geodesists

An intense beehive of activity from miners, loggers, ranchers and farmers swept over the flanks of Mt. St. Helena from 1875 to 1900. During the same time period a small, dedicated group of scientists from the U.S. Coast and Geodetic Survey were intent only on the summit. Packing crushing loads of specialized equipment and personal gear, they set up primitive camps on top for months at a time, often into the rainy season. Their purpose was to establish a network of precise triangulation from summits all over northern California.

To accomplish the task, headquarters were set up on one peak while a second party made its way to a distant height. There, by means of sunlight on mirrors, a heliotrope could send a powerful beam many miles, even through smoke and haze. Back on the first peak, a precision instrument called a *theodolite*, essentially a telescope, would take the reading. In conjunction with a third peak reading, geodesists could determine a mountain's height, longitude and latitude. Some of the peaks triangulated from Mt. St. Helena were Ross Mountain in Sonoma County; Mt. Tamalpais; Mt. Diablo, 66 miles southeast; Round Top, 146 miles east in the Sierra; Sutter Buttes, Snow Mountain and Mt. Sanhedrin in Mendocino County; Mt. Lassen,140 miles northeast; and Mt. Shasta, 192 miles north.

The men assigned to the mountain tops were of rare character, able to endure great hardship and privation. One report says it took nearly three weeks to haul gear to Snow Mountain's 7,000 foot summit, due to deep snow and a succession of storms. The mercury fell below freezing every morning, and a constant fire was kept throughout the day.

Another year, on Snow Mountain, the "heliotroper," though alone and snowed in, bravely kept his post and showed signals when practicable. By this steadiness Mr. (George) Davidson was able to close observations on the lines to Round Top and Lola on the 27th of November" (1876). (George Davidson's fifty years of dedicated service with the Coast and Geodetic Survey made him an internationally honored expert in his field. He helped establish boundaries in Alaska and between the United States and British Columbia. The highest point in San Francisco, Mt. Davidson, is named in his memory.)

The April 24, 1883 edition of the *St. Helena Star* reports that Dr. McLean had spent two nights on the 14,000 foot summit of Mt. Shasta. He was the first to successfully exchange signals with Mt. St. Helena 192 miles away. This broke a previous record of 150 miles by the French in the Mediterranean Sea.

High altitude and deep snow were usually not problems on Mt. St. Helena. It was high winds, up to 100 mph, that sometimes made living difficult and scientific observation impossible. For protection, tents and instruments were placed behind crude rock walls. Just getting there was not easy. In 1891, a track overgrown with chaparral made it necessary to widen the existing southeastern spur trail. Eight days were required for repairs and encampment.

It became almost fashionable in the last quarter of the 19th century for locals to ascend Mt. St. Helena, and the Coast Survey crew was one of the prime attractions. To climb a mountain for recreation was still thought to be slightly aberrant behavior. You had to have a reason, which science provided. It was considered best to ascend the peak when scientists were there. Parties of young men and women, dressed in their Sunday best, would make a day of hiking or riding horses to the top to observe the surveyors at work.

Journalists also made the ascent, and their accounts made widely known the incredible view possible from Mt. St. Helena. On a clear day these extreme positions were visible with the naked eye: Sierra

28

Nevada peaks 150 miles to the east, at least 75 miles west into the Pacific Ocean, Point Reyes Lighthouse and San Francisco about 70 miles south, and Mount Shasta 192 miles to the north.

The rumor is often afloat that Mt. St. Helena has the most extensive view of any peak in the country. This claim has likely been confused with Mount Diablo, 66 miles south. Although shorter than Mt. St. Helena at 3,849 feet, its position on the edge of the Central Valley makes 300 continuous miles of the Sierra Nevada visible. William Brewer, who climbed Mt. Diablo with the Geological Survey in 1861, estimated the

> "extent of land and sea embraced between the extreme limits of vision amounted to eighty thousand square miles, and that forty thousand square miles, or more, were spread out in tolerably plain view - over 300 miles from north to south, and 260 to 280 miles from east to west, between the extreme points."

In a recent publication, *California Mountain Ranges*, Russell B. Hill has stated that from the summit of Mt. Diablo, forty thousand square miles embracing 35 of 58 California counties are visible. He goes on to say that apart from Mount Kilimanjaro in Africa, Diablo has the best view in the world. The Kilimanjaro statement is a curious one often found in the literature, but whose source is elusive.

I asked John Werminsky of California State Parks and Recreation in Sacramento about it. Werminsky is currently writing a book on Mt. Diablo after many years of experience there. He considers the Kilimanjaro statement unverified. In the 1870's, a subjective claim like this was easy to make and hard to refute. Today, with sophisticated computer technology, determining which peak truly has the 'best' view is objectively possible, as long as terms are defined.

Whether we consider 'best' to be the total number of square miles in view, or farthest distance to each of the four compass points, Mt. Diablo has Mt. St. Helena beaten hands down. Diablo's position on the edge of the great Central Valley is superior, in terms of visible square miles, to St. Helena's surrounding mountainous terrain. And, although the view of Mt.Whitney to the south is blocked by the intervening Great Western Divide, the Divide itself is seen 205 miles from Diablo on a superb day. That's 13 miles further than St. Helena's view of Shasta. Does that make Mt. St. Helena the third best view in the world? That claim can't be made without further data. We can say, though, that both peaks have pretty damn good views.

The U.S Coast and Geodetic Survey, through the dedication of its employees, established a network throughout the U.S., the National Geodetic Reference System. It consists of one million precisely located points, a common base for geodesists to make measurements of longitude, latitude, height and gravity. Surveyors, cartographers and building contractors use NGRS every day of the year.

Wildfire

Disastrous fires on Mt. St. Helena on a regular basis were probably not a concern for the Wappo. Dry years and lightning strikes were a real threat, of course, but the Indians annual 'controlled' burns prevented understory buildup that leads to dangerous 'crown' fires. With the extirpation of the Wappo, the ecological makeup of the forest changed quickly. Just how quickly was illustrated by Joaquin Miller, the celebrated 'poet of the Sierra'.

He lived with the Indians of Mt. Shasta when they were still in possession of their native land. The forests then were wide open, a man on horseback could ride anywhere with ease. A generation later he returned to the scene of youthful adventures, to find the forests choked with chaparral and deadwood, no longer a pleasant parkland.

Yolande Beard, in *The Wappo, a Report*, describes the 1850's as these natives' single, most devastating decade. Let's assume then, that by 1860, annual burns were no longer an event on Mt. St. Helena. In the next 40 years, fires were reported but not in conflagratory terms. Helen Goss, who describes life at the Great Western Mine in *Life and Death of a Quicksilver Mine*, says the mining town inhabitants feared fires originating in the Chinese camp more than woodland fires. By the turn of the century, however, enough downed wood and underbrush would have accumulated for a potentially disastrous fire. In fact, in 1908, a major fire swept the thickly forested slopes of Mt. St. Helena's northwest side. Bob Smith, whose family has owned the Trout Farm property in this area since 1898, says it was the last major fire on this side to date.

30

Claude and Clara Russell, homesteading in Troutdale canyon, were caught in a battle for their lives in 1929. It was a year unlike any old timers could recall, well into November and not a drop of rain had fallen since spring. It started when a cigarette was tossed out on the Ida Clayton Road. A dry, north wind fanned the flames into Calistoga in a few hours, charring the whole south side of the mountain. In Troutdale canyon, the Russells' few buildings and orchard were besieged by fires, first upcanyon, then below. Escaping embers and rolling, flaming trees set new fires periodically. At times it seemed they were surrounded by the inferno.

In those days, fire fighting volunteers were not just sideline helpfuls, but often the main force. If you were driving over the mountain and were pulled over and asked to assist, you went! All able-bodied men on the mountain were out fighting the prolific blaze, including Claude Russell. His wife, Clara, was providing food and coffee night and day for the exhausted men . For three days, their homestead was constantly in danger, the Russells getting two or three hours of sleep a night. One evening, the fire burning downcanyon blocked access to the highway. If it had continued in their direction, their only safety was to flee upcanyon where the fire had already left the terrain a smoking ruin covered deep in ash.

Although the 1929 fire had started on the north side, it was saved from much damage by unvarying north winds. The rest of the mountain was torched. The Russells' auto bridge over Troutdale Creek was destroyed, but they rebuilt and stayed on many more years. Up the road, the landmark Mt. St. Helena Inn, belonging to the Patten family, had been spared, but Harry Patten's home close by was gone. Official information is scarce, but oldtimer, Earle Wrieden of Middletown, believes it was worse than the 1964 Hanley fire.

Further confirmation comes from Don Martinelli, who served with the California Division of Forestry for 38 years. He believes fires in the 1920's and 30's were able to burn longer and farther, without the high number of roads and firebreaks we have today.

The Hanley fire is the biggest inferno in local contemporary memory. It started at 10 a.m. on Saturday morning, September 19, 1964. Some have said it started with brush burning, others from an escaped campfire, but neither is likely because its point of origin was far off the road under the Palisades. More probably it was a burning projectile or a lone hiker throwing out a cigarette, but the cause was never determined. Nearby, a bar and restaurant called *Hanley's on the Mountain* provided the name.

Spud Hawkins was there Saturday night, September 19. Spud was born within earshot of the Old Toll Road in 1912. His first memory is the sound of the horses' hame bells as the animals brought the heavy freight wagon up the steep and dusty grade. Hawkins spent most of his life on or near the mountain and fought fires for close to 40 years. According to him, the Hanley should never have been more than a one day fire. He believes proper monitoring of fire breaks was neglected. In the aftermath of the blaze, there was some legal action charging negligence but it was dismissed through lack of evidence.

Fire chief Don Martinelli, on the other hand, has told me, men were on the fire continuously from its inception. The *Saint Helena Star* of September 24 reports the same. And, contrary to popular opinion, he said the fire was never under control, or even well contained. A fire break had been constructed below it, but night, and rocky terrain made an upper fire break impossible. When 'Santa Anas' blow at hurricane force, there is little man or machine can do.

On Sunday, the winds really picked up and were clocked at 100 miles per hour on the summit. The fire was quickly out of control and stayed so until winds died down three days later. Besides burning the south face of Mt. St. Helena, it spread in two fiery arms south and west. One burned along the ridge tops of the Howell Mountains within three miles of Pacific Union College at Angwin. The other burned along Rincon Ridge to the outskirts of Santa Rosa, 8 or 10 airline miles away. Over 50,000 acres were burned in all, destroying 150 structures, including the historic Tubbs mansion outside Calistoga. The north half of Calistoga was evacuated because of falling firebrands and dense smoke, and some homes on the outskirts were burned. Governor Pat Brown, touring the site, soon declared it a federal disaster area.

A minor controversy surrounds the Tubbs mansion, a stately Victorian built in the 1880's. The local tourist attraction had been

32

burning for some time before firefighters arrived. It was hot enough by then to explode the windows. Strangely, none of the adjacent property was touched by flame. Speculations were soon flying that the main fire was used as a front to burn the "old lady" for insurance reasons. Nothing came of it.

The Hanley is known as the worst fire hereabouts, but it is not the biggest in this century. One fire in the thirties, reputedly burned nearly 30 miles, from Mt. St. Helena to Napa along the hill crests. Large however, does not equate to worst in people's memories. The reputation of a fire grows with the number of people and structures endangered. In 1900, a fire in the Oakland hills would have been just a spectacular brush fire. In October, 1991, it became the costliest fire in state history. A Hanley-type fire burning on the outskirts of Santa Rosa today would have similar consequences.

One might assume after the 1964 holocaust that nothing was left to burn. One year later, almost to the day, a fire broke out on the Foote property near Knight's Valley. The 12,000 acre fire actually reburned recently scorched areas, although the main body of the fire was further west. The 1970's were relatively quiet, but the eighties again saw two fires in consecutive years. Fifty acres were consumed in June, 1981 when arcing power lines sent sparks into the dry grassland below. A PGE spokeswoman said the problem was exacerbated by a marksman taking potshots at line insulators.

The last major fire on Mt. St. Helena struck on September 9, 1982, when high winds again caused power lines to arc. An oak tree on the north side of Silverado Ranch caught fire first, then it spread to a nearby building. The flames shot downslope so fast, they left an adjacent building untouched. As in the Hanley fire, the blaze reached Tubbs Lane outside Calistoga, before a wind shift pushed it right back up the mountain. Convict crews constructed a fire break down the length of the ridge leading to the middle peak. It was effective and the north side was saved once again. Most of the fire affected land on the mountain's south slope, torched just 18 years before by the Hanley fire.

A thousand firefighters battled not only flames but 90 degree heat, 60 mph winds, rough terrain and nests of yellow jackets. The insects were uncovered while cutting 10 ft. wide firebreaks. OUCH! Firefighters kept the damage to 4,000 acres, but the four day battle was not cheap. Taxpayers supplied a half million dollars for the effort.

Despite the devastating appearance after a fire, nature uses it as an effective tool for the health and diversity of wildlands. Fires may be more severe than in aboriginal days, but plants have evolved supreme adaptations. Some species of chaparral survive the worst fires by re-sprouting from a fire-proof knot at the base of the trunk called a *burl*. After the 1982 fire I remember walking cross country with ease in upper Kimball Canyon. Five years later the same slope was a nearly impenetrable thicket. Another example of adaptation is the Knobcone pine, absolutely needing fire to reproduce. The hard, closed cones of the Knobcone must have a hot fire before they will open to spill seeds.

All life increases in diversity after a fire. Animals move more freely and seeds lain dormant for decades will sprout with temporarily decreased competition and increased sunlight. As we have seen, the hotter, drier south side of Mt. St. Helena is the most vulnerable to fire. But the wetter, wooded north slopes are by no means immune. It's true, sun exposure is less acute and a thick accumulation of duff keeps the soil moist most of the year. Nevertheless, there is a window of danger, usually late summer, when the north slopes are vulnerable.

Controlled burns are a way to remove underbrush from mature forest with 'cool' fire, and avoid hot, so-called crown fires. Controlled fires are not undertaken on a regular basis on Mt. St. Helena at this time. Both Division of Forestry and State Parks find higher priorities elsewhere in the state. It seems though only a matter of time before fire strikes the north slopes. If the dense leaves and underbrush that keep the soil cool should ever dry out, say for example, in a prolonged drought, the resulting fire would be the worst ever seen here. Reviving the old Indian tradition of annual burns would seem desirable. Unfortunately, after nearly a century of debris accumulation, a Catch-22 situation has developed in which the risk of a control burn escaping is extremely high.

Resorts of Sorts

Alexander Badlam, a nephew of Calistoga's founder Sam Brannan, began the tradition of the private, summer retreat for San Francisco's prominent and wealthy. Badlam is best known as founder of the Silverado mine in 1872. By the mid 70's, he chose Mt. St. Helena's shady northeast side to locate his Troutdale estate. Trout fishing was popular then as now, so Badlam constructed fish ponds for guests' entertainment. As a joke, he rigged a scarecrow human figure complete with fishing pole and line. When guests came, he feigned surprise at this 'intruder' and threatened to go down and shoot the 'poacher!'

Nearby was another Badlam property, called Arcadia. It was later sold to Adolph Sutro, who made a fortune in the Comstock Lode of Nevada. Toward the end of Sutro's career, he was mayor of San Francisco. Arcadia had extensive fish ponds where, Norman Livermore remembers, enormous sturgeon were raised. The actress, Ethel Barrymore, paid a visit to Arcadia in 1910 when, oddly, her hosts took her underground in the abandoned tunnels of the Mirabel mine.

Just a bit east of Arcadia was Dr. James Blake's tuberculosis sanitarium. His ideas of fresh air and moderate exercise as cure were thought peculiar at the time but soon were standard practice. His personal reputation was a bit tarnished by his relationships with women, (he had a paramour he lived with), but professionally he was well-respected. Uphill from Blake was the Victorian farmhouse known as Wildwood. It was owned by the Van Ness family, prominent lawyers in San Francisco. Nearby Van Ness creek was named for them as well as Van Ness Boulevard in San Francisco. Reputedly, at one time, they raised 150 Irish water spaniels at Wildwood

All of these properties- Arcadia, Troutdale, Van Ness, Blake's- were eventually acquired by the Livermore family. Blake's sanitarium is, in fact, at the heart of the Livermore's 8,000 acre Montesol ranch. The Livermore saga began here when Horatio Putnam Livermore bought eight acres next to Dr. Blake's, to be near his wife, a patient at the sanitarium. The year was 1880, the same year Stevenson was living at Silverado mine. Although Stevenson never mentions it, he may have met Mattie and Horatio Livermore on a visit to see Dr. Blake.

Mattie was too far advanced with tuberculosis to benefit from Dr. Blake's help, and died soon after. Horatio, however, was pleased with the area and climate and brought his children back to the mountain every summer, starting a family tradition that continues unchanged over 100 years later. It was his second wife, Helen, who named the ranch, *Montesol,* meaning "mountain of the sun". Some acres were cleared for English walnuts and fruit trees, and eventually Horatio's son, Norman, brought it financially aboveboard.

The Livermores have a long history of prominence in social, political and professional life. The scion of the family on the west coast, Horatio Gates Livermore, built the American River's first dam at Folsom. Horatio Putnam Livermore founded Montesol and pioneered in several industries. Horatio's only son, Norman Banks Livermore, was a civil engineer, decorated by the French government in World War I and later president of the California Academy of Sciences. His wife, Caroline Sealy Livermore was primarily responsible for preserving Angel Island in San Francisco Bay as a state park. Livermore Peak is named for her.

Today, Montesol is a partnership run by democratic vote of the five sons of Norman and Carolyn Livermore. Each has chosen a field of endeavor that takes him far afield, with Montesol as the lodestone or glue that holds them together.

Norman Jr. is a businessman, once serving as state resources director under Governor Reagan. Putnam is a lawyer in San Francisco, Robert a farmer-rancher, George a designer, and John a mining geologist in Reno. John carries on the tradition of his father as a trustee of the California Academy of Sciences.

It is almost an axiom that 'land empires' like Montesol, established with much effort and will, are quarreled away by the founder's descendents. But a spirit of cooperation has kept this institution together. The spirit of generosity helped to found Robert Louis Stevenson Memorial Park, with Norman Sr. donating the first 40 acres in 1949. In the future, Livermore holdings may help to dramatically increase the size of the now named, RLS State Park.

Silverado Ranch

Contrasting sharply with Montesol is the checkered, but colorful history of Silverado Ranch. Its many owners down the years have been financiers, miners, squatters, dude ranch operators, rock 'n roll artists, (and their manager), corporate executives, and finally the

36

state park system. Today, Silverado is destined to be the hub and center of RLS State Park.

Silverado began as the first big silver strike of the northern Coast Ranges. By 1874, the second largest town in Napa county graced the southeast slopes of Mt. St. Helena. Borlandville soon became Silverado, a boom town of 1500 miners bursting with energy and gold lust. A month after its founding, a miner was murdered over a misplaced bottle of whiskey. The silver vein ran out before investment money could be recouped, and Silverado was a ghost town by 1877.

When Robert Louis Stevenson sojourned here in the summer of 1880, Silverado's owner by default was squatter extraordinaire, Rufus Hanson. With his wife and her brother, they occupied the sole remaining structure, the Silverado Hotel. Hanson's reputation as a deer hunter comes to us partly through his nickname, "a hundred bucks a year Hanson". In *Silverado Squatters*, Stevenson has high praise for the grave and compassionate Rufe:

> "A perfect unoffending gentleman in word and act... he was fit for any society but that of fools."

But Stevenson's character assessment turns critical on Mrs. Hanson:

> "Her noisy laughter has none of the charm of one of Hanson's rare slow-spreading smiles; there was no reticence, no mystery, no manner about the woman: she was a first class dairymaid, but her husband was an unknown quantity between the savage and the nobleman."

Stevenson reserves his worst judgement for Mrs. Hanson's brother, Irvine. Here he compares Rufe and his brother-in-law:

> "And it seems to me as if, in the persons of these brothers-in-law, we had the two sides of rusticity fairly well represented: the hunter living really in nature; the clodhopper living merely out of society...Irvine had come scathless through life, conscious only of himself, of his great strength and intelligence; and in the silence of the universe, to which he did not listen, dwelling with delight on the sound of his own thoughts."

The Hansons were forced to leave when Dan and Mollie Patten purchased Silverado townsite along with 500 acres in 1884. The Pattens moved the Silverado Hotel to the Toll House flat to replace the original Mt. St. Helena Inn, burned a year before. Rufe died a few years later in the Sierra Nevada foothills.

Very little is known concerning the old Silverado townsite for a period of forty years after the Silverado Hotel was relocated. It is said that a family named Peterson lived here around the turn of the century. The main house has been remodeled and is still in use. During remodeling, an old newspaper from the 1890's was found inside a wall, likely dating this structure at a hundred years. A hoary, twisted grapevine nearby has the appearance of a century's age.

In the 1920's, "Captain" George Dyer, a wealthy San Franciscan, built a beautiful estate for himself and his wife at Silverado. Most of the buildings now on the site date from this era. A mutual acquaintance of the Dyers, Wanda Jarvis, owned the Yellowjacket Ranch just over the ridge above Knight's Valley. George and Wanda soon fell in love with each other. Together, they constructed a horse trail to connect the two ranches, most of which is still passable. Every weekend, on the pretext of equestrian recreation, George would ride out to see his paramour at the Yellowjacket. The trysts were extremely discreet, and he never gave away telling clues like driving his automobile to the ranch.

About 70 years earlier, another love triangle had played its final hand at the Yelllowjacket Ranch. It ended in the revenge killing of Major Harry Larkyns by photographer, Edweard Muybridge, for philandering with his wife. The modern love triangle was resolved more peaceably with Captain Dyer eventually divorcing his wife and marrying his lover.

Before World War II, a newcomer, Arnold W. Meiners, acquired the Dyer property and outfitted it as a dude ranch. The heavy metal ore carts (skips) seen today were brought from a mine in Arizona by Harry Patten and used for 'atmosphere.' One of the favorite activities for guests was to ascend Mt. St. Helena on horseback. They took Dyer's trail out to Red Hill, then past Turk's Head up a steep canyon and ridge to the fireroad.

Meiners continued to snap up property from neighbors until 1949, by which time he had nearly a dozen parcels. Then mysteriously, he dispatched them all and moved to southern California by 1951. His name remains his legacy, clearly printed on the U.S. Geological Survey's *Detert Reservoir* topographic map.

Through the fifties and early sixties, it continued as a dude ranch with several owners. By the sixties, a new breed was in the real estate market for country property. The San Francisco based, rock and roll group, *It's A Beautiful Day*, (era diehards will remember 'White Bird') purchased Silverado as a quiet retreat from the rigors of concert touring. Many of the Dyer era buildings were still in good shape, including the pool and the tennis court. This was the height of the hippie era, and at Silverado it was in full flower. The laid back scene included psychedelic wall to wall murals, sunbathing and skinny-dipping at the pool, and by today's standards, a few innocuous drugs. The band found musical inspiration here while ignoring the more mundane details of day to day life.

This idealistic period came quickly to a close due to bad management and a lawsuit over rights to the band's name. By 1973, *It's a Beautiful Day* was gone and the band's ex-manager , John Walker, was in sole possession of the ranch. He was short on cash though,

Rock group, "It's A Beautiful Day." From left, Patti Santos, Val Fuentes, David LaFlamme, Hal Wagonet, Linda LaFlamme, Mitch Holman

39

and brought on Thomas J. Wenaas as a partner. When Park Ranger Bill Grummer first met Wenaas, he was surprised by the small 'arsenal' of guns stowed in the trunk of his car. "Sometimes," he said, "target practice at the Silverado Ranch sounded like a *war zone.*"

Thomas J. Wenaas was president of F.P. Lathrop Corporation, responsible for the dramatic makeover of Emeryville and the St. Helena Hospital expansion. He was quite the favorite of owner, Pierce Lathrop, who had no son, and was heir apparent of the corporation. Wenaas began investing in the ranch site: $176,000 for a two-story retreat house made of logs with a huge stone fireplace, and $300,000 for an access road past Turk's Head to Red Hill.

Meanwhile, John Walker was preparing for marriage. The ceremony was to take place on a nearby bluff with a marvelous view of the entire Napa Valley. A colossal party was planned and as the guest list was burgeoning, Wenaas suddenly posted notice that he was no longer responsible for Walker's debts. In Walker's place stepped John J. Corniata, an attorney with Lathrop Corporation . Corniata lived in the clubhouse while preparing plans for an underground house near Red Hill.

While upgrading of the ranch continued, Wenaas became socially and politically prominent in the late 70's. His wife, Carolyn, and he became the toast of Calistoga when they restored, "a la art deco", the Mount View Hotel, which, for years, arguably served the best meals in Napa Valley. The crowd at opening day, January 10, 1980, numbered in the thousands, with notables like politicians, Alan Cranston and Willie Brown, in attendance. Perhaps Wenaas's hosting of a $1,000 a plate fund-raising dinner for Lt. Gov. Leo McCarthy had something to do with their presence. His philanthropy extended to civic projects in Emeryville, providing funds for new sidewalks, equipping playgrounds and a senior center and even band uniforms for Emeryville High School. Wenaas was living the high life many dream about, and the flow of money seemed unending.

A few months after the Mount View Hotel reopened, Pierce Lathrop dropped a legal bombshell on Thomas Wenaas. He charged that his president had embezzled 3½ million dollars from both his personal and the company's bank accounts, from 1976 to 1980. Furthermore,

40

he accused Wenaas of falsifying bookkeeping records. Among the purchases made with the allegedly stolen money were a Rolls Royce, a helicopter (the helipad was at Turk's Head), a 40 foot sailboat and a fleet of antique automobiles. Records filed with the court showed some staggering monthly bills: $658 for the Rolls, $6,921 to American Express, $5,921 to Wilkes-Bashford men's store in San Francisco, and $960 to a gun dealer.

Wenaas's deceit may have been as big an *emotional* bombshell for Pierce Lathrop. Lathrop chose not to file criminal charges but simply asked Wenaas to return all the money. When the repayment schedule could not be kept, Lathrop filed a civil complaint. A foreclosure judgment in Napa Superior Court made Thomas and Carolyn Wenaas and John Corniata liable for three million dollars. By the end of 1982, Lathrop was able to foreclose on the Mount View Hotel and other properties to recoup some of the money. Corniata, Wenaas' partner, filed a cross-complaint suit, claiming he was innocent of all unlawful proceedings. His case was upheld, but the underground house, barely underway, was never completed.

As described earlier, the Silverado fire of September, 1982 added yet another complication to the Wenaas saga. Arson was at first suspected. The ranch was not foreclosed until after the fire, making insurance collection a possible motive. Then it was discovered that the electrical lines that arced in high winds were installed incorrectly by a moonlighting Pacific Gas and Electric employee. Litigation was considered at one time but charges were never filed, while questions surrounding the case remain unanswered.

Wenaas took the turn of events philosophically. In the San Francisco Examiner of November 7, 1982 he was described as "tall, soft spoken and almost courtly in manner." In the manner of a gentleman, he chose not to refute the charges, stating simply, "I can't deny that I have been a flamboyant character over the years. This is one of the prices you pay. I enjoy life. I don't believe in standing still."

Pierce Lathrop was now the new owner of Silverado Ranch but he immediately sought to sell. At the $2¼ million asking price, only developers of commercial property were interested. Fortunately, the county has strict zoning laws, so no variances were approved. The price kept dropping but no one was biting. Finally, in 1987, William Penn Mott convinced Lathrop to halve the $900,000 sum for the State Parks Foundation, which Mott directed. Four hundred fifty acres were bought for a thousand an acre, and transferred to RLS State Park.

From its birth as a mining camp, through all its incarnations over a 120 year history, Silverado Ranch has in a way come full circle. One day a State Park visitor's center will be built there, whose focus will commemorate those exciting early years.

$$\backsim \quad \backsim \quad \backsim$$

Despite the rumblings of a century and a half of progress, Mt. St. Helena maintains its wilderness links with the past. Compared with other major Bay Area peaks, like Mt. Tamalpais and Mt. Diablo, Mt. St. Helena is peaceful and little known except to local residents. I have spent whole days on the mountain without seeing another human. Many factors have been responsible: distance from major population centers; the caring and benevolence of landowners like the Livermore family and the guardianship of State Parks and Recreation; the superb abilities of plant communities to heal the scars of mining, logging and wildfire; and quirks of fate like the bumpy wagon ride of James Lick.

There were other near misses too. At one time, Leland Stanford seiously considered locating his new university in Calistoga at the foot of Mt. St. Helena. Napa Valley was deemed too remote from the Bay Area and, instead, Stanford University was built in Palo Alto.

Until 1913, a Napa Valley railroad extension from Calistoga to Clear Lake was still a company dream . They had plans to lay tracks across Mt. St. Helena's north side, paralleling the Ida Clayton Road. Their dream was doomed on June 19, 1913. On that day, a head-on train collision in Vallejo killed 13 people and injured scores. The railroad lost $100,000 in damage settlements, killing profits for the next ten years. This, along with competition from the automobile, led to its demise in 1938.

With caring and foresight, we who live in a more ecologically aware age can help maintain Mt. St. Helena's essential wilderness links with the past.

42

Chapter 2

Trails, Toll Roads, and Transportation

"California boasts her famous stage-drivers, and among the famous Foss is not forgotten. Along the unfenced, abominable mountain roads, he launches his team with small regard to human life or the doctrine of probabilities. Flinching travellers, who behold themselves coasting eternity at every corner, look with natural admiration at the driver's huge, impassive, fleshy countenance...Wonderful tales are current of his readiness and skill. One in particular, of how one of his horses fell at a ticklish passage of the road and how Foss let slip the reins and, driving over the fallen animal, arrived at the next stage with only three."

R.L.S. on stage driver Clark Foss

"Stevenson didn't lay it on none too thick. Colonel Foss weighed two hundred and sixty-five pounds, and could handle six horses like you'd handle that many cats. He would lift them right up off their feet and swing them around the corners so fast you couldn't see the leading team. He drove his stage to the Big Geysers for years, and he'd run down the last hill with a yell to wake the dead."

stageline entrepreneur Bill Spiers

The first travellers on Mount Saint Helena left little record of their passage. These wilderness denizens included coyote, deer, fox, bobcat and bear, both black and grizzly. Their only legacy, a faint network of obscure paths through the leaves fallen from low-hanging branches of tan oak and madrone. Down rocky ridgelines, or through the tangled underbrush on unhurried forest slopes, these paths can still be followed today, kept open by the mountain's latest descendents.

Long after the first inhabitants came the Indians, creating paths of their own. They had two ways to cross the mountain, by far the more popular was through the present Murray Hill pass, connecting Napa and Knight's Valleys. Knight's Valley, or Mutistul in Wappo dialect, meaning north valley, was a major trading center. Wappo would trade chunks of obsidian from nearby Glass Mountain for fish and seashells brought by the coast Pomo and tribes farther north. The other route, much steeper and longer, went through Jericho Canyon over the northeast shoulder of the mountain into Callayomi Valley. Apparently this trail was only used by hunters and small bands of travellers. Large parties wishing to reach Clear Lake took the gentler route from Napa through Pope Valley and out the present Butts Canyon.

Napa Valley was sparsely settled as late as 1848. George Yount and a few Donner Party survivors were some of the minority white settlers. The Gold Rush sparked a major new influx, and, by 1850, a need was seen for improvements to the old Indian trails. By volunteer effort, the Old Bull Trail as it came to be known, was carved out of the forest to connect Calistoga with settlements around Clear Lake. It was the official road for 18 years, impassable in the rainy season, steep, rough and dangerous in the best of times. Grades were as high as 35%, allowing only the hauling of sleds by cattle or hogs. Wheeled vehicles soon became roadside attractions.

The main use for the Old Bull Trail was to drive livestock to market. For most of the animals raised on Lake County ranchos, it was a one way trip. Hogs could take an entire day just to cover the distance from the Bradfords to the top of the grade. Between the Bradfords and Troutdale Creek, St. Helena Creek itself was the road, iron sleds clanking and scraping on the river cobbles. Even for a single man on horseback, it was an all day effort to ride from Middletown to Calistoga. It's difficult to appreciate such times today, as one can make the 20 minute trip asleep in the back of a car.

In 1868, occurred what may be the single, most influential event ever to hit Mt. St. Helena. It was in this year that John Lawley completed the toll road that today bears his name. Lawley, born in Alabama in 1815, moved to California in 1852 and became one of Napa County's premier pioneers. In his long and useful life, he was teacher, plantation manager, gold miner, warehouse merchandizer, banker, railroad trustee, mine owner, real estate mogul, speculator, capitalist, public benefactor, laissez-faire advocate and perhaps Napa's finest example of Social Darwinism in action. He made no excuses for the personal gain he derived from his enterprising hard work because the county benefited in equal measure. He left a remarkable legacy and estate for his heirs, who, as will be seen later, quarreled and squandered it away.

Upon his emigration to California, Lawley leased the Kellogg Ranch near the Bale Mill, where he met Cynthia Ann Williams. They were married in 1854 and had four children within a decade. The first three, Mary, Charles and Harry, were all born in the month of September in 1855, '57 and '59. Ada, the fourth, was born 'out of sync' in April, 1863.

John opened what was only the second warehouse in downtown Napa to merchandize grain in 1854. Wheat was already a big business in the county. Soon after, he became a trustee in the first bank in Napa. Already a successful businessman, Lawley was not content to rest on laurels. When the Berryessa brothers were forced out of their Mexican- grant rancho in Berryessa Valley for a minor debt, Lawley bought 26,000 acres for about $4 an acre. In one of the first big real estate subdivisions in Napa county, he set aside three 1,000 acre tracts for himself and his partners and sold the rest in various smaller parcels. He also made major improvements to the twenty-five mile road into the town of Napa, facilitating grain shipping. Ten years later, Berryessa Valley was a premier grain producer in the county. By 1861, Lawley had become owner and operator of the Phoenix quick-silver mine near Oat Hill. It was not a spectacular success, the larger impact being felt by his family and in-laws who all became steeped in the mining life.

After a brief flirtation with politics, he joined Sam Brannan as a trustee of a new enterprise, the Napa Valley Railroad. Dreams were hatched to bring the tracks from Napa all the way through the valley and into Lake County. Early attempts failed but Sam Brannan was adamant and eventually tracks were laid as far as Calistoga. Knowing a good thing when he saw it, Lawley applied for permission to build a toll road from Calistoga to Middletown. Such a road would be a key link between Lake County markets and the new transportation center. In doing so, Lawley launched his greatest accomplishment and the one by which he would be forever known.

In March, 1866, Lawley and his associates, Henry Boggs and William Patterson, were granted permission to build a new toll road from the bottom of King Canyon (now Garnett) to Siegler Valley in Lake County. Eventually, the route was shortened to the Bradford Ranch. Picks and shovels, sledgehammers and slipscrapers, tons of black blasting powder, and the strength and skill of men, were the only tools and means available. With these, the road became the high-tech accomplishment of its day. Grades were never over 12%, a great improvement over its predecessor. It was completed in 1868 at a cost of $15,300, and the era of the toll road was ushered in, to last nearly 60 years.

Rates of toll were established by the Board of Supervisors and revised periodically. In August, 1866, a year before completion of the road, Lawley was authorized to charge the following:

Eight horse team	$2.50
Six horse team	2.00
Four horse team	1.50
Two horse team	1.00
One horse and buggy	.75
Man and horse	.25
Loose horses, per head	.25
Loose cattle, per head	.10
Sheep and hogs, per head	.05

Price of passage was high, even by today's standards. Local newspapers of the day were full of bitter complaints about what one man labeled 'extortion'. And, although not in the charter, one old-timer told me they'd even charge a man on foot a dime to walk by! Perhaps in response to public outcry, the Board lowered nearly every one of these rates by half in November, 1873.

Many people could not afford to pay any toll and took the free, county-built Oat Hill Mine Road when it was completed in 1893. It was a much rougher road and longer. But the Old Lawley Road was shorter and beautifully maintained, so amidst grumbling, most people continued to pay its toll. An amendment to the rates came in response to a new form of transportation by July, 1908. If your automobile had a single seat in it, you paid a dollar to pass the toll gate, with two seats or more you paid $1.50.

On the mountain's north side, the old road basically followed the present highway from Middletown until the Mountain Mill House, where it scenically wound up the east side of St. Helena Creek to near the Fireroad entrance. This beautiful section of road was passable to cars until 1957, when it was closed at the request of the Girl Scouts' Camp. From here it made wide turns on the west side of the creek to the summit. These turns are still visible today as 'oxbows' of a sort.

On the south side, it followed the general direction of Highway 29, crossing and recrossing it many times until below Hanley's. Here, it veered off to follow the ridge between Jericho and Garnett canyons to the bottom. This lower section is one of the fine scenic drives of Napa County. Although paved, it narrows to a single lane in places with steep dropoffs, giving one the flavor of the old days.

Great improvement though it was, the dirt road could mire a wagon in the winter or accompany you with a dust cloud the whole way in summer. Here, from a locally published book by Paul McCarthy, called *Looking Back,* two old-timers record their version of what the road was like:

> "It was miserable and scary... in Lake County, it was so steep somebody would walk behind with a block, and stop the wheel at rest stops. Really a winding road." Thelma Tamagni

> "We used to go to Lake County when they didn't have no roads. They had a little turkey trail that went through people's back yards. It took almost all day to get to Lakeport."
> Mary Ottonello

The Calistoga railroad and the Lawley Toll Road were both completed, probably by design, in 1868. The toll road was the only way for gold, silver and quicksilver to reach the railhead. A sort of symbiotic relationship developed between the mining business and the toll road. The toll road business profited from the heavy traffic generated by the mines, and it, in turn, encouraged expansion of mining. From the hit and miss, off and on 60's, mining in Napa County became the top industry in the 70's.

Ida Clayton Toll Road

Another, 'poor relation' toll road operated on Mt. St. Helena at this time. It was narrower, less traveled, and took longer than the Lawley toll road. It had its beginnings in 1860 when an access road was built from Knight's Valley to the Ida Clayton Mine on the western slopes. Shortly after the mine closed in the mid 1860's, the road was purchased by Calvin Hall Holmes (the Foote family, direct descendents of the Holmes, own land at the bottom of the grade even today). Little traffic was seen for a decade, until the opening of the Great Western Mine revitalized this route.

On the mountain's north slope, the Great Western was showing signs of valuable cinnabar ore, rock from which quicksilver or mercury is processed. By 1875, the Ida Clayton Toll Road and Western Mine Road were joined, allowing through traffic from Knight's Valley to the Lawley Toll Road. Mrs. Ida Clayton was the road's first tollkeeper, minding the toll house in Kellogg, the town near the road's western terminus. A schoolhouse was soon located along the road, whose proprietress was the pretty and popular Mrs. Ida Clayton herself. The place is remembered as Schoolhouse Point, located a mile west of the Mayacmas crest.

When Andrew Rocca was persuaded to superintend the Great Western in 1876, Wells, Fargo payroll delivery was still ten years off. Every month, it was necessary to ride to Calistoga to pick up several thousand dollars in gold and silver coin. This was the grand era of the highwayman and Rocca trusted no one to perform this task but himself. The day and time of his departure were top secret, as was the route itself. Always, he rode under cover of night and always alone. The quicker and easier Lawley road was sometimes taken, but more often he rode the longer Ida Clayton route. He outwitted many outlaws by taking the less obvious choice.

Once, a band of robbers lay in wait on the Ida Clayton road for a whole week, knowing Rocca had to make the trip sometime near the month's end. By chance or prescience, Rocca took the Lawley road on that occasion. At the time Robert Louis Stevenson visited the Roccas, Andrew was still making his monthly night rides. Joan Parry Dutton believes that, out of this knowledge, Stevenson wrote a poem appearing in a *Child's Garden of Verses* :

> "Whenever the moon and stars are set,
> Whenever the wind is high,
> All night long in the dark and wet
> A man goes riding by.
> Late in the night when the fires are out,
> Why does he gallop and gallop about?
>
> Whenever the trees are crying aloud,
> and ships are tossed at sea,
> By, on the highway, low and loud,
> By at the gallop goes he.
> By at the gallop he goes, and then
> By he comes back at the gallop again."

Rocca never lost a single cent of the payroll on his wild night rides. In the mid 1880's, he and a partner purchased a drug store in Middletown, where a Wells Fargo office was set up. From then on, the stage, with an armed guard, brought the payroll to Middletown. From there, it was brought to the Western by stage owner, Bill Spiers, or Rocca himself.

The Ida Clayton road was a lively route for commerce and pleasure in the last 25 years of the 19th century. The Great Western, responsible for its completion, also maintained it periodically. For this service, employees traveled free. The mine opened a sawmill just over the Mayacmas crest on a year-round stream, so named, Mill Creek. Sunday excursionists from the mine used the route for access to fishing holes on Mill Creek. Fishermen, eat your hearts out- it was not uncommon to net several dozen fish on a single outing and once an angler hooked 150 trout in one day!

About this period, a story is told by Earle Wrieden about a group of men from Sacramento, stealing horses in Middletown and driving them along the Ida Clayton Road to Santa Rosa . There the horses were sold for, literally, chicken feed. People in Middletown got fed up with that and formed a posse at the next incident. Twenty men were captured, twenty men were hanged in a grove of black oaks, one and a half miles west of the pass. That place became known as Hangman's Grove. The vigilante action made a strong impression on people's minds and horse stealing was not seen for many years.

By 1900, the great ore body at the Western was about mined out and traffic slowed again on the Ida Clayton, as miners and commerce went elsewhere. Historian, Henry Mauldin, says the Wilkinson family was operating and maintaining the road after the century's turn, probably leasing it from the Holmes. Public outcry at the high toll, nothing new, grew louder as some paid up to $2.50 for a single vehicle. The original franchise stated that it was to be a wagon road with mile posts properly maintained. Critics claimed that the charter was subject to forfeiture because of non-maintenance and for charging autos, not included of course in the original wording.

The *Weekly Calistogan* charged in 1916:

> "We now have an opportunity to cancel an out-of-date, feudal privilege...Toll roads are relics of an age when it was customary to collect taxes by selling the right of collection to the highest bidder. This road is a hindrance to free inter-county trade, worse than any system of control could be. Let the franchise be delivered up and the road opened to the people of California."

These words might be applied to the toll bridges around the Bay Area today! The road was opened to the public soon after, although it had little effect on inter-county trade. Today, it is one of the great backwoods drives, very little changed since the old days. It sees use only by the dozen or so families living on the north side, occasional bike riders, Trout Farm patrons and fun-seekers, after an occasional winter snow fall.

Toll House

The Lawley Toll Road had been in existence nearly a decade when John Lawley moved his family to the 'gap' on Mt. St. Helena. The Calistoga Gold and Silver Mine had gone bust and nearby Silverado was now a ghost town. The original two-story toll house had been built about 1873 by a sea captain, William Montgomery, during the Silverado boom.

Affable L. M. Corwin was a business partner in the venture, and landlord until 1880 when he sold his interest in the place to Lawley and moved to Calistoga. From *Silverado Squatters*, Robert Louis Stevenson gives us a clear vision of the setting:

> A water tank, and stables, and a grey house of two stories, with gable ends and a verandah, are jammed hard against the hillside, just where a stream has cut for itself a narrow canyon, filled with pines. The pines go right up overhead; a little more and the stream might have played, like a fire hose on the Toll House roof. In front the ground drops as sharply as it rises behind. There is just room for the road and a sort of promontory of croquet ground, and then you can lean over the edge and look deep below you through the wood. I said croquet ground not green; for the surface was of brown, beaten earth.
>
> The toll bar itself was the only other note of originality; a long beam, turning on a post, and kept slightly horizontal by a counterweight of stones."

The toll house nearly burned a few days before Stevenson arrived. The Saint Helena Star of June 4, 1880, reports a fire started there early on a Sunday morning. It was extinguished in time. A disaster at this time would have impacted his visit severely, perhaps even making his stay impossible. The next time, in February,1883, a fire was not controlled and the whole building burned to the ground. A defective chimney flue was the cause. Dan and Mollie Patten escaped but all their clothes and property perished. It cost them three to four thousand uninsured dollars. A few months before, a barn had met the same fate. A temporary toll booth was established a mile down the hill, perhaps at the Martz place.

Meanwhile, plans were laid for a new toll house. By 1884, the Pattens owned 500 acres on the mountain including the old Silverado townsite. The Silverado Hotel was moved to the new location to become one wing of the new Mt. St. Helena toll house. It was a long, one-story, rambling affair with a bar on the south side, dining room and living room in the center, and rooms to rent on the north.

John Lawley

*Section of Lawley Toll Road;
Table Rock in the background*

Fossville, in Knight's Valley

Toll House
R.L. Stevenson wrote about.

Original two-story toll house located at top of the Lawley grade, burned to ground 1883

Ranch style toll house, built 1884, demolished 1953.

A covered porch ran the entire distance in front. Next to the toll house and a little bit east, was a water trough and the tiny toll booth where money was actually taken. Across the road, a new barn was built in the grove where picnic tables now reside. The Silverado Hotel sign was painted over to read Mt. St. Helena Inn.

The appearance of the toll house was constantly changing and evolving as many improvements were made over the years to prop up the ailing wood structure. In the 1920's, additions included a walk-in refrigerator, a 110 volt lighting plant, and a bathhouse. These were made in an effort to counteract a dwindling business due to the toll road closure in 1924.

After 1930, Mollie Patten's son, Harry, and his family moved into the toll house to become proprietors. Two factors influenced this change, one was Mollie's illness and hospitalization. The other was the burning of the younger Patten's home at the old Guile place, one mile south.

Harry's daughter, Betty Patten Johnson, recalls those days as a young child at the toll house with fondness. Occasional guests ran the gamut from salt-of-the-earth deer hunters, to the famous, like the actress, Olivia de Haviland. Betty was part of the party that guided Miss de Haviland on horseback to the summit of Mt. St. Helena.

Many guests came from San Francisco simply for a week or two of relaxation and quiet. They would sit on the porch, just as Stevenson did, perhaps play croquet, but generally do very little. Sometimes they would stir themselves to take the trail up the creek to the Silverado mine. The more adventurous would hike good trails out to Bear Valley to the east.

Other times were not so pleasant. Rattlesnakes might slither into the dining room while guests and the family were taking their meal. Harry would excuse himself from the table, chop off the snake's head, then casually toss the critter outside and return to his dinner, all just a part of the down home service at the Mt. St. Helena Inn.

Lively times were also furnished by Tom Marts and his nephew, Johnny Smith, who rented rooms at the inn. They made a living as woodcutters and hunters, exhibiting a fondness for alcohol when the day was over. On days when the hunt was successful, they would take

54

the deer down to Hanley's to get it weighed, then spend the evening getting toasted at the bar. They would manage to stay on the saddle long enough to get home, usually late at night, but cries for help would find them on the ground between the legs of the patient horses. Harry would have to drag them to bed and stable the horses.

In 1942, the Toll House stood deserted for the first time since it was rebuilt 58 years earlier. The Pattens could no longer make a living there and moved to Napa. Two years later, a committee was formed to raise funds for a state park. One of the goals of this group was to turn the Toll House into a museum, mainly to house Stevenson memorabilia. In the meantime, vandals were at work, smashing windows and scrawling grafitti on doors and walls. The Patten's storage shed on 'Silver Street' was also vandalized and many mementos from the Toll House were wrecked for the sake of destruction rather than thievery.

An earlier article in the Oakland Tribune on the Old Toll House describes how Anne Roller Issler and others planned to preserve the area as a state park. It went on to say:

> "Mortgages, as well as the weight of years, now rest on the Toll House roof. Those who would visit the place had best go soon, for there is a chance, unless Mrs. Issler's campaign bears fruit, it will go the way of many another reminder that has served for so much firewood, or been transformed enthusiastically and fantastically into a modern and jimcrack hot dog stand."

A hotdog stand would have at least saved the building. By the early 1950's, vandals had pulled the supports away from the front porch roof and collapsed it. State park officials decided in 1953 that the building was unrestorable, took photographs for the record, and tore it down. It's regrettable that funds were never raised for its restoration when there was time.

Today, state law prevents the dismantling of historic buildings without a thorough review process. Expensive studies and reams of reports are turned out before a decision is made. By today's standards, the toll house would have been worth saving. If it had been saved, the weight of its historical significance might have given impetus to implementation of the General Plan for Robert Louis Stevenson State

Park, now 50 years overdue.

Mountain Mill House

Built before the second Lawley Toll House , a stagecoach stop for Bill Spiers' line, and home of mountain legend, Lillie McNulty, the Mountain Mill House has weathered 110 winters, where rainfall averages close to 60 inches a year. The stately victorian is now owned by the Catherine Burke Girls' School of San Francisco, which has a ten year plan to restore the old lady, sturdy looking on the outside but a little rotten within.

Felix McNulty was part of the original crew that constructed Lawley's Toll Road. With those earnings, he bought a quarter section of land from Sam Brannan at the foot of the steep north grade, where Van Ness Creek joins St. Helena Creek. Here, he built the first house in 1873. Felix and his wife, Delia, wanted a place where wayfarers could stop for a drink, a bite to eat, friendly conversation, and a clean room for the night. Felix supplemented his income at the inn by riding the mail to the community grown up around the Oat Hill Mine. In 1881, he built the two-story, white Victorian still standing and clearly visible from the road today.

The McNultys' only son , William, was born in 1880, followed by their only daughter in 1883. Lillie was named for the Lillie family who operated a mill on St. Helena Creek next door. The Mountain Mill House derives its name from the mill. Some say that another Lillie, the famous actress, Lillie Langtry, was a guest here in 1887, the year she purchased the Guenoc Ranch in Lake County.

Lillie McNulty, spent her whole life on or near Mt. St. Helena. She became the guardian spirit of the Mountain Mill House in the same way Mollie Patten was identified with the Toll House. Most of her schooling was done on the far side of the mountain, taking the stage coach to the little schoolhouse near the present-day Christmas Tree Farm. Sometimes though, she went to Mirabel Springs, where Mrs. Charles Osgood was her teacher. (Charles Osgood was convicted in the White Cap murder case of 1890 near Mirabel and sent to San Quentin. One wonders how this affected the young Lillie. Mrs. Osgood was reportedly one of the women who made up the

56

headgear for the men, although it is said they knew nothing of their purpose).

When her mother died in 1920, Lillie and her brother became heirs of the estate. William was killed at Black Point, Marin county in 1936, in a car wreck, and Lillie became the sole heir. She was never to marry, but Lillie was not alone, because this side of the mountain was a close-knit community. The Livermores, next door at Montesol Ranch were good friends, often coming by to see her. The Russells were at Troutdale nearby and the Pattens at the top of the hill.

One person she took exception to, was Mollie Patten. Lillie reportedly was a cantankerous old lady in later years and Ivy Loeber's description of Mollie - "a weather-beaten, profane old woman in a gingham dress and apron-" might apply to Lillie as well. There was some jealousy between the women and each would accuse the other of stealing guests. The two of them, one a widow and the other a spinster, would reputedly get into verbal rows using plenty of profanity. Spud Hawkins knew both of them personally and said either of these women could "teach any kid to cuss with any cuss word there is today." He tells another story of a hungry stage driver enjoying a home cooked meal at the Mountain Mill House. After dessert, the man turns to Lillie and says "By God Lillie, that was good pie. If you didn't have them snaggy teeth, I'd kiss you!" To which Lillie replied, "You can kiss my ass!"

By the nineteen-forties, Lillie had sold the greater part of the estate, retaining the house and a few acres. In 1957, she sold the remaining acreage to the Girl Scouts of Oakland, retaining a lifelong lease. She died in 1965 at 82 years of age.

When the Mill House and property were for sale recently, the State Park considered buying it, but decided renovation would have been beyond their present resources. It was purchased by the Catherine Burke School of San Francisco, a private girl's school. In 1991, the school made the property available as a summer day camp and resident camp for young children. Bobbi Meyer, the resident manager, tells me the Mill House is slated for restoration over a ten year period. It will cost $500,000. The Burke School should be commended for this fine community service .

Mollie Patten

For nearly 50 years, the proprietress of the Toll House was Mary Frances Lawley Patten, affectionately known as Mollie. She became, after Stevenson, the most famous personality on the mountain, her name synonymous with the Toll House. Born September 13, 1855, the first child of John and Cynthia Lawley, she attended Napa Young Ladies Seminary, and, later, Mills College, receiving a first rate education due to her father's wealth and influence. Good looking, charming, and vivacious, she was the center of attention at some of San Francisco's higher social functions.

At twenty, she married Daniel Patten, the handsome, successful owner of the Aetna Mine in Pope Valley. They lived there for five years, after a year-long honeymoon trip on the east coast. They had two children, Harry, named for her favorite brother, and Mabel, who died in infancy. In 1881, the Pattens joined Mollie's parents at the Toll House, just a few months after Robert Louis Stevenson had left for Scotland. Together, the two generations ran the successful toll road and inn business. After her father died in 1906, Mollie gained firm control.

Many in neighboring counties objected to Mt. St. Helena's main route being a toll road and wished that Napa and Lake Counties would purchase this thoroughfare. Contrary to legend that John Lawley considered the toll road a family heirloom, he tried to sell it as early as 1893 and again in 1903. Although the road was kept in better condition than any county maintained roads, the local populace considered the fees exorbitant. In a letter to the Napa Register on June 24, 1893, A.L. Anthony airs a common complaint and gives us a picture of Mollie simultaneously:

> "The Toll House, which is on the line between Lake and Napa Counties is still run by Mr. and Mrs. Lawley. A daughter of this aged and estimable pair gave us just time enough to unloose our purse-strings and let loose six bits, when she complacently pocketed it and demurely reseated herself in a comfortable chair on the front porch as though nothing unusual had happened. We thought there had..."

Mollie's was a complex personality, combining generosity and stinginess, charm and profanity, a woman with business acumen yet one who left her estate heavily in debt. Cold and hungry travelers were often given aid and comfort on rainy winter nights, and often a place to stay rent free if they were penniless. If she thought you were taking advantage of her, however, she was merciless. Her many friends ran the gamut of the social ladder - truck drivers and millionaires, the unknown and the famous. One of these was Jack London, who came for stories of his favorite author, Stevenson. Mollie was not impressed by social stature or fame, so everyone was given the same fair treatment, and thus she had friends from all walks of life.

From a local newspaper in 1924, comes a story to illustrate her old world quality:

> "One Sunday, quite recently, Mollie, always the soul of hospitality, had invited in for a piping hot cup of coffee beside her cheery fireplace ever ablaze with fragrant logs of pine and pepperwood, a lady whose escort was a noted mining man. The lady looked cold despite the luxury of the great limousine, so Mollie 'carried her in to thaw out.'
>
> "During their conversation, the woman informed Mollie that she would soon wed her fourth husband. This rather startled Mollie -but not to be outdone, she informed her guest that even if she had had but one husband, she had lived for thirty-seven years 'creditably' with him. It was the woman of today versus the woman of yesterday."

One of the least known and darker chapters in Mollie's life involved an inter-family lawsuit brought against her by Charles A. Lawley, Harry B. Lawley (her favorite brother!) and Mrs. Ada Lawley Neal. Their attorney was Theodore Bell, who earlier became famous for his role in the capture of outlaw Buck English. Quoting from an article in the *Weekly Calistogan* from 1907, titled "Lawleys Bring Another Suit":

> "All parties to the suit are brothers and sisters, being the heirs of the well-known Lawley estate. For some time past trouble has been brewing among" [them] "and in May last when Mrs. Patten had her brother, C.A. Lawley arrested for threatening to kill her son, which charge was afterwards dismissed, the trouble culminated in the suit... to have the lands jointly owned by the

plaintiffs and defendant, partitioned, divided, and sold, and to compel Mrs. Patten to render an accounting of the income and profits collected from the Lawley Toll Road on Mount St. Helena during the past five years..."

"The complaint in the action... alleges that for more than five years the brothers and sisters have been co-partners in the hotel, saloon, summer resort, livery stable, cattle and stock raising and wine manufacturing business; that Mrs. Patten has been and is in full possession and control of all these co-partnership interests, and has refused to permit her brothers and sisters to participate therein..."

Even with all the varied business interests mentioned, probably not much money was being made. Mollie's contention that there wasn't enough to go around was true. Her position as the only full time resident on the estate gave her a feeling of proprietorship. Nevertheless, it was decided in court that the partnership be dissolved and that an appointed 'receiver', George W. Fee, would thenceforth distribute proceeds equally among the heirs.

Far from settling matters, that only launched what, from the records, could be called 'the Lawsuit Wars'. The next year in 1908, plaintiffs Charlie and Harry Lawley charged Mollie, her husband Daniel, and son Harry, with failure to return loaned horses and farm implements. They asked for $100 in damages. The same year Mollie filed a countersuit, charging her brothers with trespassing and illegally seizing her land. She demanded $500 in damages.

It may have been at this time that a water rights dispute erupted, culminating in a civil case in 1913. Harry and Charlie Lawley again charged Mollie and family, this time with infringement of water rights. The plaintiffs claimed sole ownership of the toll road since 1908 and as such are entitled to water access. Playing a central part in the case was a water trough, in place since 1873. Fed by a flume-supported, one and a half inch metal pipe, it tapped the creek above the toll house. Apparently the defendants had cut the metal pipe, stopping water flow to the trough. The brothers filed for $5,900 in damages. (Water rights were still a key problem to be ironed out when the Silverado mine parcel was transferred to Stevenson State Park in 1988).

60

In a surprise move in 1916, co-plaintiffs Charlie and Harry are on opposite sides of the litigational fence. Harry charged Charlie with taking toll road fees without distributing his due portion! The Lawleys and Pattens appeared in court less often after this but, after Mollie's death,13 claims against the estate were allowed in probate court. It was a confusing legal tangle that sent the best lawyers into despair. Settlement came 56 years later.

It was not the family feuds but the coming of the automobile, that changed Mollie to a hard and embittered woman. With faster transportation and the Ida Clayton Toll Road opened to the public, Mollie could see the writing on the wall. When the new highway left her inn to one side, the way of life she knew was gone. Without the toll road and with fewer and fewer guests coming to stay, income dwindled. Never one to hoard money, she now went into debt. Her granddaughter, Betty Patten, has told me that Mollie once received an inheritance of $50,000. A staggering sum of money then, it was quickly spent for improvements to the property. In conflict with her reputation as a shrewd businesswoman, she says saving money was not a part of Mollie's vocabulary.

Mollie Patten took ill in 1930, recovered partially, then suffered another stroke in February,1932. At various times, she was in the hospital at St. Helena and in the Silverado Sanitarium under the care of Alice Hawkins. She died May 24, on the mountain that she loved. Her wish to preserve the 500 acres of forest around the Silverado mine was not realized in her life but came to fruition later. A student at the University of California visited Mollie at the toll house and later gave this tribute:

> "It is nothing less than a literary calamity that Stevenson never met Mollie Patten; the impact of the two should have produced something great in literature."

William 'finest kind' Spiers

The history of commercial transportation over Mt. St. Helena can be largely but not entirely summed up in the career of one man from Kentucky, Bill Spiers. From freight wagon business owner to stagecoach entrepreneur, to motor driven bus lines, Spiers cheerfully monopolized transportation in this area for almost 50 years. By 1910, his was the largest coach and livery service in California. Without him, industry and business in Napa and Lake Counties would have been seriously retarded. Spiers however was not the first in freighting, passenger, or even auto transport. In each of these fields, others would pave the way, and Spiers would then incorporate them into his expanding business.

At nineteen, he left Kentucky with few prospects, secured a job as a woodcutter in Napa County, then as a miner at Pine Flat, west of Mt. St. Helena. The frugal Spiers saved enough money to start a freighting business in the late seventies. By then, there were several franchises hauling merchandise and textiles to Lake County and bringing wheat, tanbark, and ore back to the railhead in Calistoga.

William F. Fisher ran a successful livery out of Calistoga, as prominent a man in town as Spiers was to become later. It was while driving part-time for Bill Fisher that the paths of Spiers and Robert Louis Stevenson crossed. The two men could hardly have been more different, Spiers the pragmatic American frontiersman, and Stevenson the poet-dreamer from the Old World. In the following quote from *Stevenson At Silverado* by Anne Roller Issler, Spiers shows his provinciality when summing up Stevenson's character:

> "Fact is, I thought him kind of a fool, livin' in that old shack awritin' books! I wasn't much interested in books, nor didn't care to be. I was a few years younger than he was, but I didn't think he was hardly as smart as I which had got my diplomy back in Kintucky when I was seven and a half."

By 1878, Spiers' tireless energy and enterprise won him contracts for shipments from the Oat Hill and Great Western Mines. The *St. Helena Star* of July, 1880, records that 15 cords of tanbark from the Great Western area was being brought down to Sawyer and Company in Napa with a team of 8 mules. The trip took 5 days. With an obligation to deliver 300 cords, the contractor, probably Spiers, had his teams make no less than 20 trips to complete the contract.

In 1888, he bought out W.F. Fisher and began the Calistoga and Clear Lake Stage Line, to run for 37 consecutive years. Spiers' father had been a breeder of thoroughbreds, so, with this background and love of horseflesh, it was understandable he would go into a more glamorous line of work. Ella Spiers, his daughter-in-law, says that at one time, he owned 700 horses. Spiers saw to their care so well that most lived a long life, despite the grueling work of hauling heavy loads over the mountain.

Spiers never seemed to have enough work, so he also carried the United States mail and gradually acquired individual stage lines that served various hot springs resorts. Tourism, along with farming and mining, were the triumvirate of the economy by then and hot springs were in their heyday. Some of the resort stage lines he acquired were White Sulphur Springs, west of St. Helena and, in Lake County: Harbin, Anderson, Howard, Astorg, Spiers, Seigler, Adams, Hobergs, and Highland Springs.

Spiers' stage drivers were well-trained, venerable men and, like the owner himself, the epitome of dependability. In a business like this though, some accidents were bound to happen. On September 5, 1883, Ace Butler with four cords of tanbark went over the Great Western grade, team and all, finally stopping 50 feet downbank. Fortunately, no one was killed and only one animal was hurt. We have a wonderful description of another accident by Michael Chegywn in an article, found in the Spring 1991 issue of *Old West* magazine:

> "One of the most spectacular occurred while Joel Downey was driving a heavily loaded six-horse mud wagon north between Middletown and Lower Lake on the evening of November 22, 1913. One of the carbide 'petrolites' attached to the stage for illumination suddenly exploded, showering hot embers over the rumps of the wheel horses. The entire team spooked, taking off at a gallop. While Downey fought to slow the singed beasts, the stage caught fire. Up and down the brushy hills it went, presenting an awe-inspiring sight as it spewed flames and smoke into the darkness. Fortunately, the vehicle came to a steeper uphill grade and Downey was able to bring the team to a halt. Meanwhile, passengers had doused the blaze with blankets, but not before the coach was badly charred and the mail sacks destroyed. A male and female passenger broke their legs when they jumped from the stage as it careened along like a fiery chariot."

Tollmaster, Mollie Patten, charging a pretty penny for those days.

Spiers motor stage, circa World War I

*William Fisher, Calistoga's
first transportation mogul*

*Transportation king, Bill Spiers, whose
stock response was,"finest kind."*

65

The turn of the century brought the six and eight horse-drawn carriages into conflict with more technologically advanced machines, usually automobiles but once, a bicycle. On July 8,1900, T.C.Garner and his wife were driving a two-horse buggy (surrey) up the toll road when a bicyclist with brush tied to his wheel neared. The horses, spooked at the unfamiliar noise, jumped over the edge, badly damaging the buggy but the passengers were spared injury. They probably telephoned from the Toll House, and Bill Spiers brought them another rig to continue their journey to Lake County.

The noisy internal combustion engine was greeted with scorn by many on the mountain, who preferred the old, slower ways. Even Spiers himself tried to stay progress before he enthusiastically converted to auto buses. Once, when Norman Livermore Sr. scared Spiers' horses by driving his new auto on the toll road, Bill swore he'd shoot Livermore the next time he did it. Indeed there were incidents in which automobilists were shot at. It wasn't just noise that spooked horses either. When the Stanley Steamer was invented, it was such a quiet vehicle that passengers would walk ahead of the machine so horses wouldn't spook at its sudden appearance.

In a tables-turned situation, an automobilist was once spooked by a man with a dynamite stick in his hand. The driver was Adolph Sutro, Mayor of San Francisco and owner of Arcadia, a resort on the northeast side of the mountain. Sutro, remembers Lake County resident Earle Wrieden, had a big handlebar mustache and occasionally came into Middletown for a haircut. One day in 1915, Sutro was driving the toll road when he encountered Charles Eliot, who was working on the road. In a friendly manner, Eliot waved to Sutro, unaware of the stick in his hand. Sutro drove right off the road, evidently mistaking Eliot's intentions with that dynamite.

By 1915, the superiority of the new machine was proven and all of Spiers' Concord and mud wagons were sold to Hollywood for filmmaking. The one exception was the *California*, which can now be seen at the Sharpsteen Museum in Calistoga. Spiers took to the motor vehicle with enthusiasm, as he had with everything in life. Many oldtimers in Calistoga remember that their first ride in a car was in one of Spiers' fleet.

In the midst of all his work, he also served on the city council for many years and was mayor seven times. He was, without doubt, Calistoga's preeminent citizen. Spiers suffered a stroke in 1925 and was forced to retire. On April 4, 1931 he suffered a second, and fatal stroke, driving his Lincoln automobile down Washington Street, rolling to a stop at the town's electric train depot. Transportation of one kind or another was his theme, in life and in death. He died as he lived, in the driver's seat.

Modern Highway 29

John Lawley's Toll Road was purchased by Napa and Lake Counties in April, 1922 for $30,000. They continued to collect the toll for two years until the purchase price was re-couped. Then, it became state property. On February 1,1924, the toll house was reduced to a cultural back-water. On this day, the new state highway officially opened to the public. It was not the smooth roadway we know today, but gravelled. It would be many years before it was paved. Spud Hawkins, who has spent most of his life on or near the mountain, recalls it was built like a 'racetrack' and unwary drivers often skidded out of control on the many 'S' turns. The freshly graded slopes above the road were constantly sloughing off, causing minor and major damage. The worst slide took a month to clear, rerouting traffic back down the old Lawley grade. Eventually regrowth of the vegetation stabilized the banks.

The sound of the revved automobile engine laboring on the hill was the death knell for the toll house, but a herald for other businesses tailoring themselves to service a new kind of tourist. The days were gone when guests did little more than idle a peaceful afternoon away on the toll house porch, or play croquet in the grove. One of the new businesses was the Hawkins Mountain Inn, located just above where Hanley's is today. It featured a campground, store, and most important, a gas station.

Spud Hawkins was only a boy at the time, but he remembers the year Clear Lake was developed and parceled into a resort. Los Angelenos came in droves that summer to see their new properties. Auto cooling systems were primitive then and, the grade being steep, many radiators boiled over before the top. Young Spud made $150 in tips that summer, cooling them off with a line from a 500 gallon water tank. Automobile touring was a fairly new sport in 1924, and many with money to buy cars knew nothing of basic repair. Spud changed a lot of blown tires (poor quality rubber in those days) and became adept at carburetor repair.

The owners of Hawkins' Mountain Inn were Al and Alice Hawkins, Spud's parents. Al was a railroad man. Later he worked one of the first bus lines from Vallejo to Calistoga. He ran the first motor stage line and fast mail over Mt. St. Helena for a year before selling it in 1916. During World War I, his expertise was used to teach the French the mechanics of the railroad business. On his re-turn, he went into real estate, and along with other mountain prop-erties, obtained the land for Hawkins' Mountain Inn. Nothing is left of that enterprise today.

In the 1920's, Alice Hawkins began to care for tubercular children. Out of this concern, arose the Silverado Sanitarium. No treatment was known for tuberculosis then, except mountain air and rest to relieve a patient's suffering. Al Hawkins threw all his savings into the venture, located where Brandon's is today. In six months, he was broke, but a lumber company took over the ownership, with the Hawkins as operators.

The sanitarium was a marginal business, due to the Depression and many patients' inability to pay. Medical insurance was non-exist-ent then but the Hawkins never forced anyone to leave. One desti-tute patient stayed 16 years without ever paying a penny. The sani-tarium accommodated up to 70 people. Alice Hawkins took care of Mollie Patten here in the last year of her life. Medical advances in drugs and surgery brought the treatment of tuberculosis into the hospital by the 1930's and TB sanitariums became a thing of the past.

The site has been through two incarnations since, first as the wild and crazy Skyline Lodge and, presently, as the home of Marjorie Brandon, owner of the *Weekly Calistogan.*

The Skyline Lodge was apparently the place to be on the mountain in the 1960's. It was owned by an unorthodox couple from Texas who knew no boundaries between business and pleasure. Nick was the large-bellied host who liked to see his clients happy, serving them drinks that were nearly straight alcohol with a little mixer on top for taste. His eccentricities ran to raising the Confederate flag at daybreak and, at night, lowering it with a ceremonial gunshot. He hated wearing shirts and it's sworn that no one ever saw him with that apparel. Nick was so well-known for this that friends and strangers would present him with a shirt as a joke. Spur of the moment, long distance calls to Texas were made to talk to friends or resolve a question in debate at the bar.

No expense was spared to ensure the continuing party atmosphere. One night, a barbecue was planned at the Skyline for the Silverado Riders, a group of horseriding enthusiasts, headed by Spud Hawkins. Nick set out a large keg of beer in the yard, but when Spud went to fill his cup, he was steered inside with the admonishment " that's not for you!" Nick poured him the best imported beer, on the house, of course. Spud says it was almost impossible to pay for a drink at the Skyline if you were a local.

This sort of generosity couldn't go on, and when the Hanley fire broke out in 1964, the Skyline was on its third mortgage. By a quirk of fate, that disaster missed burning Nick's place although it started a few hundred yards away. It's alleged that, seeing the blaze was no help, he tried to set it on fire himself, not once but three times. One story says that a lit candle was set in a shoebox full of paper and placed in the dumbwaiter so all three floors would ignite. Apparently, none of the attempts succeeded. Nick's whereabouts are unknown now, but perhaps some bar patrons in Texas are having a better than average time.

Fireroad

The last major road on Mt. St. Helena was built in 1935 with the sole aim of constructing a fire lookout on top. Some claimed that it could never be done due to the steepness of the slopes. It took a government crew less than a year to build, with the help of a bulldozer that was nearly lost over the side several times. On a clear day, the wide swath and hairpin turn on the southeast side are visible in St. Helena, about 10 air miles away. For 55 years, lonely lookouts have scanned the hazy horizons during summer months to spot potentially deadly fires. But the fireroad, being the only accessible route to the summit, is less than an aesthetic route for hikers. Mt. St. Helena has been rejected for wilderness status due to the fireroad and the proliferation of communication devices on three of its summits.

By 1933, the Civilian Conservation Corps (CCC) had listed the mountain as a possible fire lookout site. The next year construction of the road was underway. The old school house site in 'Happy Hollow', a few tenths of a mile south of the pass, was the CCC's 'spike' camp. The men worked two eight hour shifts, starting at four in the morning and ending at eight at night. Betty Patten Johnson's father, Harry Patten, worked with the crew. Every weekend, Harry would take his family up to proudly show them the latest progress.

Ted Tamagni, from Calistoga, was the nervy bulldozer driver. The steep and unstable slopes took all his skill and daring to keep from toppling over. Once the dozer did get away and it took 3 days to retrieve it. Where the rocky sections made progress especially slow, dynamite was used. Here, Harry Patten's experience in mining and blasting was useful. Long switchbacks and flat hairpin turns were needed to keep the grade low for vehicles that would be hauling heavy loads of construction material for the lookout tower.

Work was almost complete by June, 1935 and only a quarter mile remained to reach the summit. Suddenly, the CCC crew was alerted that it was needed immediately in Yellowstone Park and wouldn't be back. Only a few days were left to finish the job. Ignoring the remaining survey markers, Tamagni aimed the dozer straight uphill and plowed a line to the top just before the deadline. The slope has never been altered and today, the easy-graded 6.5 mile road contrasts sharply with that last quarter mile.

Work on the tower was begun immediately by the Forestry Department. Suspended between four strong uprights, it might be called a *pole* building, (old water tanks were built in a similar way). It would sway from side to side in high winds and eventually was stabilized by four guy lines. Inside stairs went halfway up the tower, leading to a door to outside stairs, to finish the ascent. Rattlesnakes liked to congregate in the shade at the base of the stairs, calling for a light step from the ranger. Dozens of snakes were killed over the years. For

70

the same reason, a high step was necessary to prevent unpleasant surprises when entering the nearby outhouse.

As soon as the tower was finished, it came to light that the title to the land was in question. This happened when Claude Russell, who apparently owned the land, attempted to sell some parcels on top for a housing development. Years earlier, the title had been clouded, and as a favor, the Livermores cleared it up for Russell. They did ask in return, however, for right of first refusal. Years passed and all was forgotten until 1935. When the Livermores heard of the proposed sale, they reminded Russell of his promise, bought the 200 acres on the main peak, and saved it from development. Although the Livermores could have made trouble for the Forestry Dept., they gave it a one acre lease.

By coincidence, 1935 was also the year the Napa County Fair first opened. Emmy Lou Sands of Calistoga's Mountain Home Ranch, remembers the year very well. Her first husband, Bob Fouts, was a promoter who had the grand idea of a fireworks show from the summit, visible from the Fairgrounds. He engaged a local radio announcer, also coincidentally named Bob Fouts, to promote the event over the airwaves. By the night of July 4th, the entire valley was excited over the occasion. As nightfall approached, Emmy, her husband and friends gathered on top of Diamond Mountain out of Calistoga in anticipation. Although they waited until late, no fireworks were seen, even with the help of binoculars. The promotion was a bust, and an enormous disappointment for the Fouts with Bob especially embarrassed for weeks after.

The lookout tower came in for unexpected use in World War II as a spotter station for enemy aircraft. Patrols went on 24 hours each day, but none were ever sighted. In 1964, a new tower was installed. Contrary to some reports, it was not burned or blown apart by winds in the Hanley fire that year. Indeed, lookouts were stationed there throughout that holocaust. It was just time for an update. (Unfortunately, it was plunked down next to the metal plaque commemorating the Russian's first ascent in 1841, practically hiding it from view.) Wraparound windows allow a 360 degree weatherproof view that, for distance, has few rivals in the world. Lookout Bob Haggard uses only a trusty pair of WWII binoculars for spotting fires, claiming a telescope would be overkill. In fact most fires are spotted best with the naked eye.

In the days when Claude Russell owned property on the mountain, if you were a friend, you could get a key to the fireroad gate and drive topside. And when Silverado was a dude ranch, horses were ridden on the road, although the trails were preferred. Nowadays, the only horse you're likely to see is a 'shanks' mare. As for wheeled vehicles, only private landowners, California Forestry, Park Service, and communications facilities employees may drive. The public can occasionally ride in van trips sponsored by the Park for those who cannot hike the mountain. Mountain bikers are often seen making the grade also.

Commemorative marker on highway 29 just south of Middletown.

OLD BULL TRAIL ROAD AND
ST. HELENA TOLL ROAD

THE OLD BULL TRAIL ROAD RAN FROM NAPA VALLEY TO MIDDLETOWN. IT WAS BUILT BY VOLUNTEERS IN THE 1850'S. A NUMBER OF THE GRADES WERE 35 PERCENT. IT WAS AN OFFICIAL ROAD IN 1861 AND ABANDONED IN 1868. ST. HELENA TOLL ROAD ALSO RAN FROM SAME POINTS. WAS COMPLETED IN 1868. THE GRADES RAN TO 12 PERCENT. STATE OF CALIFORNIA PURCHASED FROM JOHN LAWLEY HEIRS IN 1925.

TABLET PLACED BY CALIFORNIA CENTENNIALS COMMISSION.
BASE FURNISHED BY COUNTY OF LAKE
DEDICATED MAY 30, 1950

72

~ ~ ~

One August morning, about 3:30 a.m., found me, with the aid of a head-lamp, making my way through the dark wooded first mile to the summit. Once on the fireroad, stars lit my way. The first overview of Napa Valley was surreal, like I had stepped unknowingly through another dimension and looked upon a different planet. Below, framed by the dark purplish, wooded slopes of the Howell and Mayacmas mountains, as in a bowl, was the sea fog, glowing softly, eerily white in the starlight. The lights of St. Helena and Calistoga were bright enough to shine through the fog, locating those towns precisely. The softness of the starlight, the valley replaced by the inland sea, the absolute stillness and my own solitude gave me the feeling I walked in some astral world.

Due to a temperature inversion, I wore only shorts and a tank top until reaching the summit, where a gentle but cool wind blew. My quest to see Mount Shasta was to go unrewarded that morning, but the mountain had other surprises in store. As the sun bolted over the Sierra Nevada, the fog began to stir and rise. All of Knight's and Alexander Valleys were invaded, Sonoma county and Marin as well. Suddenly, I grabbed the camera and ran to the west. The whole outline of Mt. St. Helena's shadow was etched against the white foggy billows, with the bump of the north peak like a clown's hat on top. Most incredible though, was the rainbow *halo* four times the size of the topnotch itself. Thinking it a natural phenomena, I have been told since, it is due to refraction of light through the windows of the lookout tower during the right conditions. Other lookouts will also produce this beautiful effect.

Chapter 3

Badmen:
Buck English and Black Bart

*"Like the deer on the mountain, stage robbers were
neighbors until they became game."*

Anne Roller Issler

*"I am reminded of another highwayman of that same year.
'He had been unwell', so ran his humorous defence, 'and the
doctor told him to take something, so he took the express box'."*

Robert Louis Stevenson

Introduction

In the last quarter of the nineteenth century, Mt. St. Helena was a
haven for stage robbers, both the obscure and the famous. These highwaymen, or road agents as they were sometimes called, were drawn
by the rich cargo carried by the Wells Fargo stage lines. Locked in the
express box could be several thousand dollars, payroll due workers
of the Great Western, Oathill, Bradford, and Sulfur Bank quicksilver
mines. Rock outcrops and thick stands of fir trees afforded cover for
the bandits, and places like Robber's Roost and Dusty Bend became
regular hideouts. Wild country in all directions from the lone highway allowed easy escape, even with a posse in hot pursuit. Old
newspaper accounts often relate that the rough, volcanic country of

74

Bear Valley and Oat Hill to the east was a popular escape route.

An amused, philosophic attitude was taken by locals whenever a stage was robbed. The man lightening your wallet as well as the express box could easily have been a neighbor or a congenial fishing companion. Mountain resident Rufe Hanson, who helped track down robbers of the Lakeport stage, only to find one an acquaintance of his, "expressed much grave commiseration for his fate". Robberies were so common and well publicized that even a novice could take note of the methods and fool the victims into thinking he was an experienced road agent.

Such was the case on June 23, 1888, when a stage driven by E.B. Stoddard was held up near the Bradford mine by a lone gunman. At least $2000, meant for the Great Western mine, was taken but the passengers were left unmolested. The robber was described as a "very rough individual," who surprised the driver by calling him by name and asking him to "give his regards to the boys at Kelseyville." The *Calistogan* of June 27th describes the aftermath:

> "In twenty minutes after the robbery, men were in pursuit and his trail was found and followed a short distance; but on account of the roughness of the country there his tracks were soon lost. Men have since been in pursuit, but the fellow will not be found. He's too old at the business to be easily caught."

Indeed the man did escape and the crime remained unsolved. Much later, a man, well known locally, went temporarily insane when a bottle was broken over his head in a barroom fight. While recovering at Napa State Hospital, he admitted to the above robbery. He had owed money to a woman con artist, who goaded him into the crime, coached him on the technique, and then took all the money. It was his first and only robbery, but since he was judged insane at the time of his confession, he could not be arrested. He lived lawfully on the mountain for many more years until his death. Every time a stage was held up from then on, the man came under suspicion, only to prove his innocence.

A genius I.Q. was not required to know when the stage was worth robbing. All that was necessary was to lounge around Calistoga when the heavy express box was transferred to the stage. Quoting Florence

Rocca, sister of Helen Rocca Goss, historian,

> "The messenger and a helper would come to the stage lugging the heavy box, grunting and puffing to advertise to the world what a back-breaking load they had. The box was locked, of course, but the bandits simply shot off the lock when they did get it. It would have been quite easy for a man on horseback to get out of town ahead of the stage and lie in wait for it. And that is what probably happened when the stage was held up."

Three men who hadn't figured this out robbed the Harbin Springs Stage on June 30, 1890, settling for money and watches from the passengers. (The driver was A.R. Palmer who also drove the stage when Buck English pulled his last holdup five years later). The *Napa Weekly Register* reported that, on the same day, Sheriff McKenzie captured them by lying in wait at the pass on Murray Hill, between Napa and Knight's Valleys. The bandits confessed immediately, saying they were novices, forced into the situation by poverty, and would plead guilty.

Unlike today's heartless thieves, highwaymen of that era were sometimes sympathetic to those they robbed. This was never more true than on September 14, 1899 when H.T. Quigley was held up driving Spiers stage at Dusty Bend, one and a quarter miles south of the toll house. Listening to the pleas of some of his poorer victims, the outlaw actually returned their money and valuables. He made away with $12.25 from the passengers and $50 from the express box.

Quigley made a phone call from the toll house for help, identifying a local resident, Joe Weir, as the outlaw. Blood hounds seemed to confirm this testimony as they traced the scent straight to Joe's house nearby. Despite Joe's vehement claims of innocence, he was arrested that day. By the following week, however, the prosecution's evidence was growing thin, and on the September 29th hearing, Joe Weir was triumphantly set free, amid widespread sympathy from the court crowd. The case remained a mystery.

Then, five months later, on March 2, 1900, another robbery took place only 100 yards from the previous site. Driving the stage again was the unflappable A.R. Palmer. Mrs. T.C. Van Ness, wife of the prominent San Francisco lawyer, traveling to her summer home on the mountain, was one of the unfortunate passengers. The *Napa Daily Journal* of March 6 reported that the search for a lone robber, covering northern Napa Valley and Lake County, had proved futile. The suspect was quite ingenious in his method, covering his hands with charcoal, averting his face from the driver's gaze, and using explosives to break the padlock on the express box. Students take note-- on his escape route toward Oat Hill, he scattered cayenne pepper in his tracks so that the bloodhounds refused to continue! It rained that night and further pursuit was useless.

The man disappeared until the end of the month when San Francisco police officer, P.A. Gillsen, on a trip to Mount Hamilton, arrested Horace Woods, a "tramp". He was believed to be the lone highwayman who held up the Calistoga stage on March 2. No other news items were found on this incident by the author. Personally, I'd like to believe a man as fastidious in his trade as Horace wouldn't be caught so easily, much less labeled a tramp.

A horse proved no match for an auto, so with the advent of the new machine, the highwayman era quickly came to a close. Having "eulogized" the more obscure of the profession, we return to the famous and the near famous, Black Bart and Buck English.

Charles E. Boles, alias Black Bart

Black Bart is this country's most famous stage robber. Whether he ever pulled a heist on Mt. St. Helena depends on whom you choose as a reference. Several old timers who lived on the mountain swore he did. But historians generally agree he never got closer than the Lakeport-Ukiah stage line. In his eight year career from 1875 to 1883, it is known that he robbed 28 stages all over Northern California, making fools of the Wells Fargo detectives and winning the admiration of the press for his daring ways, his chivalry to women, and his sharp-tongued poetry. After his release from San Quentin in 1888, he is suspected of two more holdups, some say on Mt. St. Helena. After that, he disappeared into history, and a reward is still out for information on his whereabouts.

Bart was nearing fifty years of age when he made a career change from school teacher to highwayman. His liberal education, knowledge of current affairs, dapper appearance and polished manners allowed him to pass in respectable society without notice. Doubtless these characteristics enabled him to escape the scene of the crime many times, as no one suspected him of wrongdoing. And yet, he was equally at home in the country, a thorough mountaineer and veteran walker, who always put 12 to 15 miles between himself and the robbery before asking for a meal at a lonely villa or ranchhouse. He was proud of his conditioning and claimed no one his equal in making quick time over mountains and steep grades. Eschewing horse travel, he always won the gamble that pursuers would lose his light track before overtaking him. Like his contemporary, the great alpine explorer, Sir Francis Younghusband, fifty miles was just a long day's walk.

From the start, he showed great inventiveness in disguising his identity and intimidating his victims. On July 26, 1875, he stopped his first stage, driven by John Shine, near Copperopolis in the Sierra foothills. Bart wore a white linen duster, a flour sack with cut eye holes, and socks over boots to disguise his footprints. Levelled at the driver was a double-barrelled shotgun. So, apparently, were six more guns in some rocks by the roadside. After noting that, Shine quickly threw down the express box.

A woman in the coach threw out her purse, but Bart gave it back, saying he was only interested in Wells Fargo money. When Shine returned to the scene later, the six "guns" were still in their same position. Bart had jammed long sticks of wood into the rocks as a ruse!

By the fourth holdup on August 3, 1877, Bart had thoroughly identified with his new character role, giving himself his infamous alias and leaving the first of his well-received poetry. Adding two verses at a later date, the poem eventually read like this:

> "here I lay me down to Sleep
> to wait the coming morrow
> perhaps Success, perhaps defeat
> And everlasting sorrow
> I've labored long and hard for bread
> for honor and for riches
> But on my corns too long you've tred

You fine haired sons of Bitches
let come what will I'll try it on
My condition can't be worse
and if there's money in that Box
Tis munny in my purse
Black Bart
The Po8

Bart's career continued brilliantly and detectives could not unearth a single telling clue. From 1877 to 1882, he ransacked Wells Fargo boxes and mail pouches near Fort Ross, Quincy, Covelo, Yreka, Redding, Weaverville and Marysville. On January 25th,1882, the stage of the Ukiah to Cloverdale line was robbed. He was believed to cross Clear Lake at the 'narrows' and pass Bartlett Springs on his way to Colusa. Then, later in the year, on November 24, he took the express and mail from the Lakeport to Cloverdale line, escaping towards Lower Lake. This is the closest Bart got to Mt. St. Helena, if we are to believe the documented record.

At least three respected old timers, however, have different stories to tell. One of them is Lily McNulty. According to the 1977 Centennial edition of the *Weekly Calistogan,* Lily McNulty, whose parents founded the Mountain Mill House, was interviewed by the newspaper's editor in 1929. She told a story her parents told her, that sometime in 1882-3, Black Bart robbed the stage of the express box and registered mail, one half mile up the road from her house. The line was owned by W.F. Fisher, the stage driven by Wash Gwynn. Tacked on a nearby tree was the following message- "Here I stand quietly waiting for the stage that is hardly worth robbing. Catch me if you can. - Black Bart." The note can hardly be called poetry and is probably a variant of a poem attributed to Bart after his release from prison in 1888:

> "So here I've stood while wind and rain
> Have set the trees a' sobbin'
> And risked my life for that damned stage
> That wasn't worth the robbin'."

James Hume, Bart's arch enemy and the man credited with bringing him in, declared the handwriting a hoax. Bart's luck finally gave out with his last holdup of November 3, 1883. He had a premonition it would be his last, held on the exact same location as his first, eight years earlier. Surprised by resistance, he dropped several personal items in his hurry to leave, one the handkerchief with the laundry mark by which he was eventually tracked to his residence on Second Street in San Francisco. He served only four years, two months in San Quentin.

Released on January 23, 1888, he spent two weeks in the city, then, according to James Hume, made his way to the San Joaquin Valley, leaving Visalia under the name M. Moore. In his room at the Palace Hotel were found two pairs of cuffs with the same laundry mark, F.X.O.7. He is variously said to have left the country (bound for Australia, Mexico, Japan, or China) or that he rejoined his wife and four daughters in the midwest, whom he had deserted years earlier.

Ella Spiers, daughter-in-law of Bill Spiers, the local stage line magnate, doesn't believe he left the state so fast. In 1888, the year Spiers acquired the Calistoga-Clear Lake stage line, he was robbed at gunpoint near Lover's Leap on the Lawley toll road. His deringer was no match for the "big old long pistol" held by the bandit, so Spiers was forced to throw down the strong box. Ella was told by her father-in-law that the man was Black Bart.

Another old timer, Clarence Myers, who drove the Calistoga-Clear Lake stage for Spiers for many years, claims he "knowed aplenty" stage robbers in his time, including Black Bart. Historian, Anne Roller Issler, who interviewed Meyers, said he "often" met Bart travelling over the mountain. Positive identification, though, was impossible, since no one ever saw Bart's face during a holdup.

The truth of his presence on Mt. St. Helena may never be known. Certainly the proximity of his home in San Francisco and his penchant for long, hard traveling make it a good guess that Bart knew the area and used the Lawley road on occasion. Whether he staged a robbery here is still open to debate. What is known is that Bart disappeared soon after leaving San Francisco and no one heard from him since. In 1991, a $1000 reward was offered by historian Bruce Devine for information as to Black Bart's final fate.

Black Bart. Knowledge of his whereabouts could still net a $1,000 reward.

Buck English, Mt.St.Helena's most notorious bandit.

Buck English

There could be no more perfect recipe for making a miscreant than the family life of Lawrence Buchanen "Buck" English. A feud of the Hatfield/McCoy type raged between the Englishes and the Durbins for years, despite the fact that Buck's father was married to Pauline Durbin. Three of Buck's brothers died violent deaths, by lynching and knife and gun fights. B.F. English, the father, made a thirteen-year old Buck swear to kill Parry Durbin, his brother-in-law, to avenge the death of Parry English. Robbing his first stage at 22, Buck was in and out of prison most of his adult life, but managed to die a natural, albeit premature, death in 1915. On the way he became Mt. St. Helena's most infamous highwayman.

He was born November 10, 1853, in Oregon, the tenth of eleven children. Family roots were in Kentucky and Missouri but, like many others, the Englishes pioneered in the West looking for better opportunity. The bad winter of 1861-2 was cause for bankruptcy, and may have spurred David English into road agentry, for which he was lynched in Lewiston, Idaho. The next year, they moved on to settle in Solano County, California, near Cordelia. In 1865, downtown Cordelia was the scene of a full-scale English-Durbin shoot-out, in which Parry English died, B.F. English lost an eye and Charley English was partially crippled in one arm. Three years later, in Napa's Spanish town, the third English brother to die, Dan, was killed in a racially motivated dispute. Charley was again shot up, and again survived, with a scarred face and the other arm crippled as well.

In 1870, they moved to Anderson Springs, Lake County, to avoid more bloodshed. Lake County was sparsely settled then, so the Englishes found a niche for themselves and prospered. Despite their rough ways, they, especially Buck, were generous with those they liked and many friends were made. Henry Mauldin, Lake County historian, tells the story that one winter, the Thorne family was desperately poor, but asked the young man to a meal anyway. Seeing they had only coffee and biscuits to eat, he promptly went out, shot another man's hog, and offered it to the Thornes. They fared considerably better after that. Loyal friends like these would keep mum when, later, Buck was in trouble with the law.

From petty thievery, English made the jump to big time crime by stopping the Calistoga-Lakeport stage in 1875. His efforts went unrewarded however, the express box yielding only two brass castings. Fond of making grandiose statements, he claimed the day would come when he would "make Wells Fargo weep". In the meantime, he robbed several Chinese miners on the road. Buck intensely disliked the Chinese, and mistreated them at every opportunity. The law looked the other way in these cases, due to widespread anti-Asian sentiment.

The English boys (Eugene, the youngest, and Charley) branched off into cattle and hog rustling too, and earned the formidable ire of the Great Western Mine superintendent, Andrew Rocca. Hearing gunshots one evening, Rocca found a swaggering Buck showing off his marksmanship by shooting a handkerchief out of the hand of a friend, scaring passersby.

The old world Italian gave the group a verbal lambaste like they had never heard before. Startled, they left immediately. Soon sworn enemies, Buck sent a boastful message through an intermediary that he would "tan Rocca's hide and make shoe strings out of it!" Soon after, cattle started disappearing from the Great Western property.

Unmoved by the threat, Rocca began accumulating evidence on the English gang. Eventually Buck was arrested on rustling charges and sentenced to San Quentin for the first time on October 25, 1876. Good connections and a good attorney got him released after serving less than a year of a two and a half year sentence. Nonetheless, he was in and out of jail for the next six years.

During his times of freedom, English expanded his activities to horse stealing and perhaps murder. According to Henry Mauldin, Buck shot and killed a man in an argument at the Middletown skating rink. He also gained notoriety by besting a professional soldier in a duel in the streets of Middletown. The soldier, a Captain Goode, was seriously wounded in the arm and leg, while Buck came out unscathed.

The English boys' aversion to regular work led to robbing a white farmer of $115 near Lower Lake. Charley was eventually brought to jail for this crime, one of the first to serve at the newly opened maximum security prison at Folsom. He disappeared into Mexico, and history, in 1885. Eugene escaped to Oregon to serve loyally in a militia under the alias Eugene Jones. Local historian, Michael Chegywn, who has researched the English family exhaustively, has conclusively traced Eugene's freedom flight to Canada. Buck was apprehended in Coyote Valley, with the tracking expertise of a Pomo Indian. He received seven years in San Quentin and served four.

Upon his return in 1882, he went straight for a while, driving the Anderson Springs/Lakeport stage line. Old man English died the next year, nearly seventy years old, and Buck drifted out of the country to Ashcroft, British Columbia. Ben English Jr., the only law abiding member of the family, had settled there in the 1850's. Buck worked on wheat and cattle ranches at this time, returning briefly to bring his mother back to Canada. One imagines she was relieved to live more quietly in the last years of her life.

English reappeared in Lake County in the mid-90's, after a stint at

Oregon State Penitentiary for robbery. The governor believed his plea of innocence and pardoned him. He showed up with a younger man, named Breckenridge, he had met while bartending in Portland. Buck's close knowledge of the stage routes was an asset in his next, and last, escapade.

In the past, his stage robberies were performed on the north side of Mt. St. Helena, near the county line. This time, on May 7, 1895, Buck again struck in the same vicinity, between Troutdale Creek and Rattlesnake Spring, within sight of the summer home of Adolph Sutro, one-time mayor of San Francisco. The six passengers - four San Francisco businessmen, a Chinese man and a young boy - were robbed of $1,000. No women were aboard so Buck had no need to display his reputed gallantry toward the fair sex. Allen Palmer was again the unlucky driver for Bill Spiers' stage line. Last robbed four years earlier, Palmer initially thought it was a joke. H.R. Goss from an unpublished biography of Andrew Rocca, relates:

> "He made a jocular reply, but one of the robbers jumped to the horses' heads, and both leveled their guns. The weapons and the profanity which accompanied a threat to blow the driver off the box took all the humor out of the situation and the driver and passengers awaited the will of the highwaymen...
>
> The highwaymen went about their work like old hands at the business, one in particular being as cool as if he was collecting taxes...
>
> The particularly cool robber is about five feet eleven inches in height, the other and shorter is about five feet eight inches. They both wore masks, and each was nearly covered with a dark gray duster, beneath which showed overalls and old shoes. They both wore black slouch hats... The taller man did all the talking as well as all the searching. They were both armed with old-style Colt's revolvers, and cursed and swore at everyone, particularly the Chinaman."

The Chinese man, in fact, was beaten and had his legal papers stolen. Palmer was then told to throw down the strong box, which was broken open with a hatchet. Inside were only worthless packages. The driver of another rig, Byrd Hunt, passed by just then and Buck greeted him by name, much to Byrd's surprise. He hurriedly moved on. Then the two men, still masked, walked off in the direction of Oat Hill. When news reached the authorities, Napa and Lake County sheriffs couldn't decide who had jurisdiction, so English and Breckenridge got a 16 hour head start. The combined force of police and citizens lost the pair for three days.

By the time the desperados had reached Berryessa Valley, their feet had given out, so they boarded the stage to Napa. English was recognized by a young farmer of the area who had known him in earlier days. He alerted the driver who telephoned Sheriff R.A. Brownlee. District attorney Theodore Bell wandered into the sheriff's office just then and was deputized on the spot. With J.N. True and Johnny Williams, the four man posse crowded into a two seated surrey to intercept the stage. They had hoped to wait in ambush on the north side of Mt. George but the stage had already topped the pass. As the two vehicles met, Sheriff Brownlee recognized the tall man beside the driver as English, holding a shotgun across his knees, and Breckenridge just behind him. "Stand them up!", he ordered, but a well practiced English blew the gun out of Brownlee's hands, destroying the weapon. An answering shot wounded Buck, but he stuck a gun to driver John Gardiner's head and shouted "drive fast or I'll blow your head off!" Another shot from Bell tore open Buck's left side, and he was seen to sag against Gardiner as the stage shot down the grade.

With Bell in pursuit, the stage rolled to a stop after the wounded bandit had fainted from pain. Breckenridge gave up without a struggle and both were transported to Napa. So ended the wildest manhunt in Napa County's history. As English lay near death, the first words he uttered to Sheriff Brownlee, when he regained consciousness were, "How many of you fellows did I kill?" Miraculously, no one had been even seriously wounded, to the outlaw's disappointment. Fifty-two buckshot were found in his body, and no one expected him to live. The Englishes though, were a tough lot, and live he did. The young district attorney Bell, only 23 at the time, prosecuted the case successfully, getting a life term for English and 25 years for the accomplice Breckenridge. Bell's career catapaulted to a large San Francisco law firm and later to California and national politics.

An attempt to break jail in Napa was foiled and the now recovered

An attempt to break jail in Napa was foiled and the now recovered English was transported to San Quentin for the last time, to serve 17 years of his life sentence. While there, he may have rubbed elbows with some of the Whitecap murder gang, Osgood, Staley, Cradwick and Blackburn. Sentenced five years earlier for a Ku Klux Klan style killing of a woman, they had committed their crime almost within a stone's throw of Buck's last holdup. In 1912, nearly 60 years of age, English was released a final time, a changed man.

It had been Buck's work, for years, to make the rounds of the prison every night and light the lamps. He instructed his successor in the task and, as he approached the gate, he looked back anxiously at the lamps of the prison yard. "I'm afraid I'll have to come back and give him another lesson," he said, as he bade his friends goodbye.

At the news of his release, Andrew Rocca, still remembering the old threat, commented to his daughter with a wry, sarcastic smile, "I wonder if he still wants my hide for shoe laces!"

Buck English was taken under the care of a patron named Luke Fay for the last three years of his life. He was buried in Colma, California in 1915.

∾　　　∾　　　∾

Despite his record, Buck English had all the makings of a first class citizen. One Sunday early in January, 1878, the faithful of Middletown became edgy when Buck walked into the little wooden church and sat in the rear pew. He and his friends listened to the 45 minute sermon politely, then headed off for a drink at one of the many saloons in town. There Buck entertained the crowd by repeating the sermon word for word, even mimicking the minister's voice and mannerisms. It was said that, by harnessing that exceptional memory through study and discipline, he could have been one of the state's smartest men. Born into the right family, there's no telling what he could have achieved. His lawless upbringing, however, practically condemned him to the life he led.

86

Chapter 4

Gold and Silver
The Mining Era

"Man will be shown counting his wealth in terms of bits of paper representing other bits of scarce but comparatively useless metal that are kept buried in strong vaults. Meanwhile, the soil, the only real wealth that can keep mankind alive on the face of this earth, is savagely being cut loose from its ancient moorings and washed into the seven seas."

John Muir in response to hydraulic mining

Introduction

In California, the Sierra Nevada gold country has hoarded most of the honors and fame as the site of the great mining period, beginning in 1849. Far less known is the fact that Mt. St. Helena was the center of one of the richest quicksilver districts in the country, and remains so on record almost 100 years later. While the fledgling agricultural business tried to get a footing, from 1870 to 1900, mining reigned as the number one industry in Napa and Lake Counties .

The period is replete with stories of entrepreneurs trying to get rich from the earth's wealth and with those using slightly easier means. Many were the stage robberies with the Wells Fargo Express box as objective, staged mostly, as we've seen, by locals like Buck English. Accidents from falls, falling objects, explosions and fire were common and health standards had yet to be established. Mining was a dangerous business, inside and out, as several documented murders will attest. Today, Napa County is in the midst of yet another mining boom, but one proceeding in a far more civilized manner.

The Mayacamas mining district, located in parts of Napa, Lake and Sonoma counties, was the second largest producer of quicksilver in the United States, credited with 455,000 flasks of mercury valued at over $15,000,000 (a flask weighed 90 pounds; 13½ were the container and 76½ pounds were mercury). Only the New Almaden and the New Idria, in Santa Clara and San Benito counties, were bigger producers. The best mines in the Mayacamas area were the Oat Hill, the Great Western, the Mirabel, and the Aetna. The Sulphur Bank, in Lake County was a major producer, and the Redington at the Napa, Yolo, and Lake County border was worth $3,000,000 by 1880. These eight mines, all in California, were the best in the U.S. Two, the Great Western and the Mirabel, are on Mt. St. Helena proper, and will be discussed in detail.

Many Napans sprinted for the Sierra Nevada gold fields in 1849, most returning empty-handed. Some refused to let the dream die and prospected in the local hills for years without much success. About 1858, a rumor spread among the population that the Mt. St. Helena area was rich in silver. It may have started when a father and son team of prospectors came across what they believed was a ledge of solid silver. Fearing claimjumpers, the potential bonanza was guarded closely while the valuable ore samples were taken to town for evaluation. The brilliant specimens turned out to be iron pyrites. Other assayers and fakes, however, were willing, for a price, to hand out a "certificate of quantitative analysis of anything from a brickbat to a lump of obsidian... showing silver anywhere between $20 and $500 per ton."

The rush was on. Every unemployed man in the county, and husband who could escape his duties took to the hills. For several weeks, the mountain and surrounds were turned upside down in the search for precious metal. At night the darkness was lit by hundreds of miners' campfires. During the rainiest part of the winter, one story goes, a man on horseback headed for the mines is informed by the sheriff that all the good claims are taken. "But damn it, isn't there anything left?" Confessing that he might find an outside claim, the man whipped his horse around without reply and "in less than two minutes you couldn't see him for the mud he raised." The excitement lasted until a local assayer, Frank McMahon, burst the bubble by declaring most of the ore worthless and, at best, contained only a trace of silver. The muddy streets of Napa got a boon when the accumulated tons of rock were recycled as paving material.

Silver was forgotten when cinnabar ore was discovered by Seth Dunham and L.D. Jones in 1860 and the first great wave of mining began in Napa County. A new road had been built from Berryessa to Lower Lake and the workmen had unknowingly pushed the bright-red ore over the side as waste. Some of it was assayed at 60% mineral. This later became the Redington mine. It was in this decade that many of the region's mines came into being, including the Yellowjacket, the Ida Clayton, the Phoenix, the Aetna and the Washington.

In the early seventies, silver was, after all, found on the southeast side of Mt. St. Helena and touched off the second wave of mining activity, as feverish as the first. The Silverado find sparked further search for silver in the hills below the Palisades. The Great Western and the Oat Hill began producing and, by 1880, the region was near its maximum production. The eighties and nineties saw an unrelenting flow of mineral from more than 50 mines, with the Mirabel and Palisades mines peaking about 1890. By the turn of the century, the exhaustion of the ore bodies and plummeting prices for precious metals shut the mines down, one by one, and the finest mining era to date came to a close.

The mines idled and decayed for fifteen or twenty years until World War I, when the price of mercury rose dramatically; it was needed for explosives. Old ore bodies were reopened and reamed, and new ones discovered. The industry was once again alive but on a much smaller scale. A whole new generation of miners appeared, working under modern and safer conditions.

Between the wars, activity stalled but World War II brought the price for mercury to a record high. By 1946 all was quiet again. The consciousness of the 1960's brought a new meaning to the word, mercury. Many quicksilver mines were located in the watershed of the newly created Lake Berryessa. Mercury was accumulating in the sediment of the lake and in the fish and waterfowl. Nearly all remnants of mercury mining activity, such as the destructive hydraulic work at Oat Hill, were abandoned.

The one exception was Bill Wilder, who continued to make a living from the earth at the old One Shot mercury mine near Knoxville. On this site on March 4, 1985, Homestake Mining Company began production of gold bars, and the fourth wave of mining in Napa County began. Through sophisticated computer technology, Homestake discovered a rich gold field composed of particles invisible to the unaided eye. A ton of rock must be crushed for every .17 ounce of gold. Nevertheless, 200,000 troy ounces of gold are produced each year, making it the fourth largest gold mine in the country.

The new technology uses cyanide to chemically release the gold, retaining the cyanide for use over and over again. The old roasting furnaces are a thing of the past now. Even Bill Wilder, the last of the old breed, has shut down his one man operation, which once stood side by side with this 20th century corporate giant.

Ida Clayton Mine

The Ida Clayton was one of the first mines to open in Napa County, shortly after the mining craze of 1858-1859. There were at least three periods of activity, all of them unsuccessful economically. Located in Rattlesnake Canyon in the vicinity of Sugarloaf Hill, its total output was perhaps only a few dozen flasks of mercury. In the 1860's, it was developed by the entrepreneurs, Stewart, Jackson and Kellogg, the latter giving his name to the hamlet in Knight's Valley, the former helping to develop it. They built a road to the mine, naming it after the local school teacher. This was the first leg of the Ida Clayton Toll Road, not completed until 1875. By the 1870's, it was owned by the Knight's Valley Land and Contract Company, with one of the original owners, W.A. Stewart, as overseer of the mine. The same company operated the Yellowjacket mine, a half mile away, and was more successful in exploiting its meagre resources. An ore furnace was built a mile and a half down the road, probably in the flat land next to Kellogg Creek. Ore was hauled in carts from both the Yellow-

90

jacket and Ida Clayton mines for processing. A newspaper account from December of 1874 , yields a clue to the temper of the day. Great activity around the two mines, including ground sluicing and the imminent use of hydraulic power, had led to talk of "moving St. Helena Mountain a little closer to Knight's Valley". Water under great pressure has the power to strip mountainsides bare. Few then considered the damage hydraulic mining brought, and the environmental movement was just a seed in John Muir's head.

After 1875, mining apparently ceased for more than a decade. In 1887, there was a minor resurgence when enough metal was taken out to pay for expenses, but predictions of a rosy future faded fast. By the 1890's, it was the property of Calvin Hall Holmes, who owned a good chunk of land on this side of the mountain, and along with his son, operated the Ida Clayton Toll Road for many years. Today, the Ida Clayton mine has long since caved into obscurity and would be well forgotten if not for its namesake.

Yellowjacket Mine

Operated by the same company that owned the Ida Clayton mine, the Yellowjacket quicksilver mine was richer than its sister. No official record of production exists but the *St. Helena Star* in October, 1875 reported 175 flasks of mercury, worth $12,000 had been shipped in the past month. Still, it was a failure and after 1875, was not worked until 1892, when C. H. Holmes was doing some exploratory mining. Speculation on reopening remained just that.

The Yellowjacket is best known, not for its cinnabar, but as the location of the murder of Major Harry Larkyns by photographer, Edweard Muybridge, to avenge his young wife's love affair with the handsome and adventurous major. The trial, held in San Francisco, became one of the most famous in early California history. Impassioned oratory by his lawyer led to Muybridge's acquittal and he went on to produce pioneering photographic work that earned him the title "father of the motion picture."

Muybridge was working in San Francisco as a photographer, when he met his future wife, then Mrs. Shalcross Stone. Flora was a "petite but voluptuous young woman with a sweet face and large, lustrous eyes," married at a tender sixteen years. Muybridge employed her as a photo retoucher and eventually, he paid for the divorce costs. When she remarried in 1871, she was twenty; he was twenty-one years older.

Harry Larkyns came from a wealthy and respectable family in England but was estranged due to an extravagant life style and spendthrift ways. After wasting his patrimony, he served with the British Army in India, traveled extensively in Europe, and served with the French in the Franco-Prussian War. He was described by an acquaintance as a gallant officer. Finally, his fortunes found him in San Francisco, working as a translator and journalist.

One fateful day in 1873, he walked into Bradley and Rulofson, the photographic firm where Edweard and Flora both worked. They all became friends and Larkyns was given permission to escort Flora to the theatre, since Muybridge was often away on business. For an entire year, Flora and the major carried on an affair under the unsuspecting nose of Muybridge. Even the birth of Flora and Harry's child, Florado Helios Muybridge, in April,1874, did nothing to raise his suspicions.

But, in October of that year, the midwife who attended Flora, went to court to collect for her services which Muybridge had to pay. Later she produced a picture of the baby with "Little Harry" written on the back and some letters sent between Flora and Harry. The whole weight of the calamity came crashing down on Muybridge at once.

That summer, Larkyns was in the Mt. St. Helena area producing a map of the silver and quicksilver mines for the San Francisco Stock Exchange. In a sublime state of jealousy and passion, Muybridge resolved to travel north that day to kill Larkyns. Apparently, before he left though, he put his will in order, expecting to be lynched by miners for the deed. At Calistoga, he was directed to the Yellowjacket in Knight's Valley, firing a shot on the way, from his Smith and Wesson five-shooter to see if it was in working order. The buggy followed the one and a half mile road off the main highway to the superintendent's house, where Larkyns was playing cribbage with some ladies in the parlor (one report says it was the Clayton house, in which case Mrs. Ida Clayton may have been present). Five min-

92

utes before Muybridge arrived, Larkyns is reported to have remarked, "should he live until tomorrow, he would be forty years old." Muybridge called the unsuspecting Larkyns out into the darkness and let him know who he was, before firing the single shot that pierced his heart. The major staggered back through the house, stumbled over the back door threshold and fell at the base of an oak, dead. Muybridge followed him part way but was disarmed by a Mr. McArthur who said he was "perfectly cool, his hand did not tremble, nor did he display any passion or nervousness whatever." When he was told the major was dead " he replied that he was sorry, and called for a glass of water. After drinking it, he sat down to read a paper, as though nothing unusual had happened."

Muybridge was completely convinced that the deed was justified, and also fully aware of the penalty he could pay. During his incarceration, he was told he was crazy, to which he replied, "he was never in a more sane condition in his life." Released in February, 1875, he at once continued with his profession, which became his sole passion and solace until he died. Flora Muybridge, denied a divorce by her husband, fell ill in March and died in July, 1875. Florado, robbed of both parents in infancy, was a gardener in Sacramento until fatally struck by a car in 1944. (For a more complete account, read Joan Parry Dutton's, *They Left Their Mark*).

The Great Western Mine

The Great Western was not only the richest producer of quicksilver on Mt. St. Helena proper, but one of the finest quicksilver mines in the United States. Over 100,000 flasks of mercury were shipped from there, valued at over $3,000,000. Only six mines in the country had a better record. Only one mine in the Mayacamas mining district, which included parts of Napa, Sonoma and Lake counties, did better. That was the Oat Hill Mine, credited with nearly 160,000 flasks of quicksilver valued at $5,000,000. The Great Western operated almost continuously from 1873 to 1911, and then was reworked when prices were favorable during the World Wars. Its best years were 1879-1881, when six to seven thousand flasks were filled each year.

The Great Western's origins go back to a man named Finley who, according to Henry Mauldin, first found quicksilver here. After five years, he sold it to E. Green, probably in 1873, when operations began in earnest. As prospects became certain, connection was made between the Western Mine Road and the Ida Clayton Road by 1875. In 1876, Andrew Rocca became mine superintendent, staying until 1900, the mine's most productive years. He was of Italian descent and had extensive experience in mining and waterworks engineering in the gold country before moving to the mountain. After a three month engagement, he married Mary Thompson, the mine schoolteacher, in April, 1880.

In June, two other newlyweds, Robert Louis Stevenson and Fanny Osbourne, were living in the neighborhood and paid a visit. RLS was well-liked by the Roccas, but Fanny was considered dictatorial, outspoken and inconsiderate. Although mining camp life may have seemed harsh to the outsider, strong community ties within created a warm and friendly atmosphere. Regular social events were held. Sunday picnics and fishing trips and Saturday night balls would bring citizens from Middletown and Calistoga, and weddings and funerals marked life's progress.

Andrew Rocca was a man of considerable energy and talent. Besides superintending 250 men and all operations at the mine, he and Mary had seven children and he also found time to entertain an almost endless stream of visitors, some of whom stayed for months. Some of the visitors included directors of other mines in the area, the Newcombs from the Oat Hill, the Grigsbys from the Palisades, and the Randols from the Bradford-Mirabel. W.F. Fisher, owner of a livery stable and stage line in Calistoga, was a guest, as were the Pattens from the nearby toll house. Mollie Patten was "known to thousands of stage passengers over the mountain for her plain-speaking, her witty if somewhat earthy sallies, her shrewdness in money matters and her genuine good heartedness". Billy Spiers came up all the time, sometimes delivering the payroll to the Western and, after 1882, freighting was so good, he installed a repair shop at the mine.

Mining has always been a dangerous business and the Western had its share of accidents and related illnesses. Andrew Rocca himself had several accidents, one a near-fatal fall. In April, 1901, a Chinese

94

workman, named Ah Lock, was killed when he fell down a mining shaft. More insidious were the toxic fumes given off by the ore furnaces. They left the adjacent hillsides barren. *Salivation* was a condition directly related to breathing mercury vapor, leaving victims with serious tooth and gum problems. The worst job at the mine was performed by *soot-men*, always Chinese, who would crawl into the hot condensers and clean out the soot, often leaving them "shaking, toothless wrecks."

Inside the tunnels, the air would sometimes get so bad during warm weather that work would be suspended. By 1890, an air compressor pumped in outside air to relieve this problem. Although forest fires were greatly feared, fires within the community were more damaging. In September,1891, a fire destroyed the fine ore furnace and repairs took two months before it could be reopened. The Chinese camps, made of whatever scrap lumber was lying around, were highly susceptible to fire. There was no central commissary, but rather, each man made dinner over his own fire, and several times the flames escaped, burning large parts of the camp. This could be particularly devastating to the Chinese worker who often stored his life savings under his mattress.

Some 200 to 250 Chinese were employed at the mine at any one time, most engaged in underground work, although some were servants to the Roccas. White workers numbered about 25, all engaged in above-ground work. Most of the Orientals or *Celestials,* as they were called, had left wives at home, but most intended to return when enough money was saved. And save they did, even on the meagre salary, usually half that of the whites. Their soft underbelly was gambling, and they often lost large sums if professional gamblers appeared. Rocca did his best to discourage gamblers, as well as prostitutes, from showing up, but usually to no avail. In 1879, anti-Chinese sentiment reached a high point when discriminatory legislation was passed by the California legislature. The Great Western was forced to let its Chinese workers go.

The president of the nearby Sulphur Bank Mine, however, purposely defied the law so it would go to court. On March 22, 1880, the Circuit Court found the law illegal and, two days later, Chinese were back to work at the Western.

Usually polite and deferential to those of another race, among themselves, the Chinese were not infrequently violent. Once, in the depths of the mine, a man tried repeatedly to light an explosives fuse that was wet, while other fuses burned. Other men, anxiously waiting in the "skip" to surface, grew nervous and left without him. The unfortunate man was able to run to safety before the charges went off. On top, he swore to kill his partner who left him to die, but the other had left the minesite never to return. The worst case of violence occurred in January, 1880, when 125 men were involved in a "bloody row" in which four or five were seriously cut. Andrew Rocca was able to break it up without firing a shot from his rifle but later he said 30 or 40 would have been killed if he had been unsuccessful. The argument started over a hat.

By the turn of the century, the Chinese were passing from the scene, to be replaced by Italian workmen. The anti-Chinese fervor, that dogged them until they left, assumed that they were replacing white Americans in the workplace by working for lower wages. What was more likely was that they performed work no one else cared to do, as is the case with Mexican labor today. So the Chinese disappeared, having done the bulk of the mining work, leaving a few businessmen rich, the timbering that made work in the mine tunnels safe, and the great stonework seen in fences, bridges and old wineries in the Napa Valley.

By 1898, Andrew Rocca was convinced the great fish-shaped ore body at the Western was played out. In 1899, he bought the Helen Mine near Pine Mountain and left St. Helena mountain in May, 1900, returning only once in the last twenty years of his life, although living just ten miles away. Final negotiating squabbles and the owners' refusal to believe Rocca's judgement that the mine was finished, left a lasting bitter impression. Cleanup operations netted some good ore but Rocca's judgement was sound. In the new century, the Western never achieved its old glory and was forced to shut down by court injunction in 1911, when charged with contaminating St. Helena Creek. In 1931, operations resumed when the New Great Western was founded, incorporating some of the old and some new tunnels.

The drop in prices at the end of WWII closed it for good.

Today, the site is easy to find, two miles up the Western Mine road from the highway, a junction known once as the "Western Gate". The road winding above the mine gives fir-spotted views into a little circular valley, now dotted with houses and gardens. On the hillside above, the scars still look fresh. (For further study, refer to *Life and Death of a Quicksilver Mine* by Helen Rocca Goss, one of the finest books of its type ever written.)

The Bradford-Mirabel Mine

Three miles east of the Great Western, as the falcon flies, is the Mirabel mine, located at the very head of the Collayomi Valley. It was the fourth largest quicksilver mine in the rich Mayacamas mining district. Only the Oat Hill, Great Western and Aetna were better, in a time when 63 mines were operating regionally. When it finally shut down in 1945, $1,200,000 in quicksilver had been produced, as well as $1,000,000 in real silver.

Nevertheless, it is best known for its connection to the notorious White Cap Murders case of 1890. For many years after, this was considered the most heinous crime in Lake County history. Despite a heavily documented book on the subject, different versions of the story abound. Even today, a hundred years later, locals in Middletown may be heard debating what really happened.

The story begins about 1861 when Edward W. Bradford and family homesteaded at the junction of St. Helena Creek and what is now Bradford Creek. They were only the second white family in the valley. The Bradfords made a living by farming and hunting, while all about them, the mining fever raged. Mrs. Bradford was a hardy pioneer woman who gave birth to twelve children (three of whom died in infancy) and all without the aid of a doctor. She also made all of the family's clothes. In 1875, a *stringer* of cinnabar was found by one of the Bradford boys in St. Helena Creek. The cows were forgotten as the whole family eagerly sought the source. Located on the east side of the creek, they developed it into what was later known as the Great Eastern. It was sold to a Captain Riley, who abandoned it after 2 or 3 years. In 1878, Edward Senior died at 54, never knowing that he had literally slept on top of one of the biggest quicksilver ore bodies in the country.

The family, grown too large for the first house, had moved into a more spacious model on the south side of Bradford Creek. From time to time, rich cinnabar float rock had been found in the creek near the first house. Evidence of wealth seemed to be everywhere but the source was elusive. Amidst a pockmarked landscape of prospecting holes, the Bradford boys decided to sink another one at the back door of the old house. Only four feet down, they found the long-sought ledge. The ore was "bright vermilion red, and almost pure mineral".

Oddly, little was done for years but show it to visitors. Then, a crude, homemade retort was constructed, and the facilities improved until, by 1888, the Bradford Quicksilver Mining Company was incorporated. By the end of 1891, they had filled 10,000 flasks of quicksilver, at which time the mine was sold for around a half million dollars.

Just a year earlier, the Bradfords were involved in perhaps the most sensational crime in Lake County history. On October 10, 1890, at a bar near the Bradford mine, called the Camper's Retreat, Helen Riche and William McGuyre were killed by a mob of eleven men. The target of the mob, Fred Bennet, escaped unharmed. The Bradfords encouraged and partially organized the action but did not actually participate. They were never implicated in the crime but the black stain on their reputation was never fully removed. Here is the setting.

The Camper's Retreat was right off the old Toll Road one mile north of the Bradford mine. The local miners patronized it for its liquor, gambling and prostitutes. The proprietors were J.W. Riche and his wife Helen, with Fred Bennet, Helen's brother, as an employee. Bennet was an unpopular man with the miners, it was said, because he treated them roughly and cheated them at cards. Another account says he was owner or co-owner of the nearby Bullion mine and was encroaching on the Bradford's property. The miners appealed to the Bradfords for help. It was then planned to tar and feather Bennet and run him out of the county.

About 9 p.m. on October 10, a group of eleven men, chosen from a larger group, advanced on the house, after freeing the horses so no one could escape. They were: William McGuyre and C.E. Blackburn, considered the leaders, Charles Osgood, B.F. Staley, Charles Evans, Henry Arkarro, August Lund, Thomas Martin, A.E. Bichard, J. Archer and Robert Cradwick. All were miners at the Bradford. All were wearing white masks with holes for eyes and nose, made by the miners' wives. These disguises were similar to the White Caps of Indiana, a group not unlike the Ku Klux Klan today. Inside, Riche was watching his wife and Bennet finish a game of cards. When the mob burst in wearing their outlandish costumes, the Riches thought it was a joke. Helen recognized one of the party and tore the mask off Charles Osgood. Someone, perhaps McGuyre, pushed her to the floor and held her down while Osgood fired four 22 caliber rounds into her chest. Many other shots were fired at this time, one grazing Riche superficially on the hip. Meanwhile, Bennet had escaped out the bedroom window and gone for help on a horse that had returned. McGuyre was shot on the front porch, some say before they entered the house, some say after, but most probably he was killed by one of his own men. McGuyre was a surly Irish miner who, apparently, was disliked as much as Bennet. Someone in the mob figured that in the confusion it was a good time to get rid of him. His wife is reported to have said that he was "the meanest man that ever lived" and that "he deserved to be shot".

When Bennet rode into Middletown, a candidate's ball was in progress and was well attended by law enforcement officials. Many in the mob were arrested that night and all within a week. Helen Riche died from her wounds, some say that night, some five days later, and some two months later. Incredibly, there are three versions of Mr. Riche's death also. Most likely he died before the trial started, in December of "apoplexy of the brain." Another indirect victim was Mrs. Riche's mother, who died shortly thereafter. Bennet left the county and his fate is unknown.

Most of the above information comes from Helen Rocca Goss's *The California White Cap Murders,* a book meticulously documented and yet widely disbelieved in Middletown today. One who takes objection to her account is Earle Wrieden, former supervisor in Lake County, whose father rode by the Camper's Retreat the day after the murder. His father was 21 at the time, living in Middletown and working at the mines. He had two days off and was riding to Calistoga to visit. On the front porch of the Retreat, he related to Earle, was not one, but three bodies, all with gunny sacks over their heads. These would be McGuyre, and Mr. and Mrs. Riche.

This same story of three killed that night was related to Wrieden by a daughter of William McGuyre, and to Mrs. Wrieden by McGuyre's granddaughter in recent times. What really happened will never be known, I suppose, until the time machine becomes as familiar a research tool to the historian as the library is today. The trial and sentencing, though, are a matter of record.

The trial, in February and March of 1891, turned into a grand spectacle. The Lakeport courthouse was jammed by spectators every day for two months. Charles Michelson from the San Francisco Examiner was one who was there:

> "There is not much in the way of entertainment at Lakeport and the Whitecap trial is to the little city by the lake what a Patti concert is to San Francisco. The courtroom is always crowded and there is a great demand for reserved seats. Young men bring their sweethearts and mothers bring their babies, and sit through the entire day listening to the story of the raid on the roadside inn and the preparations made by the raiders for their work. Opposite the jury box are ranged a number of seats. Exactly a dozen women, most of whom are young and some of whom are pretty, occupy these seats. In front and to the side of this dress circle are other chairs all occupied by females. Some of these are young girls and all are dressed out in their prettiest clothes and smartest bonnets. At first they carried the theatre-party idea to the extent of chatting pretty incessantly during the trial, but his Honor manifested a disposition to frown darkly and glower in the direction of the dress circle in a way that soon froze the conversation. Now they sit as silently as if they were entirely unacquainted with and very doubtful of each other."

Two separate trials were held, with both Staley and Blackburn convicted of second degree murder. Then Osgood and Cradwick changed their pleas to second degree murder, which were accepted. At the

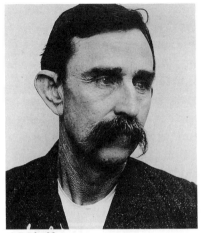
C.E.Blackburn

Robert Cradwick

Charles Osgood

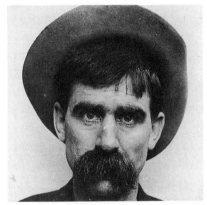
B.F.Staley

Newspaper rendition of Camper's Retreat

sentencing by Superior Court Judge R.W. Crump, Blackburn got 25 years, B.F. Staley got 20 as did Robert Cradwick. Charles Osgood, who fired the shots that killed Helen Riche, was sentenced to 12 years. All were taken to San Quentin. The other six defendants were freed with nothing more than a reprimand.

Lake County residents considered the sentencing, if anything, too light but, immediately, letters were written to the governor asking for leniency. Most of these were from members of the Grand Army of the Republic, a conservative political organization, powerful in those days. Two letters came from Alex Badlam and Horatio Livermore, who owned homes on Mt. St. Helena. Governor Markham eventually reduced Blackburn's sentence to 10 years. And, since he was the leader the other sentences seemed too severe. By 1903, all four were out of prison, never to return to Lake County.

The Bradfords had escaped criminal implication but Frank Bradford told the Burgers of Scotts Valley that it cost him $80,000 to stay out of jail. Later that same year, the Bradford Mine was sold. It was showing few signs of letup and, for many years after, it yielded rich ore. One has to wonder how much the White Caps episode affected this turn of events.

The new buyers were three men named Mills, Randol and Bell, the first syllables of their names forming the word, *Mirabel.* Change of ownership brought other changes - the Chinese were immediately replaced by white labor, a post office was dedicated in April, 1892 (only to be abolished a year later), a boarding house, office building and new furnace were built. The next seven years were the most productive in the mine's history, and a lively community of nearly 300 was formed. Miners brought their families and built cottages for them along the road. White laborers numbered 160 to 180, working the immense ore body that was 100 feet wide at the 300 foot level.

Fortunes at the Mirabel began a slow decline in 1894, when the price of quicksilver fell below $45 from a high of $52.50 during the Bradfords' ownership. The deeper the miners tunneled, the harder the rock became and the poorer the ore. Prospecting was done on minor claims in the area, like the Plymouth and Bullion, but to little avail. Then in July of 1895, the first fatal accident at the Mirabel occurred.

Thomas Habishaw was one of the oldest and most experienced miners in the district. Without warning, a large rock detached from the roof of the tunnel he was working in and crushed him and injured a co-worker, Samuel Farmer. Although the coroner's jury ruled death as accidental, his widow filed suit and was awarded $8,000. Mrs. Habishaw was a formidable woman with an iron constitution. Six of her seven children died in the diptheria epidemic of 1883; she then had six more. The Roccas remember her as having the strength of any man, a staunch friend and tougher foe. I wonder what her role was when the Mirabel appealed the case to the State Supreme Court and lost. Mrs. Habishaw enjoyed good health until she died at 96.

Early in 1898, the old Bradford mine was considered worked out and shut down. The nearby Bullion mine was worked by the same company until 1903, yielding $200,000 in silver. Then, all operations ceased. The town was immediately deserted, all buildings were torn down and carted away and, for the next 20 years, the only activity consisted of tunnels caving and filling with water.

But, like old soldiers, old mines never seem to die. In 1930, Hugh Davey found good ore in St. Helena Creek. Overcoming flooding problems, the Great Eastern was open again for the first time since Captain Riley had abandoned it in 1876. Later, the Mirabel Quicksilver Mining Company decided to take another look at the old Bradford workings across the creek. The ore body had not been completely taken after all, and a half million in silver was recovered during the war years. The price of a flask shot up to $189, enabling them to go on as the ore was gradually exhausted. Final closure was in 1945.

Quicksilver mining is a dead industry in the United States today. Whether it will ever come back, remains to be seen. What's certain is that cinnabar ore is still to be found in these hills and the right economic conditions could mean a mining resurrection. Before that happens, an environmental review would, and should, present a major challenge.

The Palisades Mine

History will do quirky things. In the case of the Palisades mine, it has ignored Napa County's most spectacularly successful silver and gold producer in favor of the Silverado, a financial bust. The Palisades yielded a total of 1,426,621 ounces of silver, 11,463 ounces of gold, 65,000 pounds of copper and a bit of lead. All told, it was several million dollars of metal. The Silverado? Just about $100,000. Not every mine can have a Robert Louis Stevenson.

The Palisades, found 3 miles north of Calistoga at the headwaters of King's Canyon (now Garnett Canyon), had an exceedingly slow start; the area was worked for almost 30 years before production was in full swing. The first claims were staked in 1859, then relocated in the 1870's as result of the Silverado mine boom with such names as the Elephant, the Helen and the Ida Easley. Long suspected to be the best of the lot, the Ida Easley failed to be properly developed by a series of owners through 1882. In 1880-1881, the construction of the Calistoga quartz mill was begun but never finished. Apparently, lack of mining experience caused these failures.

Then, in 1882, Robert F. Grigsby, whose family owned land in upper Napa Valley by the 1850's, bought the controlling interest in the mine. He knew silver mining from his days in Mexico. His partners, Johnson and Bain, were also familiar with the work. Tunneling began immediately and plans were made to build an ore processing mill. It took five years for those plans to congeal. In 1887, the Silverado mine's ten stamp mill was brought down from high on the hill to be installed at the mine, now called the Grigsby. It had to be an incredible job to haul the heavy machinery by wagon and mule down the Lawley toll road.

By 1888, the mill was churning out silver/gold alloy bars, each weighing a thousand ounces, for shipment to San Francisco. For the next four and a half years, the work never stopped. Forty-five men were employed, working shifts around the clock. A small village grew up there, with residences, a boarding house and school. In the best years, serious troubles were few. In November of 1889, two workmen, named Monroe and Smith, tried to fix the pulverizer without stopping the machinery. They were lucky to have been only caught and bruised slightly. In May, 1890, a strike was settled amicably and all returned to work. By the end of 1891, however, the price of silver was dropping, forcing the processing of only high grade ore.

104

Ironically, the efficiency of the operation may have been partly responsible for the low price, by contributing to market saturation.

By the fall of 1892, the price had dropped further and Grigsby was contemplating closure of the mine. Tragedy befell the Grigsby family in late November when their youngest son, Walter, was killed when he tripped and fell into moving mill machinery. No longer interested in the mine, Grigsby closed it in January, 1893 and moved back to Mexico.

The Palisades resurrection took nearly 40 years, but, in 1929, the Banner Development Company resumed operations. The old, ten stamp mill from Silverado was gone, but another mill used a new process called *flotation* requiring a lot of water. Over the next ten years, it was owned by 3 other companies with modest success. All structures were removed in 1941, when the mine closed down. The structure that stands today is a flotation mill, built in the 1950's, that never reached production. The mine site is privately owned now and casual visitors are seriously discouraged from sight-seeing without prior permission.

The Silverado Mine

The Silverado is the best documented mine on the mountain and well-known around the world by readers of Robert Louis Stevenson's *Silverado Squatters*. Devotees of Stevenson, from all countries, make the pilgrimage up the gently switchbacking trail to the cabin site, where he and his bride spent their honeymoon. Some will clamber up the loose talus slope to peer into the darkness of the upper mine shaft. Far fewer will scramble down the steep canyon to the lower mine tunnel, Stevenson's *Treasure Grotto*, which scholars believe was part of the inspiration for his most famous book, *Treasure Island*. It has been 50 years since any mining activity took place here, and the trees have had a century to grow up and obscure the view Stevenson once had from his cabin to the valley floor. Mostly, it's quiet and peaceful in here now, except for the occasional shouts of excited children on weekends. But, 115 years ago, this was a mining operation in full scale production, with a town of at least a thousand people, located on a flat just a few hundred yards away.

The Silverado was born in 1872, when Alexander Badlam, in the company of several others, discovered and claimed the Monitor Ledge above the Toll House flat on the southeast side of Mt. St. Helena. Badlam was the wealthy Mormon nephew of Sam Brannan who managed Brannan's Hot Springs Hotel, and lived summers at his Arcadia home on the shady north side of the mountain. Badlam took three San Francisco financiers: Archie Borman, Coll Deane, and Thomas Reynolds into partnership to form the Calistoga Mining Company (Reynolds, by the way, is the man who visited in the summer of 1880 to inspect the mine before his lease expired, to the embarrassment of squatter, Robert Louis Stevenson). They called it the Calistoga Gold and Silver Mine and it touched off a fury of prospecting, the second silver rush the mountain had seen in 15 years.

The mine employed about 45 men, but most preferred to gamble on a strike of their own rather than work for minimum wage. One newspaper of the day described the rush as:

> "An old fashioned forty-niner excitement, as to start prospectors with sledge hammers, spades and pick axes, out with lamps, in the cold drenching rain." Two or three miles along the Knight's Valley side was pockmarked with mining locations. Pine Flat was temporarily deserted. "The mountains for three miles west and east of Mount Helena were prospected in the frenzy for silver, and more, for the hoped-for flitter of real, free gold."

Once again, as in the first rush of 1859, hundreds of camp fires dotting the mountainside could be seen from the valley at night. Eventually, when no other strikes were discovered, most of these men either left or went to work at the Calistoga Gold and Silver.

It is a curious fact that the existence of the Monitor Ledge and others nearby were known for years before being investigated. As an 1875 government mining report states:

> "The existence of these ledges was known long prior to their location, as they were crossed by a well traveled mountain trail, but the presence of silver was not suspected, it being the popular opinion based on the statement of some itinerant geologist, that silver and gold bearing veins could not exist in the Coast Range."

Alexander Badlam was able to find an honest assayer who found his first samples worth $10 to $20 a ton. When the mill opened, two years later, records state the ore was worth $60 to $80 per ton. As the tunnels drove deeper, the assays jumped spectacularly, and it was not uncommon to find $1,000 a ton ore. According to Anne Roller Issler, the highest assay from the Silverado was $2,180, although one surveyor reported $3,000 a ton in his field notes of 1875. Andrew Young, the first foreman of the mine, having spent 13 years at the Comstock Lode in Nevada, said the Silverado ore was identical. A description of the ore, from Slocum and Bowen, 1881:

> "the quartz was very beautiful, being porous, or full of cavities which were lined with crystals, which sparkled like diamonds. These crystals were colored frequently with oxide of iron, and ranged from a dull yellow to a bright carmine. The silver appeared here in the form of chlorides, and the ore was sometimes quite rich."

The factory-sized, two-story, Silverado Stamp Mill was built in June, 1874 in a meadow, just below what is now the junction of the old toll road and the new highway. Springs on the slopes above, now tapped for residential use, supplied the necessary water. Upon opening, it began crushing 20 tons a day, worth $2,000 in bullion. Again, from Slocum and Bowen:

> "The ore was drawn from the mine to the mill with heavy teams. The process of gathering the silver here was similar to that practiced at any of the silver mines, and consisted of large pans, holding several barrels, called 'settlers' into which the crushed and powdered ore passed from the stamp. In these quicksilver, common salt, etc. were placed, and the whole mass set to revolving by means of a fan-wheel inside. After being taken up by the quicksilver, it was roasted, the mercury going over and leaving a residuum of gold and silver."

As the miners continued to bring out rich ore from the seemingly endless vein (hand chipped or drilled in those days) , a small city was begun on one of the few level sites the mountain offered, just south of the mine. Two hundred eighty-two lots, most of them 25 by 150 feet, were staked out in 13 blocks. Streets were 60 feet wide, sprawling up and down the mountain at all angles. They had names like Garnet, Gold, Silver and Pearl, reflecting the wild optimism of the time.

107

Fourth avenue, never constructed, was to run parallel to the stream that runs between the mine and the toll house flat.

The ore carts would run down Silver Street from the base of the ore dump, turn left at Gold Street in the center of town, left again on Market Street to the highway, renamed Main Street, and then to the Stamp Mill, ¾ mile away. Market, Silver and Gold streets are the only ones left today.

The new town of Silverado was christened on October 11, 1874. In attendance, were about a hundred people from the neighboring towns and a few from San Francisco. They gathered under a huge oak with Alex Badlam as master of ceremonies. William A. Stewart, owner of the nearby Ida Clayton Mine, made the opening remarks:

> "Surrounded by prejudice, with all the opinions of those learned in mineral formations against them, the owners of this valuable property labored steadily to convince one and all that here on the slope of our grand old mountain were hidden treasures which required but to be developed. The result convinces the most critical that hasty judgements were once again in the fault. These mighty ledges bid fair to rival the far-famed Comstock."

Badlam spoke next, predicting the town would be the second Virginia City, of Comstock fame. It was already distinguished by being "located nearer the top of a mountain than any other town in the State, and closer to Heaven than sinners usually get."

There was also musical entertainment, followed by O.P. Hoddy, (mentioned in the *Silverado Squatters* as the Toll House bartender), who made the closing speech. Soon after, the surveyor's map was filed at the County Recorder's office naming as proprietors, William Patterson, William Montgomery, (first owner of the Toll House), and John Lawley, who, six years before, had completed the toll road named after him. The next month, the Silverado Hotel was opened by Robert Thompson. It stood in the center of the mining town, one of the first major structures to be built and the last to go.

Other permanent structures appeared: Badlam's mining office, Friedburg's grocery, a schoolhouse, blacksmith shop and, of course, several saloons. The other noteworthy event was the town's first

108

murder. One month and a day after Edweard Muybridge put a hole in Major Larkyns heart at the Yellowjacket, Franklin Hadley murdered Scotty McDonald for less noble reasons. Hadley was missing a bottle of whiskey and thinking McDonald had stolen it, went to his cabin early on the morning of November 11. Scotty, unsuspecting, extended his hand in greeting. In reply, Hadley "cut him down across the forehead and face with it" (a sharp instrument), "and striking him other blows on the head that crushed through his skull in two places." Hadley was arrested that night, Scotty died later of his wounds. The newspapers called the crime at the fledgling town a "baptism in blood."

As to the success of the mine, a rumor, still floating about today, can fairly be put to rest. It stems from Stevenson's short history of the mine as told to him by locals:

> "The whole affair, mine, mill, and town, were parts of one majestic swindle. There had never come any silver out of any portion of the mine; there was no silver to come. At midnight trains of packhorses might have been observed winding by devious tracks about the shoulder of the mountain. They came from far away, from Amador or Placer, laden with silver in 'old cigar boxes'. They discharged their load at Silverado, in the hour of sleep; and before the morning they were gone again with their mysterious drivers to their unknown source. In this way, twenty thousand pounds' worth of silver was smuggled in under cover of night, in these old cigar boxes; mixed with Silverado mineral; carted down to the mill; crushed, amalgamated, and refined, and despatched to the city as the proper product of the mine. Stock-jobbing, if it can cover such expenses, must be a profitable business in San Francisco."

Stevenson himself put little faith in this story, and so have the Silverado's historians. No confirmation of this intrigue is known. The bonanza continued through 1875 but, by May of the following year, the Monitor ledge had been cut off by a fault and production suspended. Through the rest of the year, 'drifting', or tunneling to relocate the ledge was unsuccessful and, by 1877, the mine was officially abandoned.

According to the most reliable sources, $140,000 had been spent to finance the mine, but net proceeds amounted to only $93,000. The "second Comstock" had left its owners $47,000 in the red; a mighty disappointed lot they must have been. Good timber was at a premium, so buildings were dismantled and the lumber hauled away, only the Silverado Hotel, and John Chapman's boarding house were left at the mine site. The latter became Stevenson's domicile in 1880. It too, was hauled away for scrap lumber and souvenirs after the *Silverado Squatters* was published. The two-story mill still stood there, abandoned, in 1880 when Stevenson made note of it. Seven years later, its machinery was moved down the hill for use at the Palisades Mine. It is reported that an old stone wall is the only surviving remnant today.

The mining law of the day said that a company must do $100 of improvements on a property each year to maintain a claim. Apparently the owners did so in 1878 and 1879. But due to disagreements among themselves they failed to do so in 1880 and that summer, the claim lapsed. Rufe Hanson laid claim to it for a year, with Stevenson's help, but Rufe liked the thought of being a property owner more than working it. When his claim lapsed, Daniel Patten, who later would own 500 acres and the Toll House, took out a patent on the mine and claim jumping came to an end. He formed the Silverado Mining Co., after which some work was performed, then reorganized it into the Mount Saint Helena Mining Co., a corporation. Little came of this and, in 1913, Daniel Patten died. Before he did though, he passed the gold bug on to his son, Harry.

It became Harry's lifelong dream to relocate the lost Silverado vein. Some mediocre ore samples were taken to the Palisades mine for assay in the 1920's, then, around 1929, a new tunnel was dug a distance of 75 feet and an existing tunnel lengthened 90 feet. The State Minerologist Report states that Patten had 40,000 tons of $12 ore blocked out and planned to have it processed at the new flotation mill at the Palisades mine. Apparently, Harry overestimated his resources because records show no Silverado ore ever milled at the Palisades.

The Depression years put an end to any serious attempts in mining. When Mollie Patten died in 1932, she left to Harry, her sole heir, an estate heavily in debt. Harry, the dreamer, the idealist, the inventor, had little use for the business affairs of men, and chose to

110

Edweard Muybridge

Alexander Badlam

Andrew Rocca

Underground at the Silverado Mine.
The building represents the stamp
mill a mile down the road.

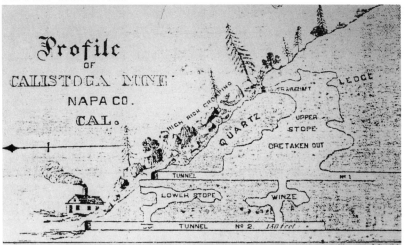

pay in land when his credit accounts came due. An acre at a time, the estate was whittled away until all that was left, was the mine site itself. Although the storage shed on Silver Street still held dynamite and fuses into the forties, they served mostly as reminders of another era.

The Pattens moved off the mountain in 1942 to make a living in Napa. Harry, who loved the mountain and knew every hill, canyon and stream by heart, never really recovered. He died in 1950, firmly convinced that the lost Silverado vein was still waiting to be found. Robert Louis Stevenson State Park became a reality in 1949 with a gift deed of 40 acres from the Livermore family. The Pattens graciously allowed hikers to cross their property but, in later years, grew worried about liability problems. At one time, it was planned to close the main shaft above the monument with dynamite but nothing came of it. With all the spelunkers, climbers, and casual hikers that have used this site, it's a wonder no one has been seriously hurt.

Finally, in 1988, after twenty years of planning, the Patten property was dedicated in a small ceremony, for inclusion in the state park. For the first time in 100 years, the Pattens were without property on the old mountain.

The potential for further mining still exists at the Silverado. Low grade ore can be found easily but the lost vein remains a question mark. The likelihood of any work occurring is, of course, very slim due to its state park status. Barring fire or Presidential edict, the most likely use in the future will be as it is today. The trees will grow, the sunlight will stream down at midday, and the quiet and peace of the forest will accompany the mine, slumbering in memories.

Chapter 5

Flora of Mt. St. Helena

There is a wonderful diversity of plant life on Mt. St. Helena, making it one of the richest sites in California. Four hundred, seventy-seven species of plants from 76 families have been identified in Robert Louis Stevenson State Park alone. For the whole mountain, the number would rise even higher. None, as yet, are listed as rare or endangered by the state or federal governments. The California Native Plant Society, however, recognizes two, the Socrates Mine jewel flower and the Rincon Ridge buckbrush, as rare and endangered in California. In addition, their watch list includes another ten plants of limited distribution.

It's easiest to understand this diverse array of greenery by dividing them into plant communities. There are four on Mt. St. Helena: oak or foothill woodland; grassland; chaparral or brushland (3 sub categories); and the forest community (also 3 sub categories). All four are what botanists call *climax communities*, the ultimate stage of development subject to change only through fire or disease.

Even though the composition within each plant community has changed somewhat in a century and a half, we are still looking at basically the same ecosystems the pioneers saw in 1850. A mixing of species will occur at community boundaries, but at a distance their distinction is evident.

There is a fifth, ephemeral community, the burn site, perhaps better thought of as a habitat. Burns, of course, can occur in any of the four major plant communities. They commonly go through two stages, pioneer and transition, before again establishing as a climax community. When the south and west slopes of Mt. St. Helena burned in September, 1982, the winter *El Nino* rains quickly followed.

Seeds of *fire annuals,* like globe gilia (Gilia capitata), long dormant in the soil, sprouted the next spring, creating a riot of color. This pioneer stage passed quickly. Buckbrush, manzanita and cham-ise resprout so efficiently from seed, burl, or trunk, that the transition stage was also fleeting. A decade after the fire, the chaparral is once again a stable climax community.

Plant Communities

Oak woodland, the first plant community, is found on the west and southwest slopes of Mt. St. Helena, below 3,000 ft. The small, sturdy, blue oak (Quercus douglasii) dominates this community. The acorns of the blue oak are a favorite food of the California woodpecker. It will lay up a store of these for the winter by drilling holes in the trunks of oak trees and placing them blunt side out, so few but a woodpecker can retrieve them. The blue oak prefers the hot, dry hillsides in company with its common associate, the interior live oak (Quercus wislizenii). Woodland manzanita (Arctostaphylos man-zanitae), can also be found here and in the chaparral community.

In wetter locations, like creek bottoms and north slopes, grows the beautiful coast live oak (Quercus agrifolia). A single tree can spread its branches 130 feet, and, in pure stands, it will form an impressive continuous canopy. The canyon live oak (Quercus chrysolepis) is aptly named, growing best on the steepest hillsides. The wood is so hard that early pioneers used it for the heads of mauls, hence its other name, maul oak. On mesas with deep soil and gently sloping hillsides is found the California black oak (Quercus kelloggii). It is easy to identify by its large, deeply lobed, bristle-tipped leaves, unlike any other western oak.

The classic oak woodland habitat on Mt. St. Helena is above Lake Ghisolfo in lower Kimball Canyon. This is in private hands and not available to the public. In fact, most visitors to RLS State Park will not experience oak woodland firsthand but see it from a distance. Perhaps some day hikers will be able to start at the base and travel through all the mountain's life zones.

The second plant community, grassland, is the least extensive of the four, found on the south and west slopes below 2500 feet. It is

114

comprised almost entirely of exotic (non-native) species, mostly European annual grasses. Native California bunchgrasses, sensitive to livestock trampling, have been replaced by aggressive, introduced varieties like bromes, foxtail, wild oats, and ripgut grass. Fortunately, clump-forming bunchgrasses have not entirely disappeared. They can still be found in out-of-the-way places, for example, on level stretches of remote stream courses.

Chaparral brushland is the dominant plant community on the upper south and west slopes of Mt. St. Helena, running right up to the 4,343 ft summit. No dark and tangled forest floor can present as formidable a barrier to travel as the prickly, clothes-rending, interlocked branches of a hillside of manzanita and ceanothus. From the early pioneers to modern cross country hikers, chaparral has been dreaded by one and all. Growing too low to tunnel under and too brittle to walk upon, a hiker's best bet is to find a ridge line to follow. There, the brush is a bit thinner, and sometimes there are rock out-crops and animal trails to make travel easier.

In Santa Barbara County, ceanothus (California Lilac) reaches its finest development, arborescent stands growing as high as twenty feet. It was here, on a hike to Cathedral Peak, overlooking Santa Barbara, that a friend and I contemplated a quarter mile of steep, trail-less hillside, covered in ceanothus, 15 feet high. To our delight, we discovered that the canopy was so high we could tunnel underneath, following animal trails quickly and easily. The dense canopy had shaded out all other plants. Hikers on Mt. St. Helena are not that lucky, due to the prevalence of ground hugging varieties of chaparral.

Locally, chaparral grows in 3 sub communities. Regular or mixed consists of *chaparral* species only. These would include 7 species of California lilac (Ceanothus), eight of manzanita (Arctostaphylos), coffeeberry (Rhamnus californica), chamise (Adenostoma fasciculatum), mountain mahogany (Cercocarpus betuloides), and the well known toyon, or Christmas berry (Heteromeles arbutifolia).

Chaparral growing on serpentine soil is the second subcategory. Serpentine soil is toxic to many plants, supporting only those tolerant of its high magnesium content. Some species like leather oak (Quercus durata) and whiteleaf manzanita (Arctostaphylos viscida), will grow naturally nowhere else. To these species, patches of serpentine are island havens, allowing them to grow where they could not grow otherwise. Serpentine soils harbor some of the rarest plants in California. This chaparral subcommunity can be found on both the north and southwest slopes.

A third subcategory is the gray pine-chaparral community. It can be found on the west, south, and north slopes. In company with toyon and Bay laurel, gray pine (Pinus sabiniana), is often found on serpentine soil. Its graceful, canting trunk grows at a characteristic angle to the slope, branching two, three or four times at midlevel. Gray pine will find enough sustenance to grow to 60 feet from nutrient-poor serpentine soil; soil where even grasses will refuse to take.

The gray pine was prized by California Indians for its sweet and oily seeds, second only in importance to those of the oak. Still known as a digger pine to most, the name has been changed, due to its derogatory insinuation. The original name, *Digger,* was given by the mountain men of the 1820's, who saw the women digging for roots. Later, the name developed a negative connotation. Gray, foothill, and ghost pine have all been proposed, with gray most commonly accepted.

The fourth, and last, plant community, the forest, is also divided into three subclasses: mixed evergreen forest, douglas fir, and knobcone pine forest.

Forests can be found on all sides of Mt. St. Helena. Often they are confined to wetter canyons and stream courses on the south and west sides, becoming the dominant vegetation type on the north and east slopes.

The mixed evergreen forest is a lush community easily seen while driving Highway 29 or the Ida Clayton road. It will not climb much above 3,000 ft. The main species are douglas fir, tan oak, sugar pine, ponderosa pine, madrone and black oak (although deciduous, the black oak is frequently found with mixed evergreen species, and sometimes in the foothill woodland community).

Tan oak (Lithocarpus densiflorus) has been called a botanical mongrel. Its flowers are like those of a chestnut, and its straight trunk is very un-oak like. But its leaves and acorn seed are those of the oak family. Some have suggested Lithocarpus is a kind of *missing link*

Gray pine with the typical high-forked trunk.

Mixed evergreen forest on the Ida Clayton Road

118

between the chestnut and oak. The bark of tan oak has a high tannin content, once sought after by the tanning industry. Trees were either cut down or, sometimes, only stripped of bark on one or two sides, allowing the tree to continue growing (reportedly, some of these can still be seen). Out of this activity came another of its common names, tanbark oak. The industry is no longer active.

Ponderosa or western yellow pine (Pinus ponderosa) is well known for its smooth, platy bark in mature trees. Sometimes these plates grow 4 or 5 feet long and a foot and a half wide. Ponderosa tolerates the widest range of soils, climate and altitude of any pine in North America. Their arrow-straight trunks up to 200 feet high have made it the most popular lumber pine. Full of light and majesty, they prefer to grow in small pure groves or singly, standing slightly apart from other trees. The ubiquitous ponderosa can be found on all sides of Mt. St. Helena.

The pacific madrone or madrono (Arbutus menziezii), was named by Father Crespi of the Portola expedition in 1769. He immediately noticed the resemblance to its close relative and sometime namesake, the strawberry tree (Arbutus unedo). Huge specimens can be seen along shady St. Helena Creek on the north side of the 'pass'. Their gnarled, picturesque trunks will grow as much as 50 feet horizontally to find enough light. The peeled red-orange bark, glistening after a rainstorm, is one of the prettiest sights in the forest. Another of its relatives in the heath family, the manzanita, has similar but darker red, skin-tight bark. The hardwood madrone makes a bright, smoke-free fire and is a wood splitter's dream. When a large tree dies, a circle of new trees, called a goosenest, grows in its place, like a redwood.

The second subgroup in the forest community is the douglas fir forest. Pseudotsuga menziezii is widely distributed to all four compass points of Mt. St. Helena, usually concentrating in steep-canyoned watersheds. The douglas fir is an immensely useful and impressive tree. It is the tallest of all North American trees, except the two sequoias, growing up to 220 feet high and 17 feet in diameter. It serves as the Western Hemisphere's premier lumber tree, and grows so fast that it is called a weed in the northwest. Identification is easiest by looking for the numerous small cones underfoot in all seasons.

Tiny bracts poking out of the scales have been likened to mice tails.

The last subgroup is the knobcone pine (Pinus attenuata) forest, conspicuously found on the fireroad below the south summit, but also occurring on the dry, rocky mountainsides north of the main peak. Small, unattractive and often growing "thick as cornstocks", the knobcone goes unappreciated by man. Twenty or thirty feet tall and six inches to a foot in diameter on the average, this anemic looking pine is actually a marvel of adaptation. It can grow on soil so poor that no other tree would survive.

The closed, curved pine cones grow in spirals of 3 to 7 attached directly to the trunk itself (most pinecones grow on branch ends). These appear after only five years of growth, but may remain for the life of the tree. In some cases, the cones never fall and are 'devoured' by the trunk. They must wait for the death of the parent tree through fire for their seeds to be released. In this way, the knobcone is like a chaparral species, indeed often sharing the same rocky hillsides. When burned, the seeds retake quickly and form dense groves. The knobcones seen from the south summit pavilion were last burned in the 1964 Hanley fire. Although diminutive, these trees represent a nearly mature knobcone pine forest.

Species of Note

Mt. St. Helena, due to its height and relatively remote setting, serves as a sort of outpost for flora geographically isolated from other stands. Following is a description of these island populations.

Sugar pine (Pinus lambertiana) finds its southernmost extension in the North Coast ranges on Mt. St. Helena. They do not reappear until Monterey County, about 200 miles south. In 1900, the well known botanist, Alice Eastwood, made a note of the small grove of sugar pines just below the main summit. Although only 40 to 50 feet high, their thick bole and flat-topped, ravaged looking crown indicated they were mature trees. Mollie Patten pointed out other specimens to her on a ridge above the Toll House Inn.

When conditions are optimal, sugar pines will grow up to 200 feet high. This makes it the fourth tallest tree in North America, the undisputed monarch of pines. With its straight, smooth trunk unclut-

120

Sugar pine, estimated to be 200 years - just below the north peak.

tered by limbs below the crown, many consider it the most beautiful pine tree. It secretes a sweet, gummy substance for which it is named. Its best known feature is the size of its cones. They will average a foot and can be two feet in length. When green, they weigh over 4 pounds - an impressive missile when falling from a hundred or more feet (they give a new twist to the word, *widowmaker*).

It was the size of the sugar pine cone, one of which was given to pioneer botanist, David Douglas, that led to its discovery and naming. He reasoned a cone so large must come from a large tree (not so logically, it turned out; the redwood has the smallest cone). He tramped into the wilds of Oregon in 1825 to find it, pursued by Indians who nearly took his life. He escaped to announce his discovery to the world, only to die a gruesome death in Hawaii soon after, trampled by a bullock, after falling into a pit meant as an animal trap.

Incense cedar (Libocedrus decurrens) like the sugar pine, will not grow farther south in the North Coast ranges. They are easily seen on Mt. St. Helena, about 4 miles south of Middletown off Highway 29. The red furrowed bark of the incense cedar is often confused with the redwood. Cedar, however, has a bright red bark while the redwood is more red-brown. John Muir was one admirer of the cedar's foliage:

> "No waving fern-frond in shady dell is more unreservedly
> beautiful in form and texture, or half so inspiring in color and
> spicy fragrance. In its prime, the whole tree is thatched with
> them, so that they shed off rain and snow like a roof, making
> fine mansions for storm-bound birds and mountaineers."

Mount Konocti manzanita (Arctostaphylos elegans), one of six species here, has its southernmost extension on Mt. St. Helena. It is named for the dormant volcano on the shores of Clear Lake in Lake County. The many species of manzanita look stunningly similar to the uninitiated, so bring along a plant expert to tell the differences.

The tallest tree in the world, the coast redwood (Sequoia sempervirens) once grew prolifically in the shady canyons on Mt. St. Helena. Now it is mostly confined to small groves in remote Rattlesnake Canyon. There, it can benefit from the life-giving summer coastal fogs, funneling in through the Russian River Valley. Mt. St. Helena

122

is about 30 airline miles from the coast, representing one of the farthest eastward extensions of redwoods in the state.

There are other species, not distinguished by geographic isolation, but of particular interest to the amateur botanist and they are noted below for their historical, cultural or botanical significance:

The first tree to leaf in the spring and the first to drop leaves by late summer is the California buckeye (Aeschulus californica). With the leaves gone half of the year, it is easy to see the shiny brown, pear-shaped fruit (2 to 3 inches long) suspended on branch ends or littered about the tree's base. The buckeye gets its name from this fruit, reminiscent of the deer's large, limpid brown eye.

The California nutmeg (Torreya californica) is a small, sparsely distributed tree with prickly foliage and a curious green fruit known as an aril. California Indians valued the wood for its strength in bow-making. As part of the yew family, it can easily be confused with the western or pacific yew, now much in demand for its bark which yields taxol, an anti-cancer drug. The pacific yew however, is not found on Mt. St. Helena.

Other trees of note are: sargent cypress (Cupressus sargentii), more prominent in misnamed Cedar Roughs near Lake Berryessa; the beautiful pacific dogwood (Cornus nutallii), whose stunning white flowers, six inches broad, will remind many of Yosemite Valley; and giant chinquapin (Castanopsis chrysophylla), smaller specimens of which can be found on the upper fireroad of Mt. St. Helena. Their seeds are enclosed by a brown, spiny, chestnut-like burr. There are also shrub forms of the live oak and interior live oak, growing 3 to 12 feet high in chaparral.

Other species of interest include spice bush (Calycanthus occidentalis), a favorite of Robert Louis Stevenson. When crushed, the leaves give off a pleasant spicy aroma, while the flowers give an oaky fragrance like an old wine barrel. Giant wake robin (Trillium chloropetalum) is found growing in moist soil under forest or brush cover in early spring. Its deep red petals contrast with surrounding, somber forest green. Surprisingly, five species of native orchids are found on the mountain, but only by the most dedicated and persistent seeker.

Appropriately, they go by such beautiful names as phantom orchid, elegant rein orchid, and ladies tresses.

Long before European varieties were planted, wild grape (Vitis californica) dangled like jungle lianas from the highest tree branches in the riparian community. Tapping underground streams in the summer, wild grape can send out twisty and curving trunks a hundred feet long. Sometimes, they will have a single point of attachment to an oak limb 75 feet above, and plunge to the ground in one fell swoop, ten or twenty feet from the trunk. They give the impression the plant grew straight up unsupported until finding a limb to grasp at last. Most likely, the vines grew up with the tree, securing a grasp on the next higher limb before the old one fell off with age. That would mean some of these agile climbers are at least 100 years and possibly up to 200 years old!

Exotics

An exotic is a botanical term for a non-native species introduced by accident or design. When they escape cultivation and are successful (called naturalizing), they sometimes become invasive. Often, native species suffer due to a competitive invader. Many national parks and land conservatories have regular programs to eradicate or control exotics in order to encourage native plants under siege. On Mt. St. Helena, there are few exotics compared to natives. Left uncontrolled, however, they could have an adverse impact on native plant communities. Exotics have shown up most prominently as escaped cultivated species in Troutdale Canyon on the northeast side, and as grasses on the southwest slopes.

The worst invader on the mountain is Spanish Broom (Spartium junceum), a tall shrub with attractive racemes of yellow flowers. Probably escaped from cultivation after Russell's Trout Farm was abandoned in the mid-sixties, it has overstayed its welcome. It now vigorously blocks a portion of the abandoned trail along Troutdale Creek and competes with native riparian vegetation. The state park is aware of the problem but is straitjacketed by a lack of funds to combat it. In its native Europe, it was used for sweeping out dwellings, hence the name.

Abandoned homesteads are likely places to find naturalized exotics and Russell's is no exception. After wading through the Spanish broom, one encounters periwinkle (Vinca major) covering both banks of a stream, annual bulbs, holly (Ilex), and next to a decomposing foundation, a loquat tree (Eriobotrya). Ahead is the main clearing and two diversion ponds made of native stone. Once they were filled with locally bred trout, awaiting many an eager fisherman. Today, the ponds are filled almost to the top with 25 years of mud and leaf mold (Russell's is state park property but access is private).

Other homesteads can be found on the mountain with clearings nearby for orchards. Here grow neglected fruit trees, unpruned for many years, still bearing a crop each year. English walnut (Juglans regia), edible fig (Ficus), and several kinds of apples (Malus) will never be invasive since they seldom reproduce without the help of man. These abandoned orchards are slowly dying, one tree at a time. Gradually they will be swallowed by the returning forest reclaiming its old land.

On the southwest slopes of Mt. St. Helena, facing Kimball Reservoir and Knight's Valley, invasive European annual grasses dominate the broad hillsides and valleys of their plant community. They were first introduced by Spanish explorers, who carried feed grain for their mules and horses. The newcomers spread quickly and were well-established before Anglo-Americans arrived. These include wild oat (Avena fatua) and several species of the Lolium genus, a type of rye-grass. Some not so welcome are bromes like ripgut grass (Bromus diandrus) and red brome (Bromus rubens), and barleys like Foxtail (Hordeum jubatum). Grass communities are well established and no plans exist at present to reintroduce native bunchgrass.

In a final footnote, an exotic from China should be mentioned, the evil smelling, tree of heaven (Ailanthus altissima). It can grow to 60 feet high, often forming screens or groves in disturbed areas and along highways, but rarely competing in an established plant community. It was first brought to the Gold Country a century ago by Chinese miners. Tree of heaven (some call it, tree from hell), can be highly invasive, reproducing at epidemic rates, by sprouts from underground roots. When handled, tree of heaven will leave you with a strong, unpleasant stink. A word of advice: use strong soap after contact.

Rare and Endangered

As mentioned earlier, as of now, there are no plants on Mt. St. Helena listed by state or federal agencies as rare or endangered. The California Native Plant Society, however, lists two species in their highest priority, Class IB, plants rare and endangered in Cali-fornia. In addition, there is one species listed as Class 3, about which more information is required, and nine species listed as Class 4, those that are uncommon but not endangered.

Socrates mine jewel flower (Streptanthus brachiatus) has only four known populations in the world. Two are on Mt. St. Helena. It was originally found near the Socrates Mine on Cobb Mountain in Lake County. A biology professor from Pacific Union College, Dr. Don Hemphill, made the first Napa County discovery. Two serpentine 'islands' on the southwest face of Mt. St. Helena harbor this rare member of the mustard family.

Rincon Ridge buckbrush (Ceanothus confusus), once called Mt. St. Helena buckbrush, is a mound-forming species, up to 18 inches high. Its distribution is limited to Rincon Ridge, northeast of Santa Rosa, and on Mt. St. Helena. In the past and even today, there is con-fusion over its identification, thus the name, confusus. A very close relative, Calistoga Ceanothus (Ceanothus divergens), also has a confined distribution, mostly in the hills southwest of Napa Valley.

Plants that are rare but not endangered include the very recently discovered Mt. St. Helena morning glory (Collina oxyphylla); two-carpeled flax (Hesperolinon bicarpellatum); nude monkey flower (Mimulus nudatus), growing in wet, gravelly or serpentine soils; rock daisy (Erigeron petrophilus); Napa wild parsnip (Lomatium repostum); Cobb Mountain lupine (Lupinus sericatus); and the tall snap dragon (Antirrhinum virga Gray), which blooms on stalks higher than a man's head. Howell's broomrape (Orobanche valida Howellii), is a parasitic plant living off its host, the fremont silk tassel (Garrya fremontii). Chaparral Lily (Lilium rubescens), adapts also to the redwood forest ecosystem, where it is called redwood lily.

126

The Russian Connection

There is a fascinating historical footnote to conclude this chapter. In 1840 and '41, Il'ia Voznesenski, a naturalist from the Russian colony at Fort Ross, collected native California plants while making the first recorded ascent of Mt. St. Helena. The collection was shipped to the Russian Academy of Sciences in Leningrad and promptly forgotten for nearly a century. In 1936, it was shipped back to San Francisco for identification. Thus, it took two world trips and nearly a 100 years for these plants to be named, just 100 miles from their origin.

Most of the plants were collected near Fort Ross and in (present-day) Sonoma County, but some could only have come from Mt. St. Helena. Voznesenski was somewhat lax in labeling his plants' locations, but some that were, had this interesting tag: "m. St. Helenae et desertum St. Rosae", the mountain of St. Helen and the desert of St. Rose. John Howell Thomas, in *Leaflets of Western Botany*, April, 1937, gives these insights:

> "In June,1841, in the heat of early summer, as Voznesenski and his party traversed the hot and desiccated country beyond Santa Rosa in his ascent of Mt. St. Helena, well might he have called it a desert. Those inhabitants of Sonoma County who now live between Santa Rosa and Mt. St. Helena would probably not be highly edified to hear their home district called the Santa Rosa Desert, but one can well imagine the feelings of Voznesenski and his companions as they traversed the brushy hills and mountains. The hardships endured and the difficulties surmounted can be vividly imagined by those who are acquainted with the region, and the label on these plants tells in one word, desertum, that the first ascent of Mt. St. Helena was not easily accomplished. It is to be regretted that no account by any member of the party who made the historic ascent is known."

Some of the plants with the desertum label were chamise, mariposa lily, yerba santa, campion, and the tall snap dragon (Antirrhinum virga Gray), the latter now on the Native Plant Society's Watch List. Some exotics Voznesenski noted, plants now considered weeds, were already established at that early date. Annual bluegrass, wild radish, mallow, and peculiar-looking tomatillo are now among the commonest, most widespread plants in the state. Voznesenski was a thorough and diligent collector, including plants that have never naturalized like the garden pea, rue, hollyhock, and tomato.

The Russian's collection contained 214 species, many unknown to science at the time. If they had been properly catalogued and named then, it would have been as important a record as any the great pioneering botanical expeditions produced. Voznesenski's name today would rest alongside famous botanists like Thomas Nutall and David Douglas. As it stands, it is merely a decent collection of Sonoma County flora, an intriguing but minor footnote to botanical history.

Dogwood

Chapter 6

Fauna of Mt. St. Helena

The greater Mt. St. Helena area has one of the best diversities of fauna in California. No one knows its full extent though, because a thorough study has never been done. There does exist a compilation of species for Robert Louis Stevenson State Park (RLSSP) by Bothe State Park ranger, Bill Grummer. It is upon that list that this chapter is based. Due to time and monetary constraints, the RLSSP list does not represent a thorough field study, but is based on a relatively small number of sightings and several independent studies. Nevertheless, given what we have, a fair idea of the range of animal life on the mountain can be achieved.

The RLSSP list contains over 200 separate animal species, including over 100 birds, 43 mammals, 17 reptiles, 9 amphibians, and 1 lone fish (rainbow trout). Also included, are nearly 60 insect species, but this number is preliminary, and would certainly rise by hundreds or even thousands with a complete survey.

Besides well-known species, like the California mountain lion, the northwestern black bear, and the great horned owl, Mt. St. Helena is home to lesser known but equally important residents like the ring-tailed cat and the arboreal salamander (a tree climber). Anyone who sees the beautiful, tri-colored Mt. St. Helena mountain king snake has made a rare, prize sighting. Two of the world's most respected raptors can also be seen by a patient observer: the rare and endangered peregrine falcon is a resident here, while the golden eagle will fly over, but does not, at present, nest here.

Such a variety of wildlife is not accidental. Mt. St. Helena is rich in 'ecotones', a term coined to describe an area where two or more plant communities meet. American Heritage Dictionary defines ecotone as, "An ecological community of mixed vegetation formed by the overlapping of adjoining communities." Wildlife biologists tell us that these transition zones are rich in wildlife, more so than in a single plant community. It makes sense, because an ecotone is basically two or more communities in one.

Ecotones are easy to find on Mt. St. Helena. For example, let's take the southwest face, from summit to base. Near the south summit, we have knobcone pine forest which soon abuts dense chaparral, giving way briefly to a pure stand of canyon live oak. Chaparral then continues on down, enclosing islands of specialized serpentine plants, and finally ending in oak woodland near the base of the mountain. Other sides of the mountain are equally rich in ecotones. The beneficial symbiosis between the plant and animal kingdoms found here will continue as long as humans keep their intrusions to a minimum.

Mammals

The Columbian black-tail deer is by far the best known indigenous mammal on Mt. St. Helena. These shy animals prefer the forest habitat for cover, but are seen foraging in woodland and chap-arral, crashing easily through dense thickets when surprised. Some species of deer migrate, but the black-tail spends its life within a mile or two of its birthplace. Deer are strict vegetarians, browsing on the tender shoots of their favorite plants like scruboak and buckbrush. They are the only large game animal left in California with a healthy enough population to justify a regular hunting season. Of course, hunting is strictly forbidden in the park.

Many may be surprised to hear that the northwestern black bear still roams the canyoned slopes of Mt. St. Helena. Its cousin, the grizzly, was probably exterminated in this region by the end of the 1870's, although rumors of the last "griz" shot hereabouts, circa 1920, persist. Since their demise, the black bear has expanded its range, moving into the grizzly's old habitat. The black bear prefers the mixed evergreen forests of the north side but has been sighted on the fireroad. The relatively mild winters here mean hibernation is unnecessary, so it is probably active year-round.

The last of the state's great land predators is the California mountain lion. It has survived, despite human predators, because of its elusive habits. In fact, some people who spend their lives in lion habitat have never seen a big cat. They will stalk the same coniferous forests and chaparraled hillsides as the Columbian black-tail deer, their chief prey. Now that they are protected by law statewide, we can expect a stabilizing or slight rise in their numbers. This may help control the sometimes volatile deer population, but pose little threat to man. Authenticated attacks on people are quite rare.

The other member of the cat family on Mt. St. Helena is the California bobcat or wildcat, also reclusive and rarely seen. It is a tremendously successful species, found everywhere in California except for parts of the Central Valley. They like wooded ravines or dense thickets in the chaparral. The bobcat uses its small size (2 ½ feet long, 15 to 30 pounds) combined with strength and agility to prey on rodents, rabbits and other small mammals in thick cover.

The gray fox is one of the larger mammals one is likely to see on the mountain. Still, its diminutive size can be surprising. The average fox is 2 feet long, less than 1½ feet high at the shoulder, and weighs 7 to 13 pounds. This allows it to travel the maze of animal trails underneath the chaparral, impenetrable to us larger life-forms. Unlike other members of the dog family, it can climb leaning trees or even low-branched vertical ones. A good place to see one is on the southwest slopes of Mt. St. Helena where the chaparral meets the oak woodland.

The other member of the dog family found here is the wily California valley coyote. Extremely adaptable, it is found in all life zones but prefers open country. The coyote, along with deer, is one of the few large animals to increase in range and population since the arrival of white Americans. This is partly a result of its intelligence and adaptibility, but mostly a result of the North American wolf's extermination, whose habitat it inherited. The majority of the coyote's diet consists of small mammals like rabbits, gophers and mice. Occasionally they kill poultry or small livestock. For this, they have been shot, trapped and poisoned despite the fact that this predation is far outweighed by their service to the rancher as a rodent exterminator. Locally, war on the coyote is negligible due to the diminishing livestock industry.

The ring-tailed cat can be distinguished from its relative, the raccoon by incomplete, black tail rings, and the lack of a face 'mask'. It is strictly nocturnal, spending the day in a rock crevice or hollow log, coming out only in the dead of night to hunt mice. It is so good at this that miners sometimes allowed ring-tails to inhabit their cabins. This led to another common name, miner's cat. They are not commonly seen on the mountain, but have been spotted on the north and south peaks.

Fourteen kinds of bats are found here, the only mammals capable of true flight. A membrane stretched between the elongated fingers is its 'wings'. It is not blind, as is commonly thought, but uses echolocation, a series of high pitched squeaks, to locate any obstacles and, probably, prey. Bats can best be seen at dusk when they come out for a brief period to snare insects. Some bats will eat fruit and the blood of other animals, but only insectivorous species are found on the mountain.

Many other mammals on Mt. St. Helena, too numerous to mention in detail, include mice, wood rats, gophers, rabbits and their predators, the California lowland mink and the redwoods long-tail weasel; insectivores like shrews and moles; and omnivores, like skunks and the marsupial Virginia opossum - the latter introduced into Los Angeles County from the east coast around 1900.

From there, the opossum has spread to most of the state, appearing in Napa County as recently as the 1970's. With its affinity for water, it will move out of the hills and into the city limits, by way of municipal waterways. Opossums are fond of making nightly raids into backyards for any leftovers to be found in the cat or dog dish. Its undiscriminating palate means it will eat nearly anything edible, one reason this newcomer is such a successful competitor. We can expect to see its numbers increase on Mt. St. Helena, and in the surrounding townships.

Perhaps the most surprising animal sighted on Mt. St. Helena was a river otter in 1985. It was seen by Jim Hench of Napa on a cold, rainy, blustery New Year's Day, as it was crossing the fireroad just below the south peak junction. The otter is presumed to have traveled up the Napa River, ascending Kimball Creek Canyon to the fireroad. Soon after, a river otter was reported swimming in a reservoir owned by the Livermores, on the opposite side of the mountain. If this was the same one, which seems likely, since otter sightings are uncommon here to say the least, then it traversed the entire mountain, an elevation gain and loss of around 6,000 ft.! Strange as it seems, this kind of behavior is not unknown. Otters will travel 50 to 60 river-miles in a year, and go overland during the mating season.

Reptiles

There are 17 reptiles listed as known on Mt. St. Helena, consisting entirely of lizards and snakes. The five species of lizards include the western whiptail, with a tail twice as long as its body, the western skink and the foothill alligator lizard.

The elongate alligator lizard is well-named, its body covered by overlapping scales that make an unnerving sound when in motion. Sometimes they slither out from under leaves or rocks in the garden and startle those whose defense mechanisms register 'snake!' for a split second.

The western fence lizard and the sagebrush lizard have been called blue-bellies, for their blue undermarkings. Almost every hiker has seen them doing 'pushups' on a rock, which I assumed was for a ventilating effect. Not true. The male will flash his blue markings as a territorial defense against other males, and sometimes for courtship displays. When defending territory, one male will attempt to get his opponent's head in his jaws and then, as if in a wrestling match, 'throw' his opponent.

Of the twelve snakes found on the mountain, eleven are non-venomous. Sometimes in the spring or summer, in the still, deep pools of a spring-fed stream, you may see an aquatic snake sharing your swimming hole. This is the amphibious version of the western garter snake, almost identical to the terrestrial garter. Docile and non-agressive, they pose no threat, making them the most popular of pet snakes.

The rubber boa, also extremely docile, is identified by its blunt tail and chocolate-brown color. The notorious boa constrictor is a larger relative. When a rubber boa is threatened by predators, the blunt tail goes up in the air instead of the head, fooling enemies into striking the expendable tail instead of the more vulnerable head area.

Another constrictor is the common king snake, one of the few animals in the world to make the rattlesnake go on the defensive. The king is nearly immune to the rattler's poison and will, in chance encounters, strangle and swallow him whole.

The rarest snake and one most prized by collectors (collecting is strictly forbidden in the park) is the Mt. St. Helena mountain king snake. Tri-colored with red, black and white bands, it can be mistaken for the deadly coral snake. It likes the mixed evergreen forest and borders of rocky streams. It is not yet listed as rare or endangered, although it is very much localized here.

The western rattlesnake (Crotalus viridus Oreganus) is the only dangerous reptile on Mt. St. Helena. Dark gray, olive or brown in color, it is powerfully built, growing to 3 or 4 feet in length. (In some other locations it reaches 5 feet.) The ominous rattling sound is made by loose rings of horn-like material on the end of its tail. Two common misconceptions should be corrected concerning these rattles. The first, is that a young rattlesnake without rattles is harmless. In fact, the young are poisonous and will inflict venom. Second, the number of rattles will tell chronological age. Again a mistake: one rattle is added each time the snake's skin is shed, which varies but can be up to three times a year. Rattlesnakes are most likely to be out in warm, but not hot weather. Watch for them sunning on trails or roads, or on rock piles (see chapter 10 for snakebite treatment).

Amphibians

Three of the four world groupings of amphibians are found on Mt. St. Helena: frogs, toads and salamanders. The fourth group, caecilians, are legless, wormlike amphibians found in the tropics. Amphibians do not have the ability to restrict body water loss and will dry out quickly and die without moisture.

The friendly and fearless rough-skinned newt, a type of salamander, can be seen by the dozens after the autumn or winter rains fall. In a contradictory manner, it often seems to be heading away from water, but studies show it will soon return. The newt won't mind at all if you pick it up for a closer look. Its bright orange under-coloring is impossible to miss. Here, from, *The Klamath Knot*, David Rains Wallace gives a vivid impression:

> "Hardly a lake in the Klamaths is without legions of rough-skinned newts - six-inch, lunk-headed salamanders with orange or yellow bellies. Their other name, water dog, attests to this abundance, since uncommon things seldom are called dogs. Newts spend spring and summer in lakes, where they breed, then take to land and spend winters underground. Rainy nights in spring and fall are times of mass newt migration during which one may stumble over a newt every few yards along a trail. A migrating newt is awesome, a rubber toy of a creature waving spindly legs as though it's a clockwork toy, but persistently climbing almost vertical slopes through a tangle of leaf litter and herbage that soon would exhaust a man of comparable size, its silver-flecked eyes unfocused on any conscious goal or reward. Spring-migrating newts seem to be moving away from the nearest body of water as often as toward it, but their numbers in summer lakes belie this impression of random movement. Experiments indicate that newts return to the water in which they   hatched, and that they often return even though blinded, mutilated, or removed some distance."

There are five other salamanders found on the mountain, including the solid-black colored black salamander, the wormlike California slender salamander, the yellow-eyed salamander, the Pacific giant salamander, one of the largest land salamanders at a foot long, and the tree-climbing arboreal salamander. The arboreals will nest and breed in their favorite tree, the coast live oak. Eggs, looking like grape clusters, are often suspended by thready filaments in the nest cavity.

The two frogs found here are: the California yellow-legged frog, never venturing far from streamside (like another water lover, the water ouzel), and the misnamed Pacific tree frog, who rarely climbs trees. As you approach a pool in following a stream course, the tree frog gives its presence away by plopping into the water. It changes color quickly, like a chameleon - green, brown or bronze. It grows less than two inches long but outsings the western toad, 2 or 3 times its size. Because it is solitary and reclusive, the best time to see the western toad is a rainy night in the spring.

Birds

A fine array of over 100 species of birds is found on Mt. St. Helena, making these aviators by far the most likely form of animal life you will see there. If occasional and rare sightings are included, the total would rise perhaps five or ten per cent. About 12% are raptors, or birds of prey, represented by hawks and owls. Other groupings include hum-ming-birds, woodpeckers, game birds, like dove, pigeon and quail, and songbirds like wrens, thrushes, warblers, finches, flycatchers and sparrows. Surprisingly, even jays and crows, with their squawking and croaking voices, are considered songbirds. Since there are so many species, only those of widespread interest are mentioned here (see Appendix C for complete list).

As its name implies, the European starling is an introduced species, brought to North America about 1890. It has naturalized successfully nationwide. Starlings will often show strong flocking behavior in which large groups wheel and turn in perfect unison. This hypnotic mass movement may be performed by as many as 100,000 individual birds. The starling can be seen all year but most commonly over the nearby vineyards in winter. Taking cover is advised when they are directly overhead!

Perhaps the best-known of all songbirds is the American robin, common enough to be sighted on most field trips. The northern mocking bird, however, is the undisputed king of song, able to mimic not only all other birds, but other animals, farm machinery and musical instruments! Its latin name, Mimus polyglottus, means *many-tongued mimic*. Look for it on Mt. St. Helena during the cool months.

A mountaineer from the Sierra Nevada, Clark's nutcracker will sometimes wander far, as on the day Ranger Bill Grummer made a rare sighting on the summit of Mt. St. Helena. Another, more aggressive member of the crow family is the Stellar's jay, differentiated from the scrub jay by its crest of head feathers. Both, along with crows, have earned their reputation as 'camp robbers.' They are very common throughout the year on the mountain.

The common raven is a large, all-black, bird preferring mountainous areas. Its rounded wings and wedge-shaped tail in flight distinguish the raven from its cousin, the crow. It will nest on 'inaccessible' cliffs. (We found a nest of three juveniles while rock climbing high on the 700' west face of Fairview Dome in Yosemite. They were ensconced in a five foot deep hole in the otherwise smooth granite, while the mother perched unconcerned downcliff, waiting patiently for us to tiptoe past.)

The American crow, on the other hand, nests in trees no great distance from the ground. It is black but with a purplish sheen, while the tail appears squared in flight. The crow is less commonly seen on Mt. St. Helena than the raven, but it also can be seen year-round. Gregarious, appearing in large flocks, they are among the most intelligent of birds. Like ravens, they are opportunistic eaters, going for carrion, fruit, insects or planted crops. (They have little fear of people, as evidenced by the one that landed noisily on top of my truck cab parked at a Baja, California beach. Someone had bandaged an injured leg with bits of old clothing. Despite the handicap, it pursued me around the vehicle squawking loudly, looking for a handout!)

One of the most agile and daring flyers is the white-throated swift. It never rests anywhere but in the nest, catching insects on the wing by the hour. Its preference for the airways not only extends to courtship displays but actual mating in flight. In the ultimate display of acrobatic sex, the male and female approach from opposite directions, join in copulation, then tumble end over end for up to 500 feet! They are often seen around their rocky home cliffs throughout the year on the mountain. Never slowing a bit, the swift will approach the entrance to its nest, a small crevice in the cliff, at terminal velocity and disappear inside, unscathed. The white-throated swift, fastest of North American swifts, will go into semi-hibernation in cool months or when the food supply is low. A good place to see one is on the main summit.

Even harder to follow in flight is Anna's hummingbird. Easiest to see while hovering, its brilliant plumage and nectar-feeding habit make it unique in the avian world. A friend of mine, who always wears a bright red cap, attracts this bird on almost every field trip.

Six species of woodpecker inhabit Mt. St. Helena, including the migratory red-breasted sapsucker, seen in the cool months. Its reputation as a destructive bird comes from pecking holes into the cambium and sap layers, often killing the tree. The species most likely seen here is the acorn woodpecker, whose energy to burn goes into pecking holes in oak or gray pine to store its favorite food, acorns of course. Why this hoarding is necessary is a mystery, since acorns have always been plentiful for squirrel, birds and men.

The reclusive pileated woodpecker can still be found in denser forests. Its size is astonishing, sometimes a foot or a foot and a half high. The pileated has been described as looking like the cartoon character, Woody Woodpecker. In real life, it is not as sociable. It does not adjust to man's ways and populations diminish along with the disappearance of forests.

Birds of prey have long established an agreeable work schedule, with owls taking the night shift and hawks the day shift. At least three species of the owl family live here: the misnamed screech owl, whose voice is really a series of soft, whistled notes; the great horned owl, whose deep and resonant, *hoo, hoo-hoo* begat the term, *hoot-owl,* is named for the 'ear tufts' raised in moments of excitement; and the pygmy owl, who stands out for two un-owlish traits: the pygmy will often hunt by day, and is not silent in flight. Most owls have downy edges on their flight feathers to dampen sound.

A fourth species, the well-known spotted owl, has been taken from the obscurity of the forest to the limelight in recent years. The spotted owl has been heard but not seen yet on a remote part of Mt. St. Helena. Since all owls are reclusive animals, identifying their calls will be the best way to 'look' for them.

Hawks, eagles and falcons are the raptors found hunting by day on Mt. St. Helena. Of the four hawks present, the red-tailed hawk is by far the most commonly seen. It is also the easiest to identify by its prominent light-orange tail feathers. The sharp-shinned hawk and its larger relative, cooper's hawk, were, along with the goshawk, once considered the most destructive to domesticated farm animals. Both were thought blood-thirsty because of kills left uneaten. Nowadays, we understand better the predator-prey relationship and the balance they achieved long before man sought to 'even' things up. The

138

northern harrier, also known as the marsh hawk, is found here only in the warm months, best identified by its habit of 'working' a field back and forth in a methodical fashion.

The dark-brown golden eagle is the largest raptor in the nation. As big as three feet long and with a seven foot wingspan, the eagle can soar many minutes without a wingbeat (in Canada, we saw one riding a thermal, with wings motionless, slowly rising until out of sight)

They will take fairly large prey, like grouse, woodchucks, rabbits, and even an occasional fawn. Eagles will also kill livestock but only those sickly or crippled. They are found year-round on Mt. St. Helena, hunting open slopes, but do not live here. One reason may be the resident peregrine falcon, who will vigorously and repeatedly drive off and even kill the much larger eagle.

Hawks are built for soaring, with ample, rounded wings but falcons are born for speed, having sharp, pointed wings and smaller bodies for increased agility. They are simply the best hunting birds in the world, as falconers knew centuries ago. Three falcons hunt the open skies of Mt. St. Helena. The American kestrel, once confusingly called the sparrow hawk, is the smallest North American falcon. It will use its perch for hunting, diving suddenly on prey, or hover over open fields until spotting mice, lizards, snakes, frogs or grasshoppers. They often nest and hunt close to roads and settlements.

The prairie falcon is much more typical than the kestrel, nesting on remote steep cliffs and hunting birds and small mammals. It is almost as fierce as its famous relative, known earlier in this century as the duck hawk. Once classed as a harmful species and persecuted by hunters, egg collectors and pigeon fanciers, the peregrine falcon has had its rightful name and reputation as a noble hunter restored.

Peregrine Falcon

The peregrine falcon is, without peer, the fastest, self-powered animal on the face of the Earth. Estimates of maximum speed range from 180 to 276 miles per hour. The 1992 Guiness Book of World Records cites a 1968 German study as proof of the bird's unrivaled superiority. When diving for prey or in courtship displays at high speed, called the stoop, a peregrine was clocked at 168 mph flying at a 30 degree angle, increasing to 217 mph at 45 degrees. At these speeds, peregrines have been known to overtake and pass small aircraft.

To sight prey from a mile away and keep it in focus at 200+ mph requires fantastic eyesight. Peregrines have what we call binocular vision- seven times the power of human eyes. Their eyesight has been compared to reading a newspaper a mile away. When the falcon spots its prey, it tucks its wings and dives. One or two pumps of the wings and maximum velocity is reached. With a stunning blow, the prey is usually killed outright. If the catch is small, it is immediately seized with powerful talons; if the prey is large, the falcon may take a turn and grab it in midair, or sometimes let it fall to the ground. It can also attack from below, rolling over at the last moment and breaking the neck of its prey with its feet. If not hunting to feed its offspring, the kill is taken to the nearest safe tree. The peregrine's favorite meal is mourning dove, rock dove, or band-tailed pigeon.

In the spring, the male and female peregrines will look for a nesting site on the most inaccessible cliff they can find. A cave or ledge with a protective overhang is sought and, importantly, a gravelly floor. Peregrines have lost the nest building instinct and scrape a small depression in the gravel to keep eggs from *taking flight* too early. Three or four, round, red-brown eggs are laid, after which incubating duties are shared by both sexes. In a little over a month, the hatchlings use a special, temporary feature on the head, called an 'egg tooth' to saw through the outgrown home. Eating constantly, they grow ten times birth size in 3 weeks. They are full grown and ready to fledge, or take their first flight, in 5 weeks. Mortality is high in the first half year, from predators like the eagle and the great horned owl. If they survive into the autumn, they will have acquired most of the skills they need to stay alive, and disperse to find their own territory. Adults may live 12 years or longer in the wild.

The word, peregrine, is Latin for 'wanderer'. When suitable habitat is not available nearby, the falcon may wander great distances to find it. Some local peregrines have been tracked to South America. Others have nested on the Oakland Bay Bridge. They are not strangers to the world's cities. In this country, skyscrapers in Los Angeles, New York, Baltimore and Washington D.C. are inhabited by peregrines, some purposely released there. In fact, man and falcon have a long and distinguished history together.

∽   ∽   ∽

For centuries, man has admired the strength and intelligence of the falcon. The sport of falconry was born in Persia, about 2,000 B.C., when it was discovered the raptor could be trained to hunt for a master. Falconry reached its apex of popularity in Europe during the Middle Ages. A pecking order evolved; only royalty could hunt with the best species of falcon. The gyrfalcon was used by the royal family, the peregrine by an earl, the goshawk by a yeoman, and the sparrow hawk by a priest. Women hunted with merlins, and the commoners had to be content with other raptors. Falconry began its long decline with the invention of guns.

The falcon's revered partnership with men was forgotten over the last several centuries. Its reputation changed to that of a destroyer, especially if one asked pigeon fanciers in England. Pigeon is the peregrine's food of choice, and it is thought to have followed its favorite prey into the cities of the world. Regular campaigns to destroy the falcon were lauded by the public, with further depredations by egg collectors. Their reputation as vermin continued as late as the mid-1960's. Nevertheless, the falcon has a wonderful adaptability and determination to persist in the face of threats to its survival. It was not until DDT was introduced into the biosphere that the falcon was threatened with extinction. DDT became widely available in 1946. It soon became science's miracle chemical that could do no wrong. It was to the mosquito what aspirin is to the headache. There are even reports of people bathing in the stuff!

Soon after, nesting failures and the desertion of long-active peregrine eyries became commonplace. A census conducted east of the Rockies in 1942, reported 275 active eyries. In 1964, there were none. In California, 200 known pairs dropped to 10 by 1970. This was not a marginal species being surveyed, but one found on every continent in the world except the Antarctic; a long- lived bird with a low mortality rate after the first year; a species equally at home at sea level or at 13,000 feet in the Himalaya. It took about twenty years but by 1970, DDE, a breakdown product of DDT, was determined to be the culprit.

DDE will cause a thinning of the bird's egg shells so that they can break under their own weight before the eyas, or young, can hatch. Since the peregrine is at the top of its food chain, it is at the greatest risk. In 1972, DDT was banned and the peregrine was placed on the federal list of rare and endangered species the following year.

Through a program of captive breeding and releasing at centers in Ithaca, New York, Boise, Idaho and Santa Cruz, California, the peregrine has made a stunning comeback. From ten pairs in 1970, 120 pairs are flying the California skies today. Recovery is occurring more slowly in the Rockies and the eastern U.S.

More sobering, though, is the continuing presence of DDE in the environment. The situation on the Pacific Coast is the most disturbing. Here, the too-thin eggshells of shore-dwelling peregrines make human intervention compulsory for its reproduction. The migratory nature of the coast peregrines means they winter in South America. There they become contaminated with DDT where it is still used as a legal pesticide.

In the North Coast Ranges and Mt. St. Helena in particular, the situation is better. Direct intervention has not been necessary and hatching rates have been high. One of the reasons is the non-migratory habits of the local peregrines and their prey.

Nevertheless, according to Dr. Monte Kirven, professor and wildlife biologist, DDE levels in peregrine eggshells on Mt. St. Helena have not dropped significantly in over a decade. Kirven has studied these birds in the field every summer for 13 years, working for the Bureau of Land Management. He says eggshell thicknesses were 16% lower than normal in 1977 and they were the same in 1991. Until peregrines can reproduce without our help, the recovery program can not be considered complete.

Why then, with the non-migratory habits of local peregrines, are dangerous levels of DDE still affecting their eggshells? A 1985 report by the California Dept. of Food and Agriculture has shown that DDT is a stubbornly persistent chemical. Of the 99 soil samples taken in 32 California counties, all contained varying amounts of DDT. Illegal use of DDT was ruled out. In 1983, of 90,000 pesticide use inspections, none involved DDT. In addition, there was concern over the chemical, dicofol, in commercial use known as Kelthane. In the field, Kelthane can be a direct source of DDT and DDE. However, after monitoring, levels of DDT found in Kelthane were too low to account for DDT residues.

In 1991, for the first time since 1977, Mt. St. Helena's resident peregrines failed to raise a single eyas. It has been documented that, as peregrines grow older, they can concentrate higher and higher levels of DDE in their bodies. The reason for this recent hatching failure can best be explained by the persistence of DDT in the environment. It has been nearly 20 years since the nation-wide ban on this chemical. We can only hope its disappearance will come soon.

The fate of the peregrine falcon is still uncertain. Loss of habitat, such as encroaching hillside vineyards, is a serious threat on Mt. St. Helena, as is human intrusion. Uninformed landowners and hikers can disturb nesting falcons enough to cause hatching failures. The best thing we can do is give the falcon the space it needs to survive. The peregrine needs lots of open space; it will defend up to eight square miles of territory. Education and a benevolent attitude from land owners and visitors is a paramount need, as is the establishment of a Peregrine Falcon Habitat Protection Area.

People first noticed peregrines on the mountain in the 1890's. It is probable they have lived on Mt. St. Helena for hundreds, perhaps thousands, of years. Peregrines have their own sense of history, and return year after year to the same eyrie. It is my hope there are enough of us who care to see this magnificent bird of prey inhabit its ancestral eyrie for many more millenia. The solution is simple. It takes a lot of effort to alter a landscape, but very little to leave it alone.

Chapter 7

Volcanic, But Not A Volcano

"Generations of geologists have been driven to despair by the scrambled rocks of the Coast Ranges. Rocks that are both complex and nondescript, that clearly defy some of the most basic and dependable principles of geology, that lack vital kinds of evidence and - to add the cruelest insult of all - are very poorly exposed. If all rocks resembled these, the science of geology could never have been developed. Geologists have needed every insight they could gain from study of simpler rocks elsewhere to reach some broad understanding of the chaotic jumble of broken and disordered rocks that are the Coast Ranges."

Alt and Hyndman, *Roadside Geology of Northern California*

A few miles southwest of Mt. St. Helena, on Petrified Forest Road, is the Petrified Forest, one of the finest examples of a Pliocene redwood forest in the world. Here, ancient redwoods were toppled by herculean ash flows, (similar to Mt. St. Helens), buried, and turned to stone. They were discovered in the 1850's, but not excavated until 1871 by Charles "Petrified Charley" Evans, while clearing his field. The following year, they were turned into a tourist attraction and, in 1880, visited by Robert Louis Stevenson. Today, it is still popular with tourists worldwide, although typically neglected by locals.

In the most recent pamphlet circulated by the owner of the Petrified Forest, the first sentence reads: "Over three million years ago the volcano, Mt. St. Helena, erupted 7 miles northeast of here." Despite the fact that, as early as 1905 and continuing to the present, every geologist to study the region has found no evidence to suppose Mt.

144

St. Helena was a volcano, the widespread myth persists today. It is the purpose of this chapter to explain how and why it is volcanic, but not a volcano.

History of Geologic Thought on Mount Saint Helena

The problem may have begun with State Geologist, Josiah Dwight Whitney, the first professional geologist to write concerning Mt. St. Helena. Whitney was well respected in his time, so his beliefs tended to become dogma. Unfortunately, many of his pronouncements have proven wrong. In his technical *Geological Survey of California* and also in the popular *Yosemite Guidebook,* Whitney declared the Yosemite Valley a product of a great, sudden downdrop of the earth's crust. His *catastrophism theory* was rendered obsolete by a sheepherder/mountaineer named John Muir, who proved the slow, steady grinding of glaciers was the cause.

In 1865, Whitney published his well-received *Geological Survey of California.* It is of interest not only for its volcano theory but for a curious report of a localized explosion:

> "Another fact, connected with the volcanic character of the rocks of Mount Saint Helena was testified to by a number of independent and reliable witnesses at different places in this vicinity...in December, 1859 a tremendous explosion was heard in the mountain, like the discharge of heavy artillary, causing a distinct vibration of the ground like an earthquake, except that the cause seemed to be local and was referred by all to the mountain itself, where the noise seemed to originate and from which in all directions, for many miles, it was distinctly heard. It is not unlikely that it may have been caused by the falling of heavy masses of rock in some of the subterranean cavities which we know to exist in these volcanic regions."

[Strange as the report of an 'explosion like heavy artillary' is, it would not be the only one. Similar events occurred in 1878 and again in 1943. From the *Weekly Calistogan* of January 1, 1943, we have reports from residents of mysterious rumblings, accompanied by flashing lights and soaring fragments. The noise seemed to come from the heart of the mountain, sounding like 'big guns'. Neither the Army nor the Navy reported gunnery practice in the area. Several faults are known to exist on the mountain, possibly indicating shifting fault planes, but the origin of these mysterious rumblings remains a mystery].

Further on in his report, Whitney states that the volcanic material spread over the country to the east and southeast appears to have originated from Mt. St. Helena. Here then, may be the beginnings of a misunderstanding spanning two centuries. In all fairness to Whitney, the fault may lie less with him, who only indicated a possibility of the volcano theory, and more with journalists who ran with the idea and never looked back.

Only eight years after the Whitney paper, *Bancroft's Tourist Guide to Napa Valley* touted Mt. St. Helena as an extinct volcano. It was doubtless in its affirmation that eruptions from the mountain had felled the Petrified Forest. Newspapers, magazines and county histories all expounded this idea until it was firmly set in the public's mind. They pointed out the flat summit as evidence that the volcano had blown its top in some distant geological age. Despite the lack of any hard evidence, the 'bowl' between the north and south peaks was confidently spoken of as the remains of the old crater.

In 1885, California's State Mineralologist, Professor Hanks, reported the existence of a geologic phenomenon on the highest peak. From the *St. Helena Star* of September 18:

> "...he found a second 'Giant's Causeway' of five sided basaltic columns, covering an extent of many acres. The formation of the columns he pronounced to be most perfect, being of a pale greenish-yellow color, and presenting a beautiful appearance. The entire summit of the mountain is composed of this formation, and the professor expresses great surprise that attention has not been called before now to this wonder of nature..."

The original Giant's Causeway Professor Hanks refers to is a startling gridwork of six-sided basaltic columns, each 10 to 50 feet thick in Northern Ireland. The 'basalt' columns on Mt. St. Helena are actually made of andesite, mineralogically different but indistinguishable to the casual observer. The columns extend down the north side of the peak, 'buttressing' the main summit. On the summit, only the tops of

Giant's causeway on north summit. Andesite columns form an interesting gridwork.

these columns are seen. The professor's columns are not as 'perfect' as he describes, but one can still step from stone to stone as if on a path made by giants.

In 1904, the United States Geological Survey commissioned Vance C. Osmont to conduct the first major study ever to include the Mt. St. Helena area. The landmark work covered the Sonoma and Napa valleys over a two year period. It was already known that the Franciscan assemblage, or complex, were the 'basement' rocks for this part of Northern California. On top of these, Osmont identified three distinct layers of volcanic rock.

The bottom layer, he called the Mark West andesite, varying in thickness up to 1,500 feet. Next came the Sonoma tuff (rock formed of compacted volcanic fragments), as thick as 1,700 feet in places. Finally, on top of it all, is the St. Helena Rhyolite, as much as 2,000 feet deep. Total depth at any one place was 4,000 feet, or about the height of Mt. St. Helena above sea level. Simple in theory, in the field this sequential layering was not always so obvious.

These layers varied wildly in depth, from a few feet to several hundred feet within a short stretch. Sometimes, they were missing altogether, or interbedded with other materials, so that later researchers tended to downplay the three-fold distinction and treat them as one layer.

Osmont estimated the age for the Sonoma tuff at mid-Pliocene, and late-Pliocene for the St. Helena Rhyolite. That dates the youngest rocks at around 3 million years, just before the great mountain building era of the Pleistocene. Despite the pervasive presence of volcanic rock, Osmont could find

"no evidence of its ever having been a volcano. No crater, or residual neck, or heterogeneity of material is present. On the contrary, it is made up of even, well defined flows of lava, which frequently show evidence in columnar structure of having cooled as surface flows."

What Osmont did find as a clue to its origin was an important fault on the western flank of the mountain. When he looked at Mt. St. Helena from the south, the shape suggested a fault block.

"The straight line of the top sloping gently to the eastward, and the precipitous descent to the west, have all the appearance of a tilted block with a fault escarpment."

148

A hike down the southwest ridge between Knight's and Napa Valleys confirmed his first impression. He estimated the throw of the fault had elevated Mt. St. Helena 2,500 to 3,000 feet. Cobb Mountain, to the north, was also part of this action. Uplift had to occur after most or all of the St. Helena Rhyolite deposition.

After Osmont's study in 1905, very little was published on the mountain's geology for the next 45 years. The incredible complexity of northern California geology would continue to baffle geologists right up to the re-introduction of plate tectonic theory in the 1960's. Few were the economic incentives for studies. After the local quicksilver boom of the late nineteenth century, Mt. St. Helena had little to offer. Grant money went to studies of places like the southern California coast ranges where oil was prevalent.

If the professionals were not interested, students from UC Berkeley were. Beginning around 1948, a storm of graduate students took to the Napan hills, spending whole summers in the field, fighting impenetrable brush and dessicating heat in pursuit of Masters Theses. Typically, four students would be assigned to cover one *section,* each taking a quarter of a standard 15' USGS topographic map. One student was W.H. Carter, who took the northeast corner of the Calistoga quadrangle.

He was impressed with the great thickness the volcanic rock attained on the east flanks of Mt. St. Helena, in the vicinity of the Livermore property. Although already deeply cut by erosion, it still completely covered the older rocks (this fact is important when we later muse on where all the building material for Mt. St. Helena came from).

When Charles Weaver did a major study of the northern coast ranges in 1949, he relied on Osmont's pioneering work for the Mt. St. Helena area. He noted the great variation in form and thickness of Osmont's three volcanic strata: the Mark West andesite, Sonoma tuff, and St. Helena rhyolite. Insisting that they should be treated as one single geologic unit, he applied the term, *Sonoma Volcanics.* Weaver was able to date the lowest layer at early Pliocene or younger. The most interesting idea he proposed was a possible location for the source of the Sonoma Volcanics. This he suggested was 3 miles southeast of Napa -- where the basalt rock quarries are today.

Two years later, O.E. Bowen, in very certain terms, reconfirms Osmont's convictions that the mountain was not a volcano. In a compendium of works entitled, *Geologic Guidebook of the San Francisco Bay Counties,* Bowen touches on the relationship between Mt. St. Helena and the Petrified Forest near Calistoga:

> "The tree trunks all fell in approximately the same direction
> and may have been blown down in an ancient volcanic blast
> or blasts; but the popular idea that the trees perished in some
> fiery cloud sweeping down from the slopes of Mount St. Helena
> is false. Mount St. Helena is built up of a series of folded lava
> flows and originated in the same way as any other fold mount-
> ain, that is by warping of the earth's crust. It is not the root of a
> former volcanic vent and did not get its height from volcanic
> activity. "

Included in the same guidebook is an article on volcanic rocks by C. W. Chesterman. He also debunks the volcano theory and suggests a source for the Sonoma Volcanics:

> "Mount Saint Helena is made up of volcanic and sedimentary
> rocks. True, it resembles an extinct volcano, but it owes its
> elevation to mountain-building processes rather than volcanic
> activity around some central vent... In all probability most
> volcanic rocks in the San Francisco Bay area came from fissure-
> like vents which now are covered by volcanic debris. Some of
> these vents might well be located in the northern Mayacamas
> mountains, southeast of Mount Saint Helena, where considerable
> amounts of andesitic agglomerate and breccia are exposed."

Chesterman refers here to the Palisades, a prominent band of cliffs northeast of Calistoga. For years they have been popularly thought to be the site of the old volcano that felled the Petrified Forest. Lake County historian, Henry Mauldin, has likened these cliffs to an old crater rim and called the area behind them 'Greater Mt. St. Helena'. Kay Archuleta in *The Brannan Saga* has also pointed out the shape of Bear and Cub Valleys behind the Palisades as evidence of an old crater. Although the verdict is not yet in, recent professional opinion indicates this is unlikely.

The Palisades and Mt. St. Helena were the setting for a University of California Master's Thesis in 1953 when W.H. Crutchfield submit-

150

ted his *Geology and Silver Mineralization of the Calistoga District.* The report centered on two mines, the Silverado on Mt. St. Helena, and the nearby Palisades Mine. Crutchfield called attention to nearby dike-like masses of rock where gold and silver had been deposited.

The special conditions needed to form these precious metals were present during the recent Pleistocene epoch. The many faults and fissures in the area provided the avenues for its formation. This is the way it works: water and hydrogen sulfide run through these passageways in the rock, dissolving and taking along minute quantities of gold. This scavenging action, under the right conditions, will concentrate gold or silver in sufficient quantities to make it economically valuable. Precious metals will not always be concentrated in fissures where siliceous (quartz) solutions have become encrusted. But it is the first sign a miner will look for.

By 1971, a compendium of articles, edited by UC Davis geologists, Jerry Lipps and Eldridge Moores, was published. Entitled *Geologic Guide to the Coast Ranges, Point Reyes Region,* it applied the revolutionary plate tectonics theory locally.

Mt. St. Helena appeared to be southernmost in a series of rhyodacitic conical peaks stretching from here to Clear Lake. The farther north one went, the more recent the volcanics became. Thus, within a short distance, one successively encounters Mt. Cobb, Mt. Hanna, and finally, Mt. Konocti, which still retains its original volcano form.

Superficially, it appears volcanic activity is moving north under the earth's surface. In reality, it's just the opposite! The hot spot from deep in the earth's mantle remains relatively stable, while the 'earth' itself is moving large distances. Here, the great North American tectonic plate is moving south, while the Pacific plate, on the other side of the San Andreas fault, is moving north. Pinnacles National Monument, west of Hollister, was once over this same hot spot, some 20 million years ago.

Lipps and Moores concluded by saying that the Clear Lake area mountains, Konocti and Hanna, were certainly vent volcanoes. If Mt. St. Helena was not a volcano, it had to be close to the source, because the top member of the Sonoma Volcanics (St. Helena Rhyolite) reached its greatest thickness here.

In the geologically short time since the mountain was raised, intense weathering has obscured or eradicated a lot of evidence that might have been used to learn of the Sonoma Volcanics origin. Outcrops are tough to follow and faults are buried under soft volcanic debris. Some features that do stand out though, are basaltic and andesitic dikes and plugs in the Palisades. These are probably indications of old fissure vents, avenues for lava flow.

Robert Hamilton, in a 1973 UC Berkeley thesis, noted many of these and contrasted them with their total absence on the east side of Mt. St. Helena. The closer one got to these dikes and plugs, the larger the individual rock fragments became, indicating proximity to the eruptive center. For these reasons, he strongly believed the source of the Sonoma Volcanics was the Palisades.

One old myth he put to rest was the Bear Valley/Cub Valley crater theory. These are structural basins, formed by two downwarpings of the earth during intense folding. Geologists call them *synclines*. Twin Peaks nearby is part of an anticline, or upward fold of the earth.

Except for Weaver in 1949, very few new ideas had been introduced until Ken Fox published a far reaching pioneering work in 1983. Not since Osmont's work in 1905, had so much new material been available on Mt. St. Helena. Its orientation was indicated by the lengthy title, *Tectonic Setting of Late Miocene, Pliocene, and Pleistocene Rocks in Part of the Coast Ranges North of San Francisco, California.* The mountain would now be further interpreted in the new light of plate tectonic theory.

The basic premise of his paper is founded on the existence of two separate but adjacent *structural blocks,* the Sonoma block and the Santa Rosa block (Mt. St. Helena is located in the northeasterly section of the Santa Rosa block). They show a sharp difference in the average dip or inclination of their rocks, indicating degree of deformity after deposition. The Sonoma block is inclined at only 5.8 degrees, compared to the Santa Rosa block which averages a whopping 34.5 degrees.

Geomorphically they differ too. The Sonoma block is dominated by the Mendocino Plateau, stretching from Mount Tamalpais in the south to Fort Bragg on the north. It is not a plateau in the sense most of us picture it, usually the flat top of a desert mesa. Rather, it is an

152

extensive area of rounded and table-topped summits of similar height. Even though heavily dissected by recent erosion, it was once perhaps as flat as the Sonoma Valley.

On the other hand, the Santa Rosa block, which includes the Howell and Mayacamas Mountains and Napa Valley, is broken and folded into a basin and range province. The forces that created it are still active. Eight major faults were located in the Santa Rosa block, four of which are still active. The intense shearing and folding that created these mountains is going on at an undiminished rate today.

Why the great difference between these two neighboring blocks? Ken Fox believes the answer lies far up the northern California coast at Cape Mendocino. Here, three great tectonic plates, the Pacific, the North American, and the Juan De Fuca, collide at what is called the Triple Junction. The Pacific plate is basically moving north and west, the North American plate at this point south and west (although as a whole it moves west) and the Juan De Fuca dives under the North American into a presumed subduction zone. Tremendous stresses are produced when just two plates meet. When three collide, the situation becomes a puzzle in geophysics. In this part of California, the Pacific and North American plates are basically north/south oriented. This means that the western edge of California, including San Francisco and Point Reyes, is moving north for its eventual demise in the Aleutian trench off Alaska. The eastern portion is travelling south at about 6 centimeters (2 inches) a year. The Juan De Fuca is situated in an acute angle between the two (once part of the Pacific plate, it has now separated).

As it dives northeasterly under the American continent, the Juan de Fuca plate may actually take some stress off the plate margin in a zone beginning at Cape Mendocino and ending near San Francisco. It's believed that the Sonoma block is in this zone of reduced stress, and therefore exhibits this by relatively little rock deformity. The Santa Rosa block, by it's particular position, is in a high stress zone.

Another factor that may be involved is the geothermal gradient, or relative closeness of magma to the surface. The closer the heat source, the thinner the earth's crust, creating more folding and faulting. The crust in the Santa Rosa block then, has thinned, allowing magma to well to the surface creating the Sonoma volcanics and the Clear Lake volcanics. Crustal thinning may be an additional factor in the difference between the two structural blocks.

Putting It All Together

We now know the progression of local geologic thought during the last hundred and thirty years. With this background, a composite picture of Mt. St. Helena's formation can be stitched together using the latest information. No doubt when the next revolution in geology happens, the story will change. For now though, it's unlikely plate tectonic theory will be 'displaced' in the near future.

We can go back only about 200 million years, to the Jurassic period, to the birth of the landmass known as California. At that time, the North American continent was in a head-on, east/west, slow-motion collision with the Pacific Ocean tectonic plate. The west coast of North America was somewhere in Nevada, and California was only a gleam in the eye of the Great Tectonician.

As the lighter, granitic rocks of the continent overrode the heavier, basaltic rocks of the ocean floor, the latter were shoved down into a trench system called a subduction zone. Some ocean plate rocks however were scraped off onto the continental plate as they collided, and California was born.

The ocean floor, diving into the trench system, was moving not only downward but laterally. When it sank deep enough, heat turned the rocks to magma. Heated, they slowly rose to form a volcanic 'arc', the ancestral Sierra Nevada. (Apparently the Cascades are a perfect example of how the Sierra looked 150 million years ago).

As California moved into the Cretaceous period 135 million years back, it expanded westward as new real estate was continually deposited on its shore. As the volcanic arc grew, a *forearc basin* developed to the west, made up of marine sedimentary deposits from the mountains. This would be the Central Valley. At the same time, the incipient coast ranges appeared, products of tectonic plate scrapage, elevated slightly by normal folding and faulting. Toward the end of the Cretaceous, about 63 million years ago, the great east/west plate collision came to a gradual halt, and the volcanic arc of the ancestral

154

The Geologic Time Scale

Eras	Periods	Epochs	millions of years ago
The Cenozoic	**Quaternary**	**Holocene**	**0.01**
		Pleistocene	**2**
	Tertiary	**Pliocene**	**5**
		Miocene	**24**
		Oligocene	
		Eocene	**58**
		Paleocene	**70**
The Mesozoic	**Cretaceous**		**144**
	Jurassic		**160**
	Triassic		**209**
The Paleozoic	**Permian**		**230**
	Pennsylvanian		
	Mississippian		
	Devonian		
	Silurian		
	Ordovician		
	Cambrian		**600**
Precambrian Time *About 400 million years*			

By geologic standards, Mt. St. Helena is an extremely young mountain, its oldest rocks dating back to the Pliocene epoch, only 11 million years ago.

Sierra Nevada ran out of fuel.

For the next 30 million years, scientists are unsure of what happened, but they believe it was a relatively quiet time. The volcanic arc lost some height as it eroded into an inland sea, the future Central Valley. Erosion also lowered the coastal ranges. In light of what followed, it might be said Mother Nature was simply shifting gears, and this period of quiescence was 'neutral'.

Between the Oligocene and Miocene epochs, about 30 million years back, coastal tectonic plates changed directions to move in a north/south alignment. The San Andreas fault, which actually is a whole system of strike/slip faults, is dated by Ken Fox as activating locally about 27 million years ago. (There are three basic types of plate movements: 1) pulling apart as the mid-Atlantic rise, 2) collision, as India meeting Asia to form the Himalaya and 3) strike/slip or transform as the San Andreas). Here was created the system of northwest /southeast trending valleys seen throughout the coast ranges today. One was to become known as Napa Valley.

Movement on the San Andreas and related faults slowly began to raise the height of the coast ranges that had for so long been eroding away. Sea withdrawal accompanied this action during the Miocene epoch.

With the start of the Pliocene epoch, 13 million years ago, remarkable things began to happen in northern California. Scattered but widespread volcanism laid down layer after layer of ash, mudflows and lava. There were many, minor volcanic centers (fissure eruptions) rather than a few large scale sources, as for example, in the Cascades. Periods of quiescence interrupted the action. So many different types of rock and ash were laid down in overlapping periods of time that correlating the various units is a near impossible task. The volcanic field at its greatest extent was 350 square miles. Today, due to agents of weathering and earth movement, only islands of volcanic rock remain on Mt. St. Helena and surrounding hill tops.

Four to five million years ago was the most violent eruptive period. It was not a good time to be around! Magma, under the surface at that time, was high in silica content and low in water, about the consistency of hot peanut butter. This made for highly explosive eruptions when reaching the surface (Hawaiian volcanoes are low in silica and high in water content, making them slow-flow lavas). Rhyolite ash flows were also common, producing choking gases and dust, like the Mt. St. Helens eruption of 1980.

Petrified Forest

One or more of these ash flows buried the Petrified Forest near Calistoga. The species found here is similar but ancestral to, today's redwood . The forest's state of preservation is so good it can be dated fairly precisely at 3.4 million years. Paleobotanists find it extremely important since fossils are rarely found from Pliocene rocks. The great changes in climate and topography in the Pliocene epoch have obliterated most animal and plant remains.

In principle, the process of turning cellulose to stone, *petrifaction,* can be likened to ancient Egyptian embalming. The Egyptians soaked the body in a bath of special natron salts to preserve the body. All of the body's moisture was gradually removed until it became like stone. In nature, something similar happens; the tree's organic material being replaced by silica. Rhyolite, common in ash flows locally, happens to be high in silica. Once buried, the trees are infiltrated by silica in solution, which replaces the organic material with stone, down to each individual cell.

Several theories about how the forest was felled have been trashed over the years. Originally, the idea that a volcanic blast from Mt. St. Helena was responsible, enjoyed popularity. After, it was supposedly buried by volcanic debris. Another recent idea suggests that heavy rainfall unleashed a torrent of volcanic ash and mud flows (lahar) to fell the trees. Later volcanic ash eruptions covered them. Recent field work by Elise Mattison(California's Fossil Forest; *Calif. Geology,* Sept. 1990), makes this idea unlikely. The perfectly preserved bark on many trees could not have survived a great volume of abrasive volcanic mud.

Mattison suggests two possible causes. Since most of the trees are oriented northeast 35 to 45 degrees, it may simply reflect the orientation of the slope the trees fell onto when they died. Or it may be a violent volcanic blast, similar to Mt. St. Helens, was the culprit, originating northeast of Mt. St. Helena. As she disturbingly points out,

> Locating the actual eruptive centers may be impossible because
> geologic processes have drastically changed the terrain in this
> region since the Pliocene.

Finally, different tiers of trees felled and correspondingly different ash types may indicate two events rather than one.

At the time the trees fell, the climate was more tropical, with higher winter rainfall and more rain in the summer, allowing plants like avocado to grow. Soils would form and forests would grow up in the periods of quiescence, then get blown away by volcanic explosions to become petrified later. Pebbles of petrified wood can be turned up among stream gravels around Napa and Sonoma today.

The last layer to be laid down on the mountain was the St. Helena Rhyolite, dated about 2.9 million years ago. Confusingly, it is found throughout the Sonoma Volcanic sequence, but assuredly it marks the end of the period for Mt. St. Helena. The volcanic activity then shifted north and east to Clear Lake and Mt. Konocti, where rocks have been dated as young as 44,000 years. Clear Lake volcanics were more spotty than the Sonoma sequence. The nearest they approach Mt. St. Helena is Table Mountain near Oat Hill Mine, from ½ to 2 million years ago.

The Orogenous Zone

A scant 1 million years ago there began the greatest mountain building age since the Jurassic, nearly 200 million years earlier. This is the Pleistocene epoch. Many of the great mountain ranges worldwide are products of this time. The great fault block that tilted the Sierra 10,000 feet above the Owens Valley was one. In fact, most of the mountains in California come from this time, including Mt. St. Helena.

No simple explanation can account for the origin of the mountain, but it can be described as a combination of three distinct geologic actions, folding, faulting and erosion. Imagine for a moment, the volcanic field, 350 square miles, created in the previous age. Then imagine a warping of that surface, a huge fold. One part goes up, one goes down. The up part is an anticline -- *mountains*. The part that goes down is a syncline -- *valleys*. Napa Valley is a downfold in the crust, the adjacent Howell and Mayacamas mountains are anti-

158

clines. Mt. St. Helena seems to be its own minor anticline, with bedding moving downward in all directions from the summit.

The intense folding has been accompanied by faulting: two basically rigid planes of rock moving past each other. In this part of California, all major and minor faults are probably part of the San Andreas fault, a strike/slip system. Additionally, it is described as a right lateral wrench system by geologist Ken Fox. Movement on the main fault will find a stress point, past which the two planes cannot move. This creates movement elsewhere, sort of like what happens when a jig saw puzzle is accidentally jarred. In this case, other faults are created roughly parallel to the main, usually trending northwest 30 or 35 degrees.

A geologic map will show an active fault west of Napa city. The West Napa fault can be traced along the foothill/valley boundary as far as Yountville. From here it is presumed, but not known, to extend to the town of St. Helena. Ten miles north and trending in roughly the same direction, are a series of faults on the west side of Mt. St. Helena. It's very tempting to draw a line connecting the two fault systems. If we did, we could assume the same fault that dropped Napa Valley and raised the Mayacamas Mountains also elevated Mt. St. Helena. But the evidence is not there, at least not yet.

Little has been said about the mountain's west side faults since Osmont's 1905 study, except to acknowledge their existence. There seems little doubt, though, that major uplift has occured here in the last million years, and continues into the present.

The third way to look at Mt. St. Helena is as an erosional remnant. Weathering agents are always at work to reverse the effects of mountain building forces. In the late Pliocene, as soon as volcanism came to an end, they began chipping away at the thinner edges of the lava plateau and moving inward. Mt. St. Helena's anticlinal nature and recent fault block tilting has saved it from leveling. Should the mountain building forces cease, it would soon lose its elevated status. Much of the St. Helena rhyolite on the mountain's top has already been eroded away, revealing the lower Sonoma tuff. As proof of the power of weathering agents, valley alluvium washed from the surrounding hills since the Pleistocene is, in some places, 2,000 feet thick.

The Mystery

Mt. St. Helena may look like a volcano from the south, but views from the west and east show it to be a long, elevated ridge. Millions of years of volcanic activity from a number of sources have produced the building material. Then, folding, faulting and erosion have uplifted and shaped its present form.

In 1949, Weaver proposed the quarry site southeast of Napa city as one source of the Sonoma Volcanics. But this is probably too far from our subject. Hamilton, in 1973 strongly favored the Palisades, a mile southeast of Mt. St. Helena, pointing out the existence of numerous volcanic plugs and dikes as proof. Ten years later, Ken Fox counted 28 of these to be exact, but declares them incidental. They can account for the Palisades formation, but not the great mass of rhyolitic material capping Mt. St. Helena. Having done the latest and most extensive work in this area, we must consider Fox the authority. In a phone conversation with me he hazarded his best guess.

The area east of Mt. St. Helena on the Livermore Ranch, says Fox, contains the greatest depth of rhyolitic lava in the vicinity. It also correlates well with the direction of downed Petrified Forest trees, about 35° east of north. If a volcano was once here, it was close enough to spew high quantities of rock and ash onto the present site of the mountain. Then we can only imagine that tremendous weathering agents have obscured all evidence of the volcano's former existence.

Perhaps not quite all. John Livermore, a professional geologist, lives smack in the center of the area described by Dr. Fox. The Livermore Ranch sits in a nearly circular depression, with even-sided forested slopes rising in three directions. Looking east, the effect is a little like standing in an outdoor sports arena. John believes it *may* be the remnant of the old caldera, the sunken crater that remains after a volcano has blown its top. Extensive research is still needed.

Maybe some day sophisticated gravity measuring instruments will be used to find the now hidden central volcanic vent to confirm this hypothesis. An expert on calderas might also be able confirm it through study of surface rocks or aerial photographs. The problem, as always, is funding. In the meantime, geologists will remain intrigued by the difficulties and will continue to try to piece together this intricate geologic puzzle.

Chapter 8

Robert Louis Stevenson State Park

"And there was something satisfactory in the sight of that great mountain that enclosed us to the north: whether it stood, robed in sunshine quaking to its topmost pinnacle with the heat and brightness of the day; or whether it set itself to weaving vapours, wisp after wisp, growing, trembling, fleeting and fading in the blue."

Robert Louis Stevenson, *The Silverado Squatters*

For many visitors, Robert Louis Stevenson State Park is the embodiment of Mt. St. Helena. Sometimes the two are thought synonymous. But the park's 3,760 acres cover only about 15% of the mountain's approximately 23,000 acres. Almost the entire southern approach to the park on Highway 29 is in private hands. Large expanses of land on the east, north and west are also private. If we picture the mountain in 3D for a moment, RLS Park land is like an umbrella in a windy rain that keeps the upper body dry but leaves the lower soaked. I believe the analogy has merit because, today, housing development, timbering and clearcutting for vineyards are a constant threat to the unprotected lower slopes.

Even within the park, there are major inholdings. Two hundred acres on the north and middle peaks, and 40 on the south, are not park property. Until 1988, the historical centerpiece of the park, the Silverado Mine and Stevenson monument, was in private hands also. The development of the park has been far from static, and it continues to grow and change. The park may be on the verge of acquiring land that would allow hikers to start just outside the Calistoga city limits, skirt the spectacular Palisades cliffs, and end up on the mountain's summit, all within park property.

While there has been money for land acquisition, development of visitor facilities has been sorely neglected. The Department of Parks and Recreation promised to develop facilities in 1967, when the Bureau of Land Management deeded 2700 acres to the park. That promise is unfulfilled almost 30 years later. The implementation of the General Plan, scheduled for 1996, would change all that. In the meantime, we can look forward with both hope and concern to the Park's future.

∽   ∽   ∽

Thirty-three years after Robert Louis Stevenson left Mt. St. Helena for Scotland, a monument was placed on the cabin site where he had spent his honeymoon. It was the first historical landmark placed in Napa County. The prime movers in this action were five women's groups from Napa, St. Helena and Calistoga.

On May 7,1911, nearly 400 people convened at the Toll House flat and walked along Daniel Patten's newly constructed trail for the noontime ceremony. Among the many speeches delivered was one by the vice president of the Sierra Club, Professor A. McAdie, a substitute speaker for John Muir, who was away in South America.

When the Scottish and American flags were lifted at the unveiling, the base of the monument was seen to be made of quartz rock from the nearby mine. It was capped by a slab of Scotch granite, imported from Scotland, in the shape of an open book.

Carved into the right page was one of Stevenson's poems, written for a woman whose son had tragically died as a youth. It was chosen because it was so appropriate for the author himself:

> "Doomed to know not winter, only spring,
> A being trod the Flowery April blithely for a while,
> Took his fill of music, joy of thought, and seeing,
> Came and stayed and went,
> Nor ever ceased to smile."

A dinner hosted by the Pattens afterwards was attended by half of the gathering, many of whom were living in the county when Stevenson had made his brief sojourn there.

162

The Stevenson's honeymoon cabin
may have looked very much like this.

Scene from the 1911 RLS monument dedication
ceremony. Center, Mrs.Wm. F. Fisher; right,
Mrs.Charles Armstrong.

Robert Louis Stevenson

Perhaps it was at this ceremony that the idea of a park was first conceived by Mollie Patten, innkeeper at the Toll House Inn. She confided later to historian, Anne Roller Issler, her dream of setting aside 500 acres of 'virgin' forest to the state as a game preserve. A rash of lawsuits encumbering the estate made this impossible. Mollie died in 1932, but Issler took up the dream herself. Her book, *Stevenson at Silverado*, published in 1939, attracted widespread sympathy for a park in Stevenson's honor. Already, at the fire lookout dedication on Mt. St. Helena's summit in 1935, Judge Henry Clay Gesford had expressed hope for the establishment of a national park. His mother had scaled the peak in 1853, only 12 years after the first recorded ascent.

Then, in 1944, a lumber company threatened to cut timber on Stevenson's side of the mountain. This galvanized the Robert Louis Stevenson Memorial Park Committee into birth. Some well known people got involved, including Dr. Robert Sproul, President of the University of California; novelist Somerset Maugham; Hollywood actor, Leo Carrillo; Idwal Jones, author of *Vines in the Sun*; *St. Helena Star* editor, Starr Baldwin; local historians, Ivy Loeber and Anne Issler; and local land magnates, Norman and Edith Livermore. Apparently, Somerset Maugham's participation was only superficial. The story goes that, when asked for a monetary donation, he declined, replying with a letter giving permission to sell his signature thereon!

On December 2, 1944, a gala dinner at the Park Plaza Hotel in Napa raised $7,000 - matching funds were promised by the state. Besides the sponsors already mentioned, there were: Warner Brothers Studios and Ralph Winston, the *Weekly Calistogan* editor and coordinator of the event. The next day, Robert Louis Stevenson Memorial Park was officially dedicated at the monument site. It was the fiftieth anniversary of Stevenson's death. There was only one thing missing -- land. That wasn't provided for another five years.

Norman B. Livermore, Sr., is credited with donating the first forty acres of land to the new Park in 1949, but it was his sister Edith who laid the groundwork. Edith was invalided at a young age by a tragic fall from a horse. Nevertheless, she carried on a tireless letter writing campaign to raise the necessary money and solve conflicts among the many land owners. Through her dedication and the Livermores' generosity, the park became a de facto reality.

Two years later, another 322 acres was bought by the State Division of Parks and Beaches from the Piner-Cooper estate for a bargain $10,000, a little over $30 an acre. (The Piners were a Calistoga-based family who acquired some of their property here from the Pattens. They owned a market in town and gave Harry Patten extended credit during the tough Depression years. Periodically, they had to ask for payment, and Harry, short on cash, would barter an acre or two.)

The memorial committee was full of plans and high hopes for the park. It was proposed that a replica of Stevenson's cabin be built on

164

the same spot. This was not carried out, but the same proposal is current as of this writing.

The committee also wished to see the Mt. St. Helena Toll House Inn, collapsing into crumbling decay by age and vandalism, restored as a museum. The finest collection of Stevensoniana in the world was offered by history buff, Flodden W. Heron. He insisted that a fireproof building be constructed, attended by a full-time caretaker. Alas, the new park management deemed the old Toll House beyond help, and tore it down in 1953.

The greatest expansion in the park's history was proposed during the Lyndon Johnson Administration. Then, it seemed, money was available for every cause and anything was possible. The influence of the *Great Society* filtered down to the state government level, and Sacramento made plans to enlarge and rename RLS park. The Memorial Park was to become part of Mt. St. Helena State Park and explode in size from some 300 acres to over 9,000. Two and a half million dollars were earmarked for land purchases, including Russell's Trout Farm on the northeast, Silverado Ranch, adjacent Bureau of Land Management land, and the Foote property, which ran clear down to Knight's Valley.

Development was to include hiking and riding trails, picnic facilities and campgrounds, a visitor center and interpretive displays. One of the main objectives was to move all communications towers and buildings off the south peak, and consolidate them on the main peak. Out of all these plans, only BLM land, about 2700 acres, (minus the 40 on the south peak), and Russell's land, were transferred to the new park.

How did it fail? By 1967, when the deal was completed, the political climate in America was changing. The Great Society was a vanishing dream, sunk by the morass of the Vietnam War and domestic rioting. Also, Edmund Brown's Democratic Administration gave way to Ronald Reagan's Republican Governorship, far less willing to spend money on public works. Ironically, it was Ronald Reagan who saved Knight's Valley from inundation. Knight's Valley was to be flooded, (as Berryessa valley had been in the 50's), as part of the massive Eel River reclamation project of northern California. Reagan refused to spend a dime, killing Brown's project outright. Knight's Valley wine grape growers call their land the best microclimate and soil in the Western Hemisphere. They can trace their luck to this quirk of fate.

With the two and a half million dollar allocation cut off, money was no longer available to buy private land at fair market value. The Foote property and Silverado Ranch stayed in private hands, but the BLM came through, selling their 2700 acres at $2.50 an acre. The BLM, however, retained a lease on the south peak summit. Plans to consolidate buildings and communications transmitters on the north peak were not carried out. The reason for this is not clear interwoven amid conflicting accounts.

Those who support the development on the south peak say it is the perfect harmonious use between commercial and wilderness interests. They point out the huge public benefit from organizations like the Napa county and city fire departments, radio and TV stations, microwave transmissions and even the FBI. The sacrifice of a few acres of land is far outweighed by the benefits.

Detractors argue that consolidation of equipment on one peak instead of the three that are covered today was a sensible and attainable goal. They also say that developers have made a mess on the south peak; transmitters and turrets sprawling all over the forty acres instead of being consolidated in one, low profile building, invisible from below, as originally agreed.

The pattern of land acquisition without the development of visitor facilities was to continue. Another 70 acres of BLM land was transferred in 1969, bringing the total acreage to about 3,000. That is how things stayed for the better part of two decades. With the failure to acquire the Foote and Silverado Ranch properties, the only flat, easily accessible land in the whole park was the toll house flat. This was too small for a visitor's center. The vast majority of the park consisted of steep, wild lands, making a diversity of public use difficult.

The potential for dramatic change in visitor use came with the Silverado Ranch purchase in 1987. In the mid 1870's, this site was a mining boom town called Silverado, home to 1500 miners. In five short years, it went from birth, to boom to bust; all evidence is now long evaporated. In the 1940's, it was a dude ranch, in the 70's, a

166

private retreat for a San Francisco based rock and roll band. Originally on the market for two and a quarter million, the park purchased its 492 acres for just $500,000.

Development plans were quickly drawn, with the Silverado Ranch as the hub of the park. The old townsite held room for parking, employee residences, visitor's center and much more. Only one problem existed. A General Plan for the park was not due until 1996. Without it, no development could proceed. Other parks, closer to urban areas and subject to greater resource degradation, held higher priority. So, today, six years after the purchase, all plans remain unfulfilled.

Unknown to many, the historical centerpiece of the park remained in private hands. The Silverado mine and the Stevenson monument, marking the honeymoon cabin site, 25 acres in all, was the last parcel owned by the Patten family. Once owners of up to 1600 acres on the mountain, three generations of Pattens had pioneered here for over 100 years. People visiting the monument, assuming it was on state land, were there only because the Pattens had granted easement to hikers. The Pattens had let their claim to the Silverado mine slide over the years, leaving no owner's name on any official documents. For this reason, the State was reluctant to purchase land without clear title, although the Pattens had attempted to sell it for 20 years.

Resolution came in 1988, when Napa County Land Trust took on the difficult job of disentangling the snarled web. To the Patten's amazement, their lawyers were able to thread the legal maze, and the key parcel was transferred to the park for about $30,000. It was a sad day for the Patten descendents, landless after 104 years. But they could also breathe a sigh of relief. Threat of lawsuit had been a constant worry. For years, climbers, spelunkers and casual hikers had explored the completely accessible Silverado mine area, fortunately without serious injury.

What then, of the future? While a full-fledged park is still years away, land acquisition opportunities keep popping up. RLS received a $2 million windfall in June, 1988, when California voters passed Proposition 70, the so-called *California Wildlife, Coastal and Park Land Conservation Act of 1988*. The land tracts considered top priority objectives included the rim of the Palisades, a natural geological extension of Mt. St. Helena.

Running through the heart of the Palisades cliffs is the Oat Hill Mine Road. A narrow and picturesque trail today, it once was used to carry quicksilver flasks from Oat Hill Mine to the railhead in Calistoga. If all the land tracts along the Palisades could be pieced together, RLS Park would be contiguous with Oat Hill trail. The finest hiking trail in Napa County would thus be available to the public. It would start only a stone's throw out of Calistoga, ascending the four mile Oat Hill Mine Road, where deep grooves in rock cut by freight wagons are still visible. Another five miles would then skirt the precipitous volcanic cliffs of the Palisades with views of the rugged and remote Bear Valley. Eventually it would meet highway 29 at the Mt. St. Helena trailhead.

Negotiations between the state and local landowners seemed to be going well at first, only to stall. We may expect though, the completion of this deal in the forseeable future. One part of this project, the Table Rock property was acquired in early 1993. When all comes through, the 3,600+ acre park will increase in size dramatically.

What Parks and Recreation calls a General Plan is a comprehensive document, authorizing a State park to proceed with the development of visitor facilities. Some feel the General Plan for RLS has not just been on the back burner, but off the stove and on the shelf for the last 40 years. Although now slated for 1996, if the money is not there, it could be pushed even farther back. In the meantime, some management plan was needed. It came in the form of the *Robert Louis Stevenson State Park Interim Management Plan,* issued in December, 1987. In it are some intriguing suggestions for change.

Presently, the focal point for Park visitors are two earth-surface 'parking lots' next to the Toll House flat. When the General Plan arrives, orientation will change to the old Silverado townsite, a quarter mile off the highway. Here will be room for a full scale visitor's center. Many of the buildings, dating from the 1940's will be retained or improved. Paved parking will accommodate 50 vehicles. Interpretive displays will feature the geology, fauna and flora of the park as well as its exciting gold and silver mining days. This is also an ideal site for an overlook of the entire Napa Valley, and Mt. Diablo, 66

168

bee-line miles away.

The present hiking trail to Stevenson monument is a wide, 1% grade accessible to almost everyone. It has proved too much temptation for switchback cutters. Several efforts to halt erosion have failed. The trail will eventually be eliminated and the entire hillside restored.

The new trail will start at Silverado and follow a road the miners called Silver Street. Once, heavy iron bins called 'skips' were loaded with quartz ore from Silverado mine, then rumbled down a narrow gauge track on Silver Street a half mile into town. Here, the ore was transferred to wagons and trundled a mile down the Lawley grade to the old quartz mill for processing. Much of Silver Street still looks the same as it did 100 years ago.

Hikers to the mountain's summit have one choice today, the fireroad. Someday, loop trails will provide more aesthetic alternatives. The most likely route will follow an existing road west from Silverado to Turk's Head, an arresting volcanic monolith. From here, the new trail might follow fir-lined Kimball Canyon, where the remains of navy and air force jet aircraft crashes from the mid 50's can still be found.

From here, it would traverse the chaparral-covered western slopes of Mt. St. Helena, with a falcon's eye views of Knight's Valley, and then on to the main peak. If they chose, hikers could then descend the fireroad to complete the loop.

On the wetter, east side of the mountain is the Troutdale Creek watershed, also park property. Averaging 60 inches of rain a year, the lush lower canyon is filled with redwood, douglas fir, ponderosa pine, and ferns along an all-year stream. It was once homesteaded by Claude Russell, who dreamed of running a dude ranch and trout farm. He and Spud Hawkins built a trail by hand and hard work across some of the ruggedest terrain on Mt. St. Helena. It was built to lead horse riding trips to the summit but, once finished, the dude ranch plans fell through. Russell's herd of goats were about the only travelers on it after that. Today, all traces probably have vanished under rockslides and plant overgrowth.

The public has no access to this canyon today, a private land tract lies between it and the highway. It's intriguing though, to think of the loop trail possibilities here. If a new trail was built to follow the old goat trail, and the intervening parcel obtained, a traverse of the entire mountain from Silverado to Troutdale, would lead through all four of the mountain's vegetative plant zones. From pure stands of interior live oaks along the Turk's Head trail, to douglas fir forest of Kimball Canyon, through the chaparral community on the upper slopes to the rich riparian undergrowth of Troutdale Creek - an outdoor experience like this would far exceed anything available to the public on Mt. St. Helena today.

Other possibilities suggested by the *Interim Management Plan* include a Peregrine Falcon Habitat Protection Area. Peregrines are flourishing on Mt. St. Helena, while populations in other parts of the country are recovering much more slowly. No measures are presently being taken to help the falcon here. So far, the fastest of all raptors finds enough quarry and open space to survive without much outside help. However, the balance now in its favor could easily be tipped against it by only a slight increase in human intrusion.

Mt. St. Helena's scenic vistas have been acclaimed for well over a hundred years. By its peculiar geographic position, not height, it claims a 360 degree view rivaled by few peaks in the world. This valuable resource is often degraded by air pollutants from the Bay area and the Central Valley. Most alarming though, is the threat to the short range viewshed brought on by recent clearcutting for vineyards.

A vineyard, attractive as it may look, is a direct attack on biodiversity. For a hillside vineyard, all vegetation must be removed before planting; that includes oak, fir and madrone as well as chaparral species. For maximum production from the vines, a farmer must keep all 'weeds' from competing by disking the field clean. For 'vine row' weeds, steep hillsides almost require the use of herbicides. To round out this rout, the farmer must spray insecticides to keep the vines bug-free. The end result, of course, is a monoculture, where very few species can complete their life cycle, unless it be Phyloxera, a root-eating grape louse. This relatively sterile environment will continue indefinitely, as long as the grower desires to farm.

Timbering, by contrast, is in the long and even short run, easier on the environment. As bad as it looks initially, logging will imme-

170

diately bring sunlight to encourage pioneer plant species sought by many animals and birds. This is actually to the peregrine falcon's benefit, whose prey is smaller birds. By the time it reaches its climax stage, a forest has seen many species come and go, a model of biodiversity in action. In 40 or 50 years, it would be almost unrecognizable as a log cut. On the other hand, forty years is about the life span of a dry-farmed vineyard.

Take a hike to either of Mt. St. Helena's peaks. From the south peak, an enormous scar is seen in lower Garnett Canyon, land that once was classic oak and grassland habitat. Today, the bare ground is ripped by machines into uniform terraces, awaiting the vine. Or look from the main peak to the west, where vineyard has escaped Knight's Valley and is steadily creeping up the foothills. One of these clearings, off the Ida Clayton Road, is in the Rattlesnake Canyon watershed, close to the peregrine falcon's critical habitat. An area once rich in food, the peregrine now must pass over this biological starveling.

The peregrine is not the only one dependant on biological diversity. Mountain lion, bobcat, black bear, ring-tail cat, deer, fox, coyote - the list goes on and on. Mt. St. Helena is comparatively rich in animal life. But how long can they survive? Animals cannot be expected to stay within park bounds. As we've seen, the park encompasses only a fraction of the whole mountain. Clearly if we wish to see Mt. St. Helena stay a wildlife refuge, official protection must be sought. In whatever form, the lands that encompass the mountain, summit to base, need a promise. That promise could be in the form of a land trust, wild-life reserve, or as part of the state park. Protection needs to come quickly. It's been said that, in as little as thirty years, land in California will be so expensive that it will simply be unobtainable.

I lived in Santa Barbara when it was still possible to see a wild condor in the nearby mountains. It lent a mystery and attraction to the area not otherwise known. The condors have only begun to be reintroduced to their native habitat, after a long captive breeding program brought about by their near extinction. The success of the program is not yet proven. After a close call in the 1970's, peregrine falcon populations have rebounded in most parts of the west. This is especially true in the Mt. St. Helena and Palisades area, perhaps one of the best best falcon habitats in northern California.

One summer day recently, a friend and I were in a remote part of the park. Suddenly, as we were leaving, something rocketed over his head. It was going so fast he didn't know whether it was natural, manmade, or alien until it stopped in a tree a mile downslope, just seconds later. Then he realized it could only be a peregrine. I was just around a corner and missed the whole thing. Since that time I have seen these exciting birds at close range. The welfare of the peregrine and the integrity of Mt. St. Helena will always be foremost in my mind. Whether the peregrine goes the way of the condor, or remains for our children to see, is up to every one of us.

Turk's Head as it appears today on the southwest face of the mountain.

Chapter 9

Places on a Landscape

Mountains are the beginning and the end of all natural scenery.

John Ruskin

Introduction

When I was in fourth grade we were asked to compose an imaginary essay on an Old West town and how it was named. I chose Hangtown. Devising some childishly elaborate plot, a whole gang of bad guys eventually met their fate, swinging from a row of gallows.

Ever since then, names of places have intrigued me, never more so than on Mt. St. Helena. In fact, one of the first conceptions of this book was simply as a place names guide. I thought there might be some good stories behind the names. But first, the boundaries had to be drawn.

How do you define a mountain? Where does it end and the next mountain begin? This is the task I set for myself concerning Mt. St. Helena. Using maps, common sense and intuition, the answer was both easy, and difficult, depending on which side of the mountain was studied.

Four U.S. Geologic Survey 7.5 minute series maps were employed, Mt. St. Helena and Detert Reservoir quadrangles, and small slices of the Mark West and Calistoga quads. From these, a single reproduction was made. On it, I wished to draw a line encircling the extreme limits of the mountain. But where?

On the south and west, the boundary seemed clearly defined by the foothills that fronted Napa and Knights Valleys. Somewhat arbitrarily, I drew a connection through Murray Hill, where Hwy. 128 crosses from Napa to Sonoma County.

The eastern boundary was not so obvious. Here, at around 2500 feet, Mt. St. Helena merged with the Palisades, a series of volcanic cliffs that make a natural geological extension. Should they be included? Part of the Palisades is Table Rock, the largest rock mass in the area, and prominent from the Old Lawley Toll Road. Behind the Palisades is the Oat Hill mine area, which has strong historical connections with the mountain. Its quicksilver mines shipped millions of dollars of mercury over the mountain's toll road. Yet, ultimately, I decided this area was so rich in lore it needed a book of its own. And, except for the pass on Hwy. 29, deep canyons north and south of it defined the eastern mountain. Winding through the canyons was the highway, which made a good working boundary.

On the north, it was tougher still. A series of ridges and valleys made it possible to draw the line in several places. I finally drew a *half-arch* that roughly follows Foote Creek north past Chalk point and Pilot Knob to the Mayacamas crest. Then, northeast along the Great Western Mine road. Features like Lindquist Ridge and Hoo-doo Creek seemed to properly belong in Dry Creek watershed.

So the perimeter line was closed, forming a slightly skewed rectangle. The area is eight miles long and 5 1/2 to 6 1/2 miles wide, about 36 square miles in all or about 23,000 acres. Nearly every place name appearing within these lines was selected, 30 in all. In addition, I couldn't resist including two not appearing on the map, for their historic significance. How these places were named and their relation to the mountain is the subject of this chapter.

Bradford Creek: An intermittent stream with its headwaters on the northeast side of Mt. St. Helena. It joins St. Helena Creek at the head of Callayomi Valley.

It is named after the Bradford family who homesteaded here in 1861. (See chapter 4, The Bradford-Mirabel Mine.)

In 1895, Jake Ivec, an immigrant from Eastern Europe, filed a homestead claim deep in Bradford Canyon. His was a small clearing east of Sacre Gap, under the dark ramparts of Tom Dye Rock. There was room enough for a one-room cabin, a vegetable garden, a peach orchard, and an old horse. Nearby were not one but two springs to fill his cistern. Most of the year he lived a solitary life, prospecting for minerals. But, for two months every year, he worked for the Livermores, earning $50 a month. In 1924, Jake's place burned and he was left destitute. At Jake's request, the Livermores bought his 100 acres so he would have something to live on. His fate after that is unknown.

Today, little evidence remains of these pioneers. Deer browse the meadow where Ivec once lived and, at the Bradford mine site, tunnels are caved-in and filled with water, and almost all evidence of the mining town is gone.

Chalk Point: elev. 2,242 ft. Seen from the north summit of Mt. St. Helena, the bald, snow-white rock of Chalk Point stands out prominently from the surrounding forest green. From the wide turn-out at Fisher Point on the Ida Clayton road, it appears as it really is, a low, sway-back saddle.

Just as there is no 'point' at Chalk Point, neither is the rock true chalk (the consolidated remains of microscopic plants and animals). It is instead a volcanic ash (rhyolitic tuff) of violent origin like much of the upper mountain. Chalk Point represents one of the last gasps of the *Sonoma Volcanic* field as it moved north and died out, giving way to the much more recent Clear Lake volcanics.

An abandoned track leads to and away from the saddle, indicating it may once have been a four-wheel drive road. The extreme narrow width of the saddle, in some places barely 6 feet wide, may have once provided some thrilling travel.

Flag Peak: At 2,960 feet, Flag Peak is easily visible from Middletown, or from the summit of Mt. St. Helena, two miles due north. It was not named as the recipient of some 19th century patriotic flag raising, an event that occurred on nearby Sugarloaf. According to Earle Wrieden of Middletown, a large fir or pine on the summit is missing branches on one side so that in profile it resembles a flag.

Foote Creek: A spring-fed, perennial stream originating near Chalk Point and joining Redwood Creek* in Knight's Valley. It was named for the Foote family, descendents of the Holmes, who homesteaded here, well over a hundred years ago. Gil Foote died just a few years back. His grandfather was C.H. Holmes who owned 2,800 acres of prime farm and grazing land at the foot of Mt. St. Helena.

In the 1960's, the Foote property was slated along with other land to become part of the state park. That would have more than doubled its acreage to 9,000. This part of the deal fell through and only land of the Bureau of Land Management was transferred.

*Topographic maps from 1915 locate the Holmes residence between Foote Creek and LaFranchi Creek right off the highway. It also shows that Redwood Creek was called Holmes Creek in those days. Some time between 1915 and 1959, the name was changed to Redwood.

Garnett Creek: A seasonal stream, Garnett begins just above Table Rock and joins the Napa River north of Calistoga. Garnett Canyon was originally called King Canyon for a miner who lived there.

Lower Garnett Creek is the site of the Palisades Mine, the richest gold and silver mine in Napa county until Homestake began mining near Knoxville in the 1980's. Its heyday was over by 1893 but, by then, it had shipped a million dollars of gold and silver bullion.

It was a common practice to name a creek after the property owner living at the foot of the canyon. Records show that by the early 1880's, Garnetts owned this land. At the base of Mt. St. Helena, where the modern grade turns steeply uphill, John K. Garnett owned many acres of prune orchard until 1945. He was called "one of the finest men in the county" by old timer, Spud Hawkins. Garnett operated his farm with little profit during the Depression, hiring men who otherwise had no means to support their families.

Goat Roost Rock: Clearly seen from the main summit, Goat Roost Rock sits atop a ridge at a lofty 3,263 feet, overlooking Rattlesnake Canyon. It is thickly wooded until near its top. The north face is even more impressive, there being half a dozen huge monoliths of rock fused together, with trees sprouting from their 'heads'. Goat Roost Rock can be seen from the Ida Clayton Road.

There are no goats native to the California coast ranges, but old accounts give evidence that large herds of domestic goats were kept in the surrounding area. Claude Russell kept a large herd in Troutdale Canyon. They would sometimes climb a rough trail to the summit. It's not hard to imagine a few strays becoming separated from the main flock and becoming feral.

Grizzly Creek: An intermittent stream with headwaters on the northeast flank of Mt. St. Helena. It joins St. Helena Creek at the extreme southern end of Callayomi Valley, just south of the Bradford Creek junction. In all probability, it was named for the bears that once roamed here in high numbers, reports say well into the 1870's. Lake County was known as a bear hunter's paradise, and grizzlies were often seen by travelers and residents, lolling in the stream bottoms on hot summer days.

According to Erwin Gudde from *California Place Names*:

> "Grizzly is a name given to 200 places in California, mostly in the Sierra. This does not mean grizzlys were less common in the Coast Ranges. Prospectors used the term for any bear, whereas farmers knew the difference between a black or brown bear and a grizzly."

Earle Wrieden related an interesting story about Grizzly Creek. Once, on a hunting trip in this canyon at around 2000 foot elevation, he noticed that the surface stream had disappeared. He investigated and heard it echoing in an underground passage 20 feet down. Volcanic rock is not as well known as limestone (karst) topography for underground rivers and caverns, but one spectacular example can be seen at Pinnacles National Monument near Hollister.

Ida Clayton Road: This former toll road traverses the north and west slopes of the mountain to connect Highway 29 with Knight's Valley. It was always second choice to the Lawley Road and today sees even less traffic. Today, the road is a delightful drive, bike ride or walk with very little traffic. It is mostly used by the few residents, visitors to Smith's Trout Farm, and by sledders and tobogganers when winter snow falls. (See chapter 2, Ida Clayton Toll Road.)

Jericho Canyon: Jericho has been the key to travel over the mountain's east side since prehistoric times. Indians first used this canyon when traveling between Clear Lake and Napa. The Old Bull Trail, a volunteer effort, widened the way but basically followed the same route. By 1868, the Lawley Toll Road followed Jericho Creek at the base but soon diverged east up the ridge between Garnett and Jericho canyons. Since 1924, the modern highway has climbed Jericho's western upper canyon.

Not one clue has turned up to explain why it was so named. Perhaps a person 'of the faith' who settled here found significance in it. In the *Old Testament,* Jericho was the first city to fall to the Israelites when they came out of the desert and entered the Promised Land.

Kellogg: Nothing is left today of the town of Kellogg, although the most recent topographic maps show it located at the junction of Franz Valley Road and Highway 128. It was named for F.E. Kellogg, who was instrumental in several endeavors here, including developing the Ida Clayton Mine and Toll Road.

Another of its developers, William A. Stuart, tried to promote the town with a half column ad in the St. Helena Star of April, 1875. It promised that:

> "The townsite of Kellogg will be offered for sale by the most popular auctioneer in the country, in town lots of different sizes, and all the avenues are being surveyed eighty and one hundred feet in width. Lots for churches, school houses, store, stables and dwellings have already been spoken for, but no reserves will be made... The water attractions of Kellogg are recognized by all as second to no situation on the coast- eight millions of gallons of the purest mountain water, having its source in the never failing springs of Mt. St. Helena, pass daily through the flumes and ditches of the Company during the summer months, and the streams adjoining the town abound in mountain trout."

The town never grew to the size envisioned by its promoters. For many years of this century only a store and a post office remained. The Kettlewells, related to the man who founded Franz Valley, lived in the converted post office. These buildings were abandoned before they burned in a 1968 fire and only empty fields remain today.

Kellogg Creek: Runs through Rattlesnake Canyon in the wildest and least known part of the mountain. A perennial stream throughout most of its course, it begins on the Sonoma side of Sacre Gap, running south past Sugarloaf Hill, then southwest to join Yellowjacket

Surviving remnants of the town of Kellogg, circa WW1.

The Ida Clayton road captures snow almost every winter.

Creek, where they form Redwood Creek near the newly built, Peter Michael Winery.

Kimball Canyon: On the southwest flank of the mountain is Kimball Canyon, a steep, rugged, chaparral-choked defile, few people follow today. Kimball is the ultimate source of the Napa river, although the porous, volcanic soil of Mt. St. Helena also discharges water at many springs. Hikers on the fireroad between the north and south peaks, pass right over the head-waters of Kimball Creek. From here the stream runs south except under Red Hill, where it jogs east. Before it can spill its waters onto the Napa plain, it is stopped by Kimball Canyon Dam forming Lake Ghisolfo, the municipal water supply of Calistoga. Kimball Canyon is named for the Kimball family, who owned property at the foot of the canyon.

Mayacmas Mountains: Mt. St. Helena marks the southernmost reach of this range, although common usage has extended the name to include the mountains separating Napa and Sonoma valleys. The Mayacmas range forms the divide between the headwaters of the Russian River and Clear Lake. They were supposedly named for the Indians (Wappo, a division of the Yuki) living on the western slope of the divide. However, north of Mt. St. Helena, resided the northern (Mishewal) and central (Mutistul) Wappo. The southern Wappo (Meyahk'ama) for whom the range was named, lived south of the Mayacmas divide in Napa Valley. Meyahk'ama in Wappo language means "water going out place" for the tide waters south of Napa.

The historical evolution of the name is as follows: In 1836, the name, Serro de Los Mallacomes (serro meaning peak) was shown on a diseno (sketch) of the Caymus grant. By 1841, the name was Mallacomes y Plano de Agua Caliente, or Moristul.* By the turn of the century, the Geographic Board made Miyakma the official name but reversed its decision in 1941 to Mayacmas. (In Wappo language, Meyahk'ama is spelled without an 's', designating both singular and plural usage.

*The Mark West Springs 7.5 minute quadrangle from 1978 shows the name as Mallacomes or Moristul y Plan de Agua Caliente.

Mill Stream: Soon after making the transition from the Western Mine Road to the Ida Clayton Road, the source of the year-round flowing

Mill Stream will be found. The sawmill that supplied the Great Western Mine with lumber was located here. In eight short miles to the mountain's base, Mill Creek flows into three other creeks, Briggs, Mayacma and Redwood. *California Place Names* historian, Erwin Gudde says about 100 such names in the state are called Mill, all as far as could be ascertained, because of mills that had been situated there.

Mountain Mill House: Not found on standard topographic maps, it is included here due to its historical significance. The old Victorian can be seen right off the highway, 2 miles north of the 'pass', and just south of the confluence of Van Ness and St. Helena Creeks.

Today it is owned by the Catherine Burke School of San Francisco, a private girl's school. Recently it has been opened to groups for summer camping. Plans for extensive renovation will hopefully save Mt. St. Helena's oldest and grandest landmark from the same demise as Lawley Toll House.

Pilot Knob: Incredibly, there are two pilot knobs within a mile and a half of each other on the mountain's north side. One is in Sonoma, one in Lake County. The one most easily visible from the north summit is in Sonoma, 2,258 feet high. Gudde, in *California Place Names* has this to say -

> "It was a favored name with overland immigrants, prospectors and surveyors for a landmark which would 'pilot' them in the right direction. In California, at least twenty orographic features are called pilot peak, hill or knob".

Rattlesnake Canyon: A major watershed on the north side of Mt. St. Helena, rich in plant and animal life. It is drained by Kellogg Creek, which ends in Knight's Valley. Rattlesnake Canyon was, no doubt, named for frequent sightings of the venomous but shy reptile. Most old timers have a personal rattlesnake story to tell. Gudde reports there are 200 such place names on state maps, and local maps would show even more.

At the time of this writing, the southern part of Rattlesnake Canyon is in state park territory, while the northern is in private holdings. The *Robert Louis Stevenson State Park Interim Management Plan* done in 1987, shows interest in including all of the canyon in the park. Many hurdles would have to be negotiated, like finding willing sellers and sufficient funding, but the logic of a whole rather than a parceled canyon is undeniable.

Rattlesnake Spring: Two and a half miles north of Robert Louis Stevenson State Park, there is a dependable, year-round supply of fresh, spring water. It is a popular stop in summer to cool overheated radiators and fill water jugs. In a unique little book by Gary Vann, *To Take The Waters*, the author states the water flows by natural pressure and will vary from season to season.

Rattlesnake Spring comes out of the Troutdale watershed, so it has no hydrologic continuity with Rattlesnake Canyon. Ongoing analysis by the county indicates high quality water. (Other, road-accessed, piped springs in the region may or may not be.) In the not too distant past, Redwood Spring on Spring Mountain Road outside of St. Helena tested positive for salmonella. It has been routed under the road and is no longer used by the public. The spring between Pope Valley and Angwin on the Pope Valley grade is still of good quality.

Red Hill, elev. 2156 ft.: Easily seen from the vicinity of Bubble Rock, it is located on the prominent ridge dividing Napa from Knight's Valley, about 300 feet lower than Turk's Head (see below). Red Hill is named for the red, weathered serpentine on its east slope. When serpentine is 'fresh' it gives a green, waxy appearance, the toxic properties of the rock allowing few plants to grow. Areas like these can be seen on this side of the mountain, supporting a few digger pines and low growing shrubs. Over the years, serpentine turns reddish and less toxic, allowing denser stands of chaparral to grow. Red Hill is slowly being covered by this vegetation. Eventually, the reason to name it so may disappear.

Robert Louis Stevenson Memorial State Park: Named in honor of the Scottish author who spent a seven-week honeymoon near the Silverado Mine. It began modestly with a deed of 40 acres by Norman Livermore in 1949. There have been five expansions since then, the largest in 1967, when the Bureau of Land Management sold 2700 acres to the Park. The most recent was in 1988, when the Patten Silverado mine property was acquired. Presently, there are over 3,600 acres. Expansion is likely in the future.

182

About 30,000 people visit each year, most for historical reasons, but many come for the summit view, one of the world's finest.

Sacre Gap: The Gap is Mt. St. Helena's own *Continental Divide.* You can see it clearly from the north summit and from Middletown. It splits the headwaters of two major watersheds, Kellogg and Bradford Creeks. Standing on the Gap and facing west, all the rain that falls in front of you will run down Kellogg creek through Rattlesnake Canyon, join Redwood Creek in Knight's Valley, thence to Maacama Creek, where it joins the Russian River east of Healdsburg and eventually meets the Pacific Ocean at Jenner. All this flow is generally west.

All the rain that falls to your back, however, will flow east down Bradford Creek, north as St. Helena Creek, east with Putah Creek (temporarily slowed by Lake Berryessa), south with the Sacramento River, and finally west into the Bay and the Pacific. The rain falling east of Sacre Gap must go through every variation of the compass to get to the same place the western waters did by simply going west.

The origin of the name is unconfirmed but when these things were named, George Sacre was a judge in Middletown and his son, Otto, was a druggist.

St. Helena Creek: This perennial stream begins almost immediately north of the 'pass' on Highway 29. In quick succession, it gathers the waters of Troutdale, Grizzly, Bradford and St. Mary's creeks on the west, and Van Ness, Hoffman and Wilkinson on the east. Eventually, St. Helena Creek joins Putah Creek north of Middletown. The modern highway closely parallels St. Helena Creek from the Mountain Mill House, north, while the old Lawley Toll Road closely followed the creek as far as Middletown. Named after the mountain.

St. Mary's Creek: An intermittent stream beginning near Flag Peak. It joins St. Helena Creek in Callayomi Valley. The Western Mine Road follows St. Mary's for the first mile.

St. Mary's has had two different names in the past, according to the late Henry Mauldin. (His research, before his untimely death, led to an impressive 50 volumes and 15,000 typewritten pages.) Originally, it was called Hog Creek. Many years ago, mountain resident, Jim Wilkinson, had a large boar hog escape his pen and raid a neighbor's garden. Wilkinson then chased the uncooperative hog to a stream where it lay to cool off. All entreaties failed. Losing patience, he sold the hog on the spot to some Chinese, who were washing rice in the stream. At a word, they all descended on the hog at once and stabbed it to death with their knives. None of the Chinese was hurt.

Later, the creek became known as Western Mine creek for obvious reasons, still called that by some today. The present name, Mauldin found untraceable.

Sugarloaf Hill: Sugarloaf is readily seen from the Ida Clayton Road on the mountain's west side. Its distinct, rounded, symmetrical appearance comes as startling contrast to the sharp, angular, volcanic formations around it. Sugarloaf is composed of older, sedimentary and metamorphic rock with such interesting names as graywacke, chert, and greenstone, exposed after the younger volcanics had eroded away. These rocks are members of the Franciscan complex, rock that was around before the Pliocene volcanics were deposited.

The *Napa County Recorder* notes that, on July 24, 1861, a small party led by F.E. Kellogg, ceremoniously planted a flag atop Sugarloaf. A sixty foot flagstaff was hauled to the 1,717 foot summit by a three yoke oxen wagon, arriving at sunset. Their motivation was patriotism, hatred of secessionists and perhaps the flagging of Mt. St. Helena earlier in the month. Gudde, in *California Place Names:*

> "In past centuries, sugar did not come in bags or boxes, but in
> the form of a 'loaf' to the grocer who would break off pieces
> and sell it by the pound. The sight of the conoidal sugarloaf was
> very familiar and applied eventually to anything of the shape,
> then became a geographic generic name. California has around
> a hundred Sugarloafs."

Today, Sugarloaf is an attractive wooded knoll, perhaps as it was in 1861, explaining why a sixty foot flagstaff was needed. It looks down upon land on either side recently scraped clear for new vineyards, perhaps a bit worried for its scalp.

Table Rock: This is the most prominent, single rock massif in the area. Many travellers have remarked on the 200 foot cliff at the head of Garnett Canyon, including Robert Louis Stevenson and historian,

Table Rock, latest acquisition for RLS State Park.

Anne Roller Issler, both of whom called it Cathedral Rocks. It stands at its high point 2,685 feet above sea level, a lure for sightseers, hikers, rock climbers and nesting raptors. Once owned by the Hawkins family, it was sold in the spring of 1993 by the Conley family and is now part of Robert Louis Stevenson State Park.

Tanbark Canyon: Tanbark is an old name for tanoak (Lithocarpus densiflorus), as is the California chestnut oak. Tanoaks still grow in abundance as part of the mixed evergreen forest on the north side.

Tanoak bark was once harvested in this area for use in tanning leather. Earle Wrieden remembers an active industry when he was a boy. Tanoaks were harvested in Tanbark Canyon and in Dry Creek Canyon in the vicinity of Pine Mountain. He says it was not necessary for the trees to be logged but only peeled on one or two sides, so that the tree would continue to live. On the other hand, Helen Rocca Goss has written that when she was a child at the Helen mine, her favorite playground forest of tanoaks was cut down for shipment. Old news-paper stories show that stagecoach entrepreneur Bill Spiers had a thriving business hauling tons of bark over the mountain and down to Napa where it was shipped to the Bay Area.

Toll House Road: This is the longest existing piece of the original toll road completed by John Lawley in 1867. It begins two miles out of Calistoga and connects with the new highway a little more than halfway to the top. Except for asphalting and guard rails, it looks pretty much as it did in the old days. (See Chapter 2.)

An historical marker commemorating the Lawley Toll Road and the road it superseded was placed just south of Middletown in 1950 on the hundreth anniversary of the Old Bull Trail.

Tom Dye Rock, Elev. 3100 ft.: As seen from the highest peak, it lies above and to the right of Sacre Gap. Behind it is one of the best stories of all the mountain's place names. A man from Middletown spent some time in a cave here, hiding from the law. There are several versions of the story, but most agree that Charley Bates was murdered and Tom Dye was the killer.

One version was told by Henry Mauldin. According to his story, Charley Bates was a fine young man, living in Middletown, married for only a month. Due to his job at the Oat Hill Mine, inhalation of mercury vapor was giving him health problems with his teeth and gums, what oldtimers called 'getting salivated'. He went into the bar at Middletown for a cure. Earlier, Tom Dye and he had quarreled, why, no one really knows. As Bates approached the door of the saloon, Dye shot him. Bates lived only 3 hours, his wife by his side.

Dye escaped, said Mauldin, to live in a cave on Mt. St. Helena for 7 months. Friends brought food and other provisions. Allegedly, a lawyer from Middletown, Dallas Poston, offered to get Dye off the hook if he surrendered. Dye came into town, was jailed, but Poston then reneged on his promise and kept the reward money! Dye was sentenced to 15 years for murder, but served only 7 due to ill health. He returned to Lake County for his family and moved on.

The facts that can be verified, make for a markedly different story. In actuality: 1) it is unlikely Dye spent much time at Tom Dye Rock, 2) he could not have been lured from there because he was captured in Reno, 3) he served only five and a half years, not seven, 4) was released for reasons other than health, and 5) although he may have returned to Lake County, it was not for his family, as they had moved out years before. Here are the facts.

186

On October 1,1878, Charles S. Bates was killed in Middletown. Thomas Dye was immediately arrested and placed in the Lakeport jail. The *Weekly Calistogan* of October 9 editorialized that "If he escapes the hangman's noose, we shall wonder". On November 9, 1878, Tom Dye and W.A. Barnes were indicted for the murder of Charles Bates by the Grand Jury. Barnes is said to have encouraged Dye in the deed.

On November 27, Dye's lawyer, Rodney Hudson, was successful in having the indictment thrown out because the Grand Jury had received illegal and improper evidence. However, Dye remained in jail to answer to the next Grand Jury. W.A.Barnes was acquitted in his trial as accessory to the murder.

Dye's second trial was still pending, when he made an ingenious escape from the Lakeport jail on March 7, 1879. At the back wall of the jail was a recess, about two feet wide, extending from floor to ceiling. Jamming stove wood between the walls, Dye built a wooden 'ladder' which he ascended to an iron grate. This obstacle was bypassed by removing mortar and brick with an iron spike until a space was created to squeeze past. Finally, he cut a hole in the zinc roof with a mysteriously procured knife, and set himself free.

He was seen briefly in the foothills west of town, but the trail was soon lost. Dye vanished for over a year. Then, on August 25,1880, he was recaptured in Reno, Nevada.

Sheriff Burtnett of Lake County brought him back from Reno in a journey that took four days. Dye had been incognito for nearly a year and a half, easily encompassing the seven month period he is said to have spent at Tom Dye Rock. Local historian, Helen Rocca Goss does not concur. She thinks Dye spent most of this time in Reno, staying at the outcrop for only two brief periods. Visits to Lake County were probably to see his family. However much time he did spend on Mt. St. Helena, it was enough to create a local legend.

Letters written to family members by Dye at this time reveal a far different version of the killing than was publicized. Dye's contention was that Bates was not walking into the saloon, but came straight at him with hostile words and intent. When just a few feet away, Bates was shot in self defense. Tom's need to gather the $500 sum necessary for his legal defense was his motivation to escape. Public opinion was against him though, and may have led to juror prejudice.

Dye's long-delayed second trial got under way on November 24, 1880. Some of the more prominent witnesses were E.J. Bradford, Taylor Harbin, and J.H. Kellogg. His lawyers were Welch, Britt, Henly, and Noel. Four lawyers were apparently less effective than one, because the trial closed only two and half weeks later. On December 11,1880, Dye was convicted of second degree murder and sentenced to San Quentin for 15 years.

Public opinion was that Dye got off lightly, yet, in the wake of the case, came controversy. Only a week after Dye was incarcerated on December 16, D.B. Armstrong of Middletown, a witness in the Dye case, was charged with perjury. With bail raised to $750, his trial began a week later. Newspapers indicate that the jurors may have made their opinions known to outsiders before giving the verdict. How Armstrong's trial ended, I don't know, but the controversy eventually led to Dye's early release from prison.

Meanwhile, Dye's wife, Nancy, with her nine children, moved out of Middletown to Alameda County to be near her husband. In 1885, the State Board of Prison Directors at San Quentin commuted Dye's 15 year sentence to eight years. They gave three persuasive reasons: 1) Four jurors signed sworn statements that the verdict was a result of a compromise. They believed Dye guilty only of manslaughter, but were deceived by the jury foreman to give the higher sentence of second degree murder. 2) Dye was suffering from chronic articular rheumatism and his health would not improve in prison. 3) Dye had exhibited exemplary character while incarcerated.

Tom Dye was released from San Quentin on August 19,1886, after serving about five and a half years. Curiously, he did not rejoin his family immediately but lived and worked in Napa County for some time. He is believed to have died in Benicia in 1890.

Troutdale Creek: Flowing east through one of the wildest and prettiest canyons on the mountain, Troutdale becomes perennial around the 2800 foot level. The USGS topographic map (photo-revised 1980) shows Troutdale as intermittent after filling a reservoir by the highway. I have been told by the owners, the Livermores, that this reservoir is no longer there. It was backfilled some years ago without permission by a caretaker. Troutdale Creek is once again confluent with St. Helena Creek.

Most of Troutdale Creek Canyon is in the state park but there is no access at this time. Part of the park's expansion plan includes access to this historically significant watershed but, unfortunately, that may be years in the future.

By the 1920's, Claude and Clara Russell were homesteading this canyon, making a living by, among other things, selling goat's milk. Following the failure of plans for a dude ranch, the Russells ran a very successful trout farm in the 40's and 50's. When Claude Russell died, his second wife, Cleavee, sold the property to the state park.

Turk's Head, elev. 2,480': Not found on a standard topographic map, this landmark is included here due to its prominence in the physical and historical landscape. It is easily seen from the fire road near Bubble Rock. Turk's Head is part of the ridge that separates Knight's Valley from upper Napa Valley, with commanding views of both.

This peculiar looking rock lends itself to odd descriptions. An article in the *Napa Daily Reporter* of Dec. 25, 1890, features a sketch of the rock, calling it the 'Sphinx' and, alternately, 'Louis XI'. The drawing is a personification of a Frenchman with his characteristic cap. Other articles of this period indicate it was a regular destination for tourists staying at the Toll House, along with a horseback ride to the summit and a visit to the trout ponds of Arcadia.

Because of its red coloring, Turk's Head can be confused with Red Hill, a little way down on the same ridge. Just a few years back, a plane made a direct hit with fire retardant on old Louis' head and, so far, the rain has been ineffective in washing it off. The natural color of the rock is seen on the right or northeast side.

Western Mine Road: Two miles south of Middletown is a road junction where a prominent sign directs you to Smith's Trout Farm. Here, at what used to be called the Western Gate, the Western Mine Road leaves Highway 29 and runs for three miles to the Mayacmas crest. The continuation to Knight's Valley is called the Ida Clayton Road.

The Western Mine Road was built in 1874-1875 specifically to service the Great Western Mine, opened a year before. Free passage was given to employees of the mine in return for building the road. The last two miles to the top are still an unpaved, but well-graded gravel road. In winter, snow may stay on the ground for up to a week, requiring a four-wheel drive vehicle.

Yellowjacket Creek : Starting just under the north peak and flowing west, Yellowjacket Creek is intermittent until the 1400 foot level, where it gushes from underneath the volcanic cap all year. It flows southwest until it meets Kellogg creek near Highway 128, becoming Redwood Creek. Rumor has it that, in the old days, fishing trips were risky here because the yellowjackets were thick enough to kill.

The Yellowjacket Quicksilver Mine, never a major producer, operated for four years in the early 1870's. Its chief fame stems from the murder of Major Harry Larkyns by Edweard Muybridge, which took place here in 1874.

Artist's rendition of Turk's Head; from the Christmas, 1890 edition of the Napa Daily Reporter

LOUIS XI OR THE "SPHINK" ON MT ST HELENA NEAR THE MOUNTAIN TOLL HOUSE.

190

Chapter 10

Mt. St. Helena Summit Guide

"At daybreak the fog lies perfectly quiet like water in a calm. When the sun comes out it begins to move and climb. Mountain peaks and hills are islands until the fog moves higher and blots them out. Napa Valley on the east and Sonoma Valley on the west at last fill up, and all the islands are gone. And then if you climb higher up the mountain you look out over rolling billows. The hotter the sun the more motion in the fog, you know. On a very bright day the peak of Mount Saint Helena is reflected as though in a sea. Before such sights an old man like me takes off his hat."

Charles Lawley

Introduction

Mt. St. Helena is located at the northeastern end of Napa Valley, 80 road miles north of San Francisco, where Sonoma, Lake, and Napa counties all meet. It is prominent from many parts of the Napa Valley. Seen from down-valley, the north peak is on the left edge of the flat summit plateau, 4343 feet above sea level. The south peak, 340 feet lower, is on the right. On clear days in St. Helena, the lookout tower on the north peak and communications equipment on the south can be seen with the unaided eye.

The most popular and pleasant times to visit are the spring and autumn weekends. By rough estimate, a hundred people a day will be on the mountain at these times. Fine displays of wildflowers are to be found in the spring, while in the autumn, the reds, yellows, and oranges of the vineyards contrast brilliantly with the dark green of the evergreen forest and the gray-green chaparral slopes. Weather extremes can be pretty severe in summer and winter, but with a little preparation, they can be just as rewarding. If it's solitude you're looking for, you may be the only one hiking Mt. St. Helena on a weekday.

The summit trail is five miles long, the first mile being somewhat rough in places, the last four on a well-graded fire road. You may encounter a vehicle or two, carrying special permits to drive the road. This should happen infrequently and few people seem to mind. Most hikers' average speed is two miles an hour on the uphill, which puts them on top in 2½ hours. Descents are about an hour less, so with a lunch stop consider this at least a half day outing.

There are no services at Robert Louis Stevenson State Park and no facilities besides the picnic tables at the trailhead. No official residence for park personnel exists, but rangers headquartered at Bothe State Park do patrol here on weekends. The closest water source is Rattlesnake Spring two and a half miles down the north side. This is an excellent source of natural spring water.

Those of us who use the park often have grown accustomed to the advantages that lack of development can bring - no registration procedure, no fee to pay, and fewer visitors. The disadvantages include lack of water, no restrooms and a haphazard parking arrangement. Worst of all is the degradation to park features due to lack of enforcement capability. Vandalism has repeatedly afflicted this area.

Park rules are few and easily followed. No dogs are allowed due to their habit of disturbing wildlife (some years ago, a friend of mine brought her dog and was slapped with an expensive fine, now since doubled in price). And no overnight camping is allowed - Robert Louis Stevenson is strictly a day use park. To these could be added a voluntary ban on smoking, in light of the countless fires that have swept these vulnerable slopes. Please stay on the trail. Switchback cutting actually takes more energy and saves less time than is thought. In the last 5 years, trail degradation has increased dramatically, despite efforts to control it. This kind of thoughtlessness decreases enjoyment for everyone. Littering has increased also. You can help reverse this trend by picking up and packing out discarded trash.

Highway 29 as it begins the uphill grade to the state park.

These picnic tables at the trailhead are about the only improvements at RLS State Park.

193

Things To Look For

Gliders : The white, albatross-winged sailplanes can often be seen zipping by in the afternoon, when conditions are favorable on this side of the valley. Sometimes one flies so close you can wave to the pilot. If you'd like to see a slightly higher view than the summit affords, a cramped back seat may be purchased in one of these birds at the Calistoga airport.

Mountain Bikers : Mountain biking has arrived on Mt. St. Helena, although not with the impact seen at Point Reyes or Mount Tamalpais. To my knowledge, mountain bikers here are courteous and no unpleasant hiker/biker incidents have occurred, but it is good to be aware of each other's presence.

Riders will want to have a solid rig with good wide tires because the upper road has large gravelly areas, and, everywhere, the surface can be slippery. Serious accidents have happened. A good rain will actually make the road safer by temporarily holding loose soil particles together. Moisture will quickly drain through the porous, volcanic soil. When dry, the 'ball-bearing' effect on dry roads can be treacherous.

An ascent takes an hour or so, descents about half that. Access is a half -mile north from the trailhead parking, where the fireroad, with a metal gate, meets the highway. There is parking for several cars on the highway's east side. Riding the hiking trail to the fireroad is a bad idea. The trail is too narrow for bikes and people to pass, and too steep and rough in the upper part to ride anyway. Bikes can be rented from the friendly people at Palisades Mountain Shop in Calistoga.

Rock Climbers : Rock climbing on Mt. St. Helena dates back to at least the 1960's. Information on climbing routes is mostly by word of mouth, although a brief mention has been made in Marc Jenson's *Climbing in the San Francisco Bay Region.* In addition, Jim Thornburg's, *1992 Bay Area Rock* has some useful information. Unfortunately, it also contains a number of factual errors.

There are four main climbing areas on the mountain. One is the Silverado mine's 75 foot north face. With direct sunlight only during midday hours, this is the most comfortable place to climb in the heat

194

Rock climber contemplates a steep section.

of summer. The second, and most popular site is the Bubble Rock, half a mile beyond the mine at a sharp bend in the fireroad. For hikers, this is a pleasant place to take a breather and watch the antics unfold on many spring and fall weekends. It is usually deserted in the summer due to all-day, intense sun exposure. Since this is a practice area, most climbers are content to toprope (rig a rope pulley with a secure top anchor) but some routes are climbed from the ground up, a much more serious proposition.

The third area, called the High Rocks, had waned in popularity in the last decade but recently has seen a flurry of new routes. These 'sport' climbs are of high quality and without doubt the hardest on the mountain. They are above the fireroad about a quarter-mile beyond the Bubble. The older, established routes can be of high quality or they can be lousy. These routes must be chosen carefully. The High Rocks are the highest cliffs on this side of the mountain and descents can be complex. A curious custom of climbers to personalize the climbs they make has produced such names as The Bear, Twinkle Toes Traverse, Nun's Crack, Snakeskin, and Guillotine Flake.

The Far Side is a very special area to me and one I would rather have remain unknown to the general public. Published information (some inaccurate) forces me to speak out. Located due west of the Bubble on a volunteer trail, the Far Side has nearly 40 generally high quality face and crack climbs from moderate to severe difficulty. Almost all the routes have been designed for lead climbing. This is not a "sport" climbing area but the routes are definitely sporty and emphasis is on adventure and challenge, both physical and mental. Many routes are bolted where protection was otherwise unavailable, but some routes take only natural pro.

Until recently, solitude at the Far Side was a given, weekend or weekday. Since the publication of *Bay Area Rock* the difference is hugely noticeable. Litter and improperly disposed human waste are now a problem. Please show respect for this special place. After all, it is part of the state park.

Climbing is at once exhilarating, heart-pumping, demanding, and exacting. It often requires a total commitment, unmatched by any

196

other sport. Serious accidents have occurred here in the past. Exercising good judgement through knowledge of one's limitations could have prevented most of these. The state park has had a tolerant view of climbing in the past and it is hoped they will continue to do so in the future. Please ensure continued access by climbing responsibly.

Things To Look Out For

Ticks : These tiny bloodsuckers are classified as arachnids, in a class with spiders and scorpions. Winter, spring, and early summer are the most likely times to encounter them. A good way to avoid them is to stay on the trail. Ticks like to hang out on brush and grass at the ankle or calf level. Then, when they sense a heat source, they will drop onto their prey and attach instantly.

If you are on an overgrown trail or in brushy country, don't wait to get home to check for ticks. By then, one may have its head half buried in your skin. I make it a practice to stop periodically to brush them off. That interval may be every quarter hour, or once a minute with bad conditions (once in Big Sur on an overgrown trail I had to stop every hundred feet to remove a dozen each time. A friend following came through scot-free!).

Ticks are black or red in color, about the size of a pinhead or the tip of a wooden match. They are slow moving, usually attach to pant legs first, and take a long time to decide on the next meal's location. This gives you plenty of time to avoid problems. I often wear white or light colored clothing to make spotting obvious. Do more than a cursory look if you are wearing shorts because the slow moving tick can be mistaken for a small mole.

The existence of Lyme disease in Northern California has grown from mini-epidemic to minor hysteria recently. West-coasters can breathe easy compared to our eastern counterparts. According to a 1990 report from a Santa Rosa physician, tick infection rates are six to twenty times more likely on the east coast. Sixty per cent of ticks encountered, carry Lyme disease as compared to only 1 to 2% on the west coast. In addition to that, ticks must be embedded for an average of 12 hours before infection can occur. A little common sense prevention should take all the fear out of a tick encounter.

Despite precautions, if you spend a lot of time outdoors, eventually a tick will find its way to your bloodstream. Don't panic. There are several good ways to remove them. One of the best is to cover the tick in heavy oil or vaseline for half an hour, until it suffocates. It should then be easy to remove. Another technique is to grasp the tick's mouth parts with tweezers and pull slowly until it is completely disengaged. Any parts left could cause infection. If you are out in the field and have only a match or candle, try holding it close to the affected part. The tick may disengage but this method is a last resort.

If you don't trust your medical skills or are still concerned, by all means go to a doctor. Save the tick in alcohol for identification. The small, red-bodied *Ixodes pacificus* is the only species that can transmit Lyme disease.

Snakes: There are a dozen kinds of snakes on Mt. St. Helena, only one of which is venomous, the Western Rattlesnake (Crotalus viridis Oreganus). Their most active months are April and May although, in the high summer, they might be about morning or evening. Rattlesnakes are shy creatures and will stay out of your way if you let them. Far less likely to be encountered than ticks, you may never run across one as a casual hiker. Then again, you may see or hear three in fifteen minutes as occurred on a recent trip in nearby Pope Valley. Be assured that rattlers are far less common than in 1880 when Robert Louis Stevenson tried to convince us that there was a rattlesnake under every bush, with

> "the rattles whizzing on every side like spinning wheels, and the combined hiss or buzz rising louder and angrier at any sudden movement."

In the rare event of a bite, it's important to stay calm in the knowledge that few (the very young and the very old) ever die from rattlesnake venom. First, identify the reptile as venomous or not, then observe whether fang puncture marks are present. If there are no fang holes, infection is unlikely. According to Fred T. Darvill Jr. in *Mountaineering Medicine,* if the reptile is venomous and fang marks are present, about 75% of those bitten will have significant symptoms, like burning pain, swelling, weakness, nausea, and 'pins and needles' sensations.

Always controversial, the incision/suction, first aid treatment is now

198

outdated. Throw out that old snake bite kit with the small scalpel. For $10, you can purchase a small pump that draws venom from the wound safely. Administer first aid within five minutes or treatment will be ineffective. First aid kit or not, antivenin treatment at a hospital is highly recommended. If a friend or passerby can be sent for help quickly and the victim is near a road, have him/her stay put. Otherwise, walk out slowly.

Poison Oak : Not related to true oaks, Toxicondron diversilobium is common on Mt. St. Helena. It prefers shady, moist but not wet conditions, but can be found on dry chaparral slopes. Its bright green foliage makes it an attractive plant and it might be a favorite of the horticulturalist if not for its well known dermal toxicity. Bright green in spring, turning dull in summer, red in the fall, and leafless in winter, it's good to know its appearance year round. The irritating chemicals can produce a rash even when the plant is dormant.

After many cases of poison oak, I find prevention the best cure. Any contact should be washed off thoroughly with cool water as soon as possible. At home, shower in cool water first, to close the pores, then follow with soap and warm water. If your skin is sensitive and an itchy rash appears anyway, try the stoic's approach and never, ever scratch. You may find the rash gone within a week, dying from lack of attention! There are several medications on the market to relieve itching and help you in your resolve.

Heat: Most summit hikers prefer the spring and fall months, and desert the upper slopes of Mt. St. Helena in summer for the higher elevations or the ocean shore. Nevertheless, sane summer hiking is quite possible here. Try the early morning, especially when the sea fogs are covering the lower elevations. Or start at four or five in the afternoon to benefit from the cooling evening breezes. With the long summer hours it's possible to make a round trip by nightfall. If you choose to ascend on or near the full moon, your flashlight can be left behind. Ascents on the full moon have lately become popular with hikers and especially mountain bikers, who, in this way, avoid the heat problem altogether.

Wear light, loose clothing, a hat, sunglasses, a layer of sunscreen, and bring two quarts of water in your pack. Sturdy shoes or boots with vibram soles prevent skids when descending the steeper, slippery sections. When the heat waves come in, as they do periodically, usually lasting 3 days, it's best to stay off the mountain and close to a major water source. A Death Valley-like, 117 degrees was recorded in Calistoga in 1972. Usually though, five degrees over a hundred would be uncommon.

Cold: Although a modest 4,343 feet above sea level, Mt. St. Helena will experience severe weather each winter, standing squarely in the path of many wet Pacific storms. Its average annual rainfall at 59 inches is nearly twice that of many Napa Valley towns, a few miles away. One to three times a winter, it will capture snow, visible from down-valley for a few days. In a big storm recently, 3 to 4 feet of snow fell, closing the upper fire road for a week. I have seen snow patches in the shady, northern ravines 3 weeks after the last storm.

Mt. St. Helena will give you plenty of warning when weather is approaching, unlike, for example, the Cascade volcanoes where surprise storms can be deadly. Old timers say a cloud cap over the peak means rain the next day. When it does finally arrive though, watch out. A hundred inches of rain is not uncommon in a wet year. According to local author Helen Rocca Goss, the year 1908 saw 136 inches of rain at the nearby Helen Mine, 71 in one month!

One New Year's Day, I accompanied a large group on an ascent of Mt. St. Helena. The day began drizzly, increased to a steady rain half-way up, and by the top, rain was blowing sideways with visibility at a 100 feet. We ate our lunch hurriedly in the shelter of the tower and fled. Rainproofs, called Goretex, kept me dry and made the day enjoyable. Having gotten a bad rap when first introduced, quality control with their distributors has improved this product to a highly recommendable state. Water proof clothing made by other manufacturers can also be found at less than sky-high prices.

In between storms, winter can be a good time to be here. One of the best reasons to make a winter ascent is the possibility of seeing Mount Shasta, 192 miles to the north. The likeliest time to see it is when strong north winds have cleared the air. The last 1,000 feet of Shasta, a tiny white triangle, can be seen 10 degrees east of north, just to the right of a large white spot below the final ridge on the horizon. Many people confuse it with Mount Lassen, a full 35 degrees east of north. Binoculars are helpful.

When you go, be prepared. Take lots of warm, layerable clothing, wind or rain proof outer shells, and high octane food. Any time between November and May is subject to cold weather.

Things To Bring

Water: No water is available, either at the trailhead or anywhere on the hiking trail. If you discover that your canteens are empty on arrival, drive down to Rattlesnake Spring. It's found 2½ miles toward Middletown (north) at a turnout on the west side. Used by locals and travellers for many years, this natural spring water flows from a pipe the year round.

On a cool day, one quart per person is adequate, on a hot day, two quarts or more are recommended. Don't be fooled by the cool shade and the breeze that often blows through the gap at the trailhead. The drier, upper slopes can be 5 to 10 degrees warmer. Having trouble deciding whether it's a 1 or 2 quart day? At such times, I often 'camel up', downing a pint or two of water before leaving to 'saturate the cells'. In this way I avoid carrying the extra weight, and find that a drink is unnecessary for the first hour or two. If you try this method, ladies, be forewarned- no restroom facilities are found in the park.

Food: Caloric requirements vary so much between individuals that it's beyond the scope of this book to make specific recommendations. The best that can be said here is to take something- whether it's a Jethro Clampett shopping bag lunch that fills your pack or a candy bar in the back pocket, you'll probably need sustenance for the 10 mile round trip. Whatever containers you bring, take them out with you, they're a lot lighter empty than full. On cold days take extra food because you'll be burning it to stay warm.

Binoculars: A valuable accessory for spotting distant landmarks, like Mounts Shasta and Lassen, wildlife, like deer, fox and red-tailed hawks, and perhaps a friend in a hang-glider or sailplane, catching thermal updrafts rising dependably off the mountainous slopes.

Guide Books : This book is not the definitive work on birds, plants, rocks and minerals of Mt. St. Helena. For that specialty guides are needed. Several are available at the bookstore in Calistoga. The Audubon Society Pocket Guides are a good place to start. Guide books can enhance your visit by increasing awareness of the natural world. One caveat -- study creates as many questions as answers.

Summit Trail Guide To Mt. St. Helena

To find the trailhead, drive north on Highway 29 from the town of Calistoga 7.8 miles, or south from Middletown 8.2 miles, until the crest of the pass. A sign indicates you have arrived at Robert Louis Stevenson State Park. There is a large turnout on the east side and a smaller one on the west. The trail starts from the west turnout. If you park on the east, be careful crossing the highway. No one is slowing down here.

Wooden steps lead to a large, pleasant clearing. This is the site of the famous Lawley Toll House Inn, once located against the hillside just to the right of the trailhead. Some of the old foundation is still there, as well as the water trough to its left. By the early fifties it had become a victim of vandalism and old age. The park service had to tear it down in 1953, along with dreams of restoring it as a museum.

Near the toll house was the toll gate, in operation until 1924 when the modern highway closed down the toll road for good. Old photographs indicate the toll gate was secured to a large douglas fir tree on the left (south) edge of the clearing. This may be the same tree fallen against the hillside today, downed during the flood year of 1986. A remnant of the old Lawley Toll Road can be picked up on the clearing's far (north) side and traced in a loop to the new highway. To your right is a picturesque picnic area. This is the site of the old croquet ground. Although he never participated in the game, Robert Louis Stevenson enjoyed watching the toll house guests play while reading his mail on the long, covered porch.

Before starting out be sure to have a quart of water in your pack. The first mile is shady but the last four are totally exposed to the sun, wonderfully or pitilessly depending on the season.

Mile 0: At the trail sign, a short series of steps leads immediately into a cool woodland of madrone, tan oak, douglas fir, black oak, and bay. These trees are typical of the mixed evergreen plant community. In addition, an occasional dogwood flowers brightly in the spring. A small streamcourse will be seen at the first long switchback. Water flows here only in the winter and spring. It is fed by one of the many springs that flow from the porous volcanic rock of Mt. St. Helena.

Mile .25: A bench has been provided by the park for rest and enjoyment. The trail winds leisurely upward with an occasional view of Butts Canyon to the northeast until about...

Mile .50: The first appearance of smooth, red-barked manzanita indicates we are in a forest/chaparral transition zone. Just above the trail is a fine example of succession. The once-dominant manzanita is being shaded out by knobcone pine and ponderosa pine. Eventually, the manzanita will all but die out, until the next fire creates space and light for them to compete. Wetter conditions on this north slope have allowed some knobcones to grow 45 or 50 feet high.

Mile .70: The last switchback before the monument. Fine views can be had of the Palisades, craggy volcanic cliffs to the southeast. They may one day be part of the Park. Directly below is the crest of the pass. The 'sea fogs' often entirely cover the valleys of Napa and Sonoma on spring or early summer mornings, leaving only islands of the highest knobs and knolls in view. At these times, the great mass of fog will sometimes try to invade Lake County over this pass, only to disappear in wispy strands time and again, as if into the maw of some fog-eating monster.

Mile .75: In this shady dell, Stevenson and his bride, Fanny, spent their honeymoon in June and July of 1880. The inscription on the monument claiming RLS wrote the Silverado Squatters here is not quite correct. Notes he scribbled by lamplight were used to write the book when he returned to Europe.

The old assayer's cabin the newly-weds appropriated was a sloppy, two story affair plastered against the hillside above the monument, just to the left of the rock outcropping. If you're interested in what it looked like, read Arthur Orton's definitive study, *Reconstructing the Robert Louis Stevenson 'Silverado Squatters' Cabin.* The upper mine

Hikers on the fireroad.

shaft is uphill and to the left of the monument. Ore carts once rumbled down the hill on a narrow gauge rail, leaving the debris you're standing on today. At the tunnel entrance, wooden wedges, called 'stulls,' can be seen, probably placed by Harry Patten in one of his many attempts to relocate the lost silver vein. Nowadays, spelunkers occasionally explore the murky depths, and rock climbers use the 75 foot north face for practice year-round.

A rough trail leads past the mine to the fireroad but most people will want to take the regular trail from the monument.

Mile .80 :First appearance of sugar pines. The arrow-straight sugar pine is left clean and attractive because branches will break off flush with the trunk. This young pine stands next to an older douglas fir trying to devour one of Harry Patten's old trespassing signs. Here we leave the forest and enter the chaparral/knobcone pine community. A steep, erosion-marred section leads to...

Mile .85: The junction with the fireroad. To the right, the fireroad connects with the highway one and a half miles away. Stay left for the summit. Note the dramatic difference in vegetation here. Above the road is young knobcone pine forest of uniform age, below, mixed evergreen forest. The fireroad has lived up to its name.

Mile 1.0: Here is the first view of the entire Napa Valley and Mt. Diablo, 66 air miles to the south. Diablo can be seen on any clear day as the twin-summited mass on the southern horizon. It was named after a Spanish/Indian battle when allegedly the Devil himself materialized from out of the mountain to help the struggling Spaniards.

On the road ahead is the hottest and driest side of Mt. St. Helena. Many fires have burned through here in the past and no doubt will in the future. The 1964 Hanley fire swept through here, as did the most recent Silverado Ranch fire of 1982. Just ten years later, most of the evidence had been eclipsed by regrowth of the fire-adapted chaparral.

The most phoenix-like species of chaparral is Cushing's manzanita. After a fire, it re-sprouts first from a knot-like growth at its base, called a *burl*. Other species abound. Stanford manzanita has bright green, ellipse-shaped leaves, while hoary manzanita is named for the 'hairs' on its gray-green leaves. These, along with chamise, ceanothus (lilac) and toyon (Christmas berry), mountain mahogany, and coffeeberry make up the bulk of the richly bio-diverse chaparral community.

Mile 1.25: These large trees have somehow managed to escape destruction from the last two blazes. They include a bay, a canyon live oak, and a gray (digger) pine. Many 'islands' of vegetation escaped the fire's notice in 1982, far fewer in the 1964 inferno.

Mile 1.33: Here, where the road doubles back on itself is the so-called 'Bubble Rock', named for the prominent potholes on the steepest part of the face. This is a popular stop for hikers to watch rock climbers work their way up the pockmarked lava rock. Handholds may be as small as the edge of a coin, or virtual caves where a whole arm can be inserted and 'locked off' to allow a pretty fair rest, even on the slightly overhanging rock.

The rock itself is a mixture of pyroclastics and ash flow, deposited here at the end of a long period of volcanism, 3 to 11 million years ago. Compositionally, the rock is called rhyolite, nearly identical to granite with one major difference. It formed quickly on the surface, whereas granite forms below ground with intense heat and pressure, making a much harder and denser rock. Most of the 'bubbles' held pebbles and boulders of a different composition than the main rock, which subsequently weathered away. Only the tiniest bubbles are due to the presence of air pockets in the lava when it hardened.

High on the hillside above the Bubble is Hole-in-the-Rock, a striking formation. Next to it is Hailstone Rock. In the right light, this is also the best place to view Turk's Head and Red Hill, directly downslope. As you continue up the fireroad to about...

Mile 1.5: ...on your left upslope is an impressive collection of dark, volcanic cliffs called the 'High Rocks'. Ahead is more evidence that the fireroad has served as a selective barrier to fire: above, a uniform stand of knobcone pines, below only chaparral.

Mile 1.75: On the left and slightly uphill are the 'Digits', so called for their three, finger-like pinnacles.

Mile 2.0: One of several places along the trail that bay trees (Umbellularia californica) can be found. This is not the true bay, but it has even more powerful aromatics than *Laurus nobilis*. I have gathered leaves from this tree, dried and used them for cooking, and found them as good as store bought (removing vegetation inside the park

Bubble Rock; probably the mountain's most popular rock climbing crag.

boundaries is, of course, prohibited). Just ahead the road passes under the power lines that feed communications equipment on both peaks. Middletown is now in view, as well as the Berryessa Valley to the east.

Mile 2.5: At the 180 degree, nearly flat, hairpin turn, you are directly over the top of the High Rocks, seen a mile earlier.

Mile 3.0: At a bend in the road, where it passes under the power lines a second time, there is a small rock outcropping. If you scramble to the top of this modest outcrop, a fine view of a rugged, unnamed canyon is seen. Far below, a homestead can be made out, the only private dwelling within the state park.

The next quarter mile climbs steeply, often shaded by the bulk of the south peak. This section can be downright cold in winter and hold snow for a week after a big storm (cross country ski-ing is possible but ephemeral). A few douglas fir reappear on the upper slopes, reflecting the change in sun exposure. The road levels out as you reach...

Mile 3.25: ...and a first view of the main peak is followed quickly by the junction with the south peak trail. The south peak summit is only .4 mile away, often the sole destination of many hikers. It has commanding views of the Napa Valley due south, Sonoma Valley and the Pacific Ocean to the west, and the Palisades to the east. The Bureau of Land Management still owns the topmost 40 acres of the south peak and leases land to various parties who have installed communication equipment. One of the leaseholders, Telecommunications Inc., built an observation deck in 1987 for the public. It features a display showing air line miles to major topographic features.

For views of the northern state and a chance to see elusive Mount Shasta, you must stay on the road for another 1.7 miles. Stretching ahead is the surprisingly flat summit plateau, sandwiched between the north and south peaks. In the late 1800's, it was popularly and erroneously thought of as the crater of the extinct volcano.

Mile 3.75: The broad summit plateau terminates at the end of a gradual downhill and crosses a streamcourse. If any one creek can be called the source of the Napa River, this is it. Kimball Creek gathers more definition to your left and eventually feeds Lake Gisolfo, Calistoga's municipal water source. Just below the dam site, the Napa

208

River begins its journey to San Pablo Bay. On either side of the road are dense stands of manzanita.

Mile 4.0: Hairpin turn. Near the back of the wide turn are several giant chinquapin trees (Castanopsis chrysophylla var. minor). The chinquapin's flowers produce burs with long spines, enclosing one to three nuts, about ½ inch long. These may be found scattered on the ground nearby. Just ahead, unobstructed views into Lake County.

Mile 4.25: Near here, look for an odd member of the California lilac genus, Tobacco brush (Ceanothus velutinus var. leavigaatus). The sweet, sticky aroma is so powerful that all you need is a nose in working order to locate it. The leaves of tobacco brush are covered with a natural 'shellac' to retain moisture. To the southeast the waters of Lake Berryessa can be seen for the first time

Mile 4.5: Four-way junction. A rough trail on the right leads to a rock outcrop with brilliant yellow lichens. From here, you can get a spectacular photograph of the lookout tower perched on the high point, showing just how steeply the north side drops off into Rattlesnake Canyon. If you go left at the junction, one of the two middle peaks is reached. Once used for cable transmission, it was recently leased by Motorola and MCI who installed communications towers in 1992. The main road continues on to 'windy gap' with the first unobstructed views of the north country.

Mile 4.75: After miles of chaparral, this seemingly misplaced little pine forest is a startling but welcome sight. One huge, 200 year old sugar pine has miraculously survived countless fires. It is pictured on page 121. The tops of these sugar pines are flat due to their natural growth pattern and continual wind breakage. The road crosses under the power lines for a third time, leaving the pine forest behind and rises steeply to the top.

One sizzling July day, over twenty years ago, I made my first ascent of Mt. St. Helena. I had to convince my hiking partner to forsake the shade of this forest for the blistering summit with a promise of water to fill our empty canteens. Fortunately, there was a ranger on top, kind enough to replenish us from her personal water source. Tempted though you may be to stop in the shade, this is no place to quit. The summit is nearly within spitting distance.

On this last leg of the hike, you will find one of the mountain's rare and endangered species. Rincon Ridge Buckbrush (Ceanothus confusus) is a mound-forming lilac up to 18 inches high. It grows only here and on Rincon Ridge near Santa Rosa.

Mile 5.0: Summit of Mt. St. Helena. This is private land, owned by the Livermore family, but hiker access is allowed. As of 1992, lookouts have not been stationed at the tower due to the state's money crunch. It was completed right after the road was built in 1935. It's too bad the tower was plunked down almost on top of the Russian commemorative plaque because many people miss this bit of Americana.

Next to the plaque is an old California Alpine Club summit register, now out of use. The top plate was removed in 1973 by the state park, and sits upstairs at the Bothe Park headquarters still awaiting repairs. Scattered about nearby, are two U.S. Coast and Geodetic survey markers, lately marked in neon pink spray paint. Not to be outdone, the California Division of Highways has one of its own.

Where the summit slopes gently to the west, a patchwork of four-five-and six-sided columns of andesite can be found. These are close in form to basalt columns found at Devil's Postpile in the Eastern Sierra and Devil's Tower in Wyoming. A century ago, they were called a second 'Giant's Causeway'. You can step from one to another of these flat column tops, looking like they were laid by human hand. They are part of the andesitic columnar cliffs on the north side, invisible from the summit, but spectacularly evident from portions of Ida Clayton Road.

If you are lucky to be here on a clear day, some of the longest views in the United States are yours. Mt. St. Helena's modest height belies its choice geographical location. On a clear day, the Pacific Ocean's horizon can be seen 80 miles away, the Sierra Nevada crest 150 miles east, Mount Shasta 192 miles toward Oregon, and the San Francisco skyline 66 miles to the south. Point Reyes Lighthouse and the Farralon Islands beyond it are commonly seen.

Scenic vistas are easy to find on two-wheelers.

Steering and braking are problematical in snow.

211

Mt. St. Helena Chronology

3 Million years B.C. - Mt. St. Helena rises to present height

12,000 years B.C. to 1850 A.D. - Native American occupation

1823 - First sighting and naming by a white man, Father Altimira

1836 - George Yount settles Napa Valley, possible first ascent by white

1841- Russians from Fort Ross ; claim first ascent, second naming

1844 - Third naming of mountain by Yankee sea captain, Stephen Smith

1850 - Old Bull Trail built by volunteer effort over Mt. St. Helena

1853 - Russian plaque discovered, removed by Dr. T.A. Hylton

1859 - Visits by authors Richard Henry Dana and Bayard Taylor

1859 -1860 - First mining fever sweeps Mt. St. Helena

1860 - First part of Ida Clayton Road constructed to Ida Clayton Mine

1861 - Patriotic raising of Union flag on summit of Sugarloaf Hill

1862 - Brewer's Geological Survey visits Napa and Geysers

1863 - Clark Foss begins stage runs to Geysers

1866-8 - John Lawley constructs Lawley Toll Road

1872 - Badlam discovers silver at Monitor ledge, later Silverado mine

1873 - Great Western quicksilver mine underway

1874 - Mining boom town Silverado is christened

1874-5 - Ida Clayton Toll Road completed, Knight's Valley to Lawley road

1875 - James Lick decides against a Mt. St. Helena observatory

1876 - U.S. Coast and Geodetic Survey begins pioneering triangulation work

1877 - Town of Silverado is abandoned

1880 - Robert Louis Stevenson and wife honeymoon at Silverado

1881 - Mountain Mill House built by Felix McNulty

1883- Original Mt. St. Helena Toll House Inn burns to the ground

1883 - Black Bart arrested in San Francisco

1884 - Mt. St. Helena Inn rebuilt, Dan Patten buys 500 acres on the mountain

1888- Bill Spiers buys Calistoga-Clear Lake stage line from William Fisher

1888- Palisades mine starts full production, Bradford mine in full swing

1890- White Cap Murders at Camper's Retreat

1893- Palisades mine closes down in January after death of Walter Grigsby

1895 - Buck English captured after his last holdup near Mountain Mill House

1890's - Peregrine Falcons reported nesting on the mountain

1905 - First major geologic study on MSH by Osmont

Circa 1905 - First automobiles begin making an appearance on Toll Road

1906 - Death of John Lawley

1910 - Stage drivers on Lawley Road stop carrying firearms

1911 - RLS monument ceremonially placed on cabin site, Silverado mine

1912 - Buck English released from San Quentin

1912 - Exact replica of Russian plaque placed on the north peak.

1915-16 - Bill Spiers converts to auto stages, coaches sold to Hollywood

1916 - Ida Clayton Toll Road goes public

1921 - Andrew Rocca, supervisor Great Western Mine 1876-1900, dies

1924 - Modern highway opens, end of era for Lawley toll road

1925 - Bill Spiers quits business after 37 years

1929 - Biggest fire in memory sweeps Mt. St. Helena

1932 - Mollie Patten, gatekeeper, dies on the mountain

1935 - Fire road completed to top, lookout tower constructed

1938 - Smith's Trout Farm, off Ida Clayton Road, opens for business

1941-5 - Lookout tower used for spotting enemy aircraft

1946 - Russel's Trout Farm, in Troutdale canyon, opens for business

1949 - RLS State Park receives its first 40 acres from Norman Livermore Sr.

1953 - Park dismantles vandalized Mt. St. Helena Inn

1954 - Two U.S. Navy jets crash in upper Kimball Canyon, no survivors

1956 - A U.S. Air Force jet crashes near 1954 site, no survivors

1964 - Hanley fire burns 50,000 acres, summit lookout manned throughout

1964 - Modern tower replaces the old lookout

1967 - 3,000 acres from Russell and BLM added to State Park

1970 - National threat to Peregrin Falcon, no nests found on MSH

1970- Silverado Ranch is owned by rock group, "It's A Beautiful Day"

1977 - Peregrines have returned to MSH

1981 - Fire burns 50 acres of Robert Louis Stevenson Park

1982 - Silverado fire burns 4,000 acres of south face

1982 - Owner Silverado Ranch, Weenas, accused of embezzling $3 million

1986 - 492 acre Silverado Ranch sold to Park for a half million dollars

1987 - Telecommunications,Inc. builds gazebo on south peak

1988 - Patten family sells 25 acre Silverado mine inholding to Park

1988 - California voters approve $2 million for State Park land acquisition

1996 - General Plan for RLS State Park slated

Mt. St. Helena's most historic remaining landmark, the Mountain Mill House.

Flora of Robert Louis Stevenson State Park*

ACERACEAE: Maple family
1. *Acer macrophyllum*   Big Leaf Maple

AMARYLLIDACEAE: Amaryllis family
1. *Allium amplectens*   Narrow-leaf Onion
2. *Allium falcifolium*   Sickle -leaf Onion
3. *Brodiaea coronaria*   Harvest Brodiaea
4. *Brodiaea elegans*   Elegant Brodiaea
5. *Brodiaea pulchella*   Blue Dicks
6. *Brodiaea congesta*

ANACARDIACEAE: Sumac family
1. *Toxicodendron diversilobum*   Poison Oak

APOCYNADEAE: Dogbane family
1. *Apocynum androsaemifolium*   Mountain Dogbane
2. *Vinca major*   Periwinkle

ARALIACEAE: Ginseng family
1. *Aralia californica*   Spikenard

ASCLEPIADACEAE: Milkweed family
1. *Asclepias cordifolia*   Purple Milkweed
2. Asclepias speciosa   Showy Milkweed

ASPIDIACEAE: Fern family
1. *Cystopteris fragilis*   Brittle Fern
2. *Dryopteris arguta*   Wood Fern
3. *Polystichum dudleyi*   Shield Fern
4. *Polystichum munitum*   Sword Fern

BERBERIDACEAE: Barberry family
1. *Mahonia aquifolium*   Oregon Grape
2. *Mahonia nervosa*   Long-leaf Mahonia
3. *Mahonia pinnata*   California Holly grape

*compiled by Ranger W.T.Grummer

BETULACEAE: Birch family

1. *Alnus rhombifolia*   White Alder
2. *Corylus cornuta*   Western Hazelnut

BLECHNACEAE: Fern family

1. *Woodwardia fimbriata*   Giant Chain Fern

BORAGINACEAE: Borage family

1. *Amsinckia intermedia*   Common Fiddleneck
2. *Cryptantha affinis*   Common Forget-Me-Not
3. *Cryptantha flaccida*   Flaccid Forget-Me-Not
4. *Cryptantha hendersonii*   Southern Fire loving Forget-Me-Not
5. *Cryptantha microstachys*   Tehon Forget-Me-Not
6. *Cryptantha muricata*   Northern Fire Loving Forget-Me-Not
7. *Cynoglossum grande*   Hound's Tongue
8. *Plagiobothrys nothofulvus*   Rusty Popcorn Flower
9. *Plagiobothrys tenellus*   Slender Popcorn Flower

CALYCANTHACEAE: Sweet-Shrub family

1. *Calycanthus occidentalis*   Spice Bush

CAMPANULACEAE: Bellflower family

1. *Campanula angustiflora*   Short-flowered Harebell
2. *Githopsis specularioides*   Common Blue-cup
3. *Heterocodon rariflorum*   Heterocodon
4. *Nemacladus capillaris*   Common Nemacladus

CAPRIFOLIACEAE: Honeysuckle family

1. *Lonicera hispidula*   California Honeysuckle
2. *Lonicera interrupta*   Chaparral Honeysuckle
3. *Sambucus caerulea*   Blue Elderberry
4. *Symphoricarpos rivularis*   Streamside Snowberry

CARYOPHYLLACEAE: Pink family

1. *Arenaria douglasii*   Douglas' Sandwort
2. *Cerastium glomeratum*   Common Mouse-ear Chickweed
3. *Cerastium vulgatum*
4. *Lychnis coronaria*   Mullein Pink

216

5. *Minuartia californica* California Sandwort
6. *Scleranthus annus* German Knotgrass
7. *Silene antirrhina* Snapdragon Catchfly
8. *Silene californica* Indian Pink
9. *Silene gallica* Common Catchfly, Windmill Pink
10. *Silene verecunda*
11. *Stellaria media* Common Chickweed
12. *Stellaria nitens* Shiny Chickweed

COMPOSITAE: Sunflower family
1. *Achillea millefolium* Yarrow
2. *Adenocaulon bicolor* Trail Plant
3. *Agoseris retrorsa* Mountain Dandelion
4. *Arnica discoidea* Rayless Arnica
5. *Artemisia douglasiana* Mugwort
6. *Aster radulinus* Broadleaf Aster
7. *Baccharis pilularis* Coyote Brush
8. *Calycadenia truncata* Rosin Weed
9. *Carduus pychnocephalus* Italian Thistle
10. *Centaurea melitensis* Napa Thistle
11. *Centaurea solstitialis* Yellow Star Thistle
12. *Chaetopappa exilis* Meager Chaetopappa
13. *Chrysothamnus parryi* Rabbit Brush
14. *Cirsium proteanum* Indian Thistle
15. *Cirsium vulgare* Bull Thistle
16. *Erigeron petrophilus* Rock Daisy
17. *Eriophyllum lanatum* Woody Sunflower
18. *Filago californica* California Woolyhead
19. *Filago gallica* Narrow-leaf Woolyhead
20. *Filago germanica* Awn-flowered Woolyhead
21. *Gnaphalium californicum* California Everlasting
22. *Gnaphalium chilense* Cotton Batting Plant
23. *Gnaphalium microcephalum* White Everlasting
24. *Gnaphalium microcephalum var. thermale*
25. *Gnaphalium purpurem* Purple Cudweed
26. *Grindelia camporum* Common Gum Plant
27. *Haplopappus arborescens* Golden Fleece

28. *Helianthella californica*   Chaparral Sunflower
29. *Hieracium albiflorum*   White-flowered Hawkweed
30. *Hypochoeris glabra*   Hairless Cat's Ear
31. *Hypochoeris radicata*   Hairy Cat's Ear
32. *Lactuca serriola*   Prickly Lettuce
33. *Lagophylla ramosissima*   Common Hareleaf
34. *Lasthenia californica*   Common Goldfields
35. *Luina hypoleuca*   Little-leaf Luina
36. *Madia elegans*   Elegant Mountain Tarweed
37. *Madia exigua*   Small Mountain Tarweed
38. *Madia gracilis*   Slender Mountain Tarweed
39. *Madia madioides*   Forest Mountain Tarweed
40. *Madia nutans*   Nodding Mountain Tarweed
41. *Matricaria matricariodes*   Pineapple Weed
42. *Micropus californicus*   Slender Cottonhead
43. *Microseris heterocarpa*   Derived Dandelion
44. *Microseris lindleyi*
45. *Picris echioides*   Ox Tongue
46. *Rigiopappus leptocladus*   Rigiopappus
47. *Senecio aronicoides*   Solitary Butterweed
48. *Senecio eurycephalus*   Cut-leaf Groundsel
49. *Senecio greenei*   Flame Butterweed
50. *Senecio vulgaris*   Common Groundsel
51. *Solidago californica*   California Goldenrod
52. *Solidago canadensis var. salebrosa*   Meadow Goldenrod
53. *Sonchus asper*   Prickly Sow Thistle
54. *Sonchus oleraceus*   Common Sow Thistle
55. *Stephanomeria virgata*   Stephanomeria
56. *Stylocline gnaphalioides*   Everlasting Cottonweed
57. *Taraxacum officinale*   Common Dandelion
58. *Tragopogon porrifolius*   Salsify, Oyster Plant
59. *Wyethia angustifolia*   Narrow-leaf Mule Ears
60. *Wyethia glabra*   Hairless Mule Ears
61. *Xanthium strumarium*   Cocklebur

CONVOLVULACEAE: Morning Glory family
1. *Calystegia collina*   Mt. St. Helena Morning Glory

2. *Calystegia occidentalis*   Western Morning Glory
3. *Calystegia polymorpha*   Modoc Morning Glory
4. *Calystegia purpurata*   Solano Morning Glory
5. *Calystegia subacaulis*   Mountain Morning Glory

CORNACEAE: Dogwood family
1. *Cornus nuttallii*   Mountain Dogwood

CRASSULACEAE: Stonecrop family
1. *Crassula erecta*   Pygmy Plant
2. *Dudleya cymosa*   Old-Man-Live-Forever
3. *Sedum radiatum*   Narrow-leaf Stonecrop
4. *Sedum spathulifolium*   Pacific Stonecrop

CRUCIFERAE: Mustard family
1. *Arabis breweri*   Brewer's Rockcress
2. *Athysanus pusillus*   Spinepod
3. *Barbarea orthoceras*   American Winter Cress
4. *Barbarea verna*   Winter Cress
5. *Brassica nigra*   Black Mustard
6. *Cardamine oligosperma*   Bitter Cress
7. *Dentaria californica*   California Milkmaid
8. *Dentaria californica var. cardiophylla*   Simple-leaf Milkmaid
9. *Draba verna*   Whitlow Grass
10. *Erysimum capitatum*   Wallflower
11. *Lepidium nitidum*   Common Peppergrass
12. *Lobularia maritima*   Sweet Alyssum
13. *Streptanthus glandulosus*   Common Jewel Flower
14. *Streptanthus glandulosus ssp. secundus*   Sonoma Jewel Flower
15. *Streptanthus brachiatus*   Socrates Mine Jewel Flower
16. *Streptanthus tortuosus*   Mountain Jewel Flower
17. *Thelypodium lasiophyllum*   California Thelypodium
18. *Thysanocarpus curvipes*   Fringe-pod

CUCURBITACEAE: Gourd family
1. *Marah fabaceus*   Wild Cucumber, Man Root

CUPRESSACEAE: Cypress family
1. *Calocedrus decurrens*   Incense Cedar

CUSCUTACEAE: Dodder family
1. *Cuscuta ceanothi*   Canyon Dodder
2. *Cuscuta occidentalis*   Western Dodder

CYPERACEAE: Sedge family
1. *Carex globosa*   Round-fruited Sedge
2. *Carex multicaulis*   Many-stemmed Sedge
3. *Carex eragrostis*   Umbrella Sedge

DATISCACEAE: Datisca family
1. *Datisca glomerata*   Durango Weed

EQUISETACEAE: Horsetail family
1. *Equisetum laevigatum*   Smooth Scouring Rush
2. *Equisetum telmateia*   Giant Horsetail

ERICACEAE: Heath family
1. *Arbutus menziesii*   Madrone
2. *Arctostaphylos* canescens   Hoary Manzanita
3. *Arctostaphylos canescens var. candidissima*
4. *Arctostaphylos elegans*   Konocti Manzanita
5. *Arctostaphylos glandulosa*   Eastwood Manzanita
6. *Arctostaphylos glandulosa var. cushingiana*   Cushings
Manzanita
7. *Arctostaphylos manzanita*   Woodland Manzanita
8. *Arctostaphylos stanfordiana*   Stanford Manzanita
9. *Arctostaphylos viscida*   Whiteleaf Manzanita
10. *Rhododendron occidentale*   Western Azalea

EUPHORBIACEAE: Spurge family
1. *Eremocarpus setigerus*   Turkey Mullein
2. *Euphorbia peplus*   Petty Spurge

FAGACEAE: Beech family
1. *Chrysolepis chrysophylla*   Giant Chinquapin
2. *Lithocarpus densiflora*   Tan Oak
3. *Quercus agrifolia*   Coast Live Oak
4. *Quercus agrifolia var. frutescens*   Coast Live Scrub-oak
5. *Quercus chrysolepis*   Canyon Oak, Maul Oak

6. *Quercus douglasii*   Blue Oak
7. *Quercus dumosa*   Scrub Oak
8. *Quercus durata*   Leather Oak
9. *Quercus kelloggii*   Kellogg Black Oak
10. *Quercus kelloggii forma cibata*   Kellogg Shrub-oak
11. *Quercus wislizenii*   Interior Live Oak
12. *Quercus wislizenii var. frutescens*   Interior Live Shrub-oak

GARRYACEAE: Silk Tassel family
1. *Garrya fremontii*   Fremont Silk Tassel Bush

GERANIACEAE: Geranium family
1. *Erodium cicutarium*   Red-stemmed Filaree
2. *Erodium obtusiplicatum*   Short-beaked Filaree

GRAMINEAE: Grass family
1. *Aira caryophyllea*   European Hairgrass
2. *Anthoxanthum odoratum*   Sweet Vernal Grass
3. *Avena barbata*   Slender Wild Oat
4. *Briza minor*   Quaking Grass
5. *Bromus hordeaceus*   Soft Chess
6. *Bromus diandrus*   Ripgut Grass
7. *Bromus rubens*   Red Brome
8. *Cynosurus echinatus*   Dogtail
9. *Deschampsia elongata*   Slender Hairgrass
10. *Elymus glaucus*   Rye Grass
11. *Festuca californica*   California Fescue
12. *Festuca elatior*   Meadow Fescue
13. *Festuca idahoensis*   Idaho Fescue
14. *Festuca megalura*   Foxtail Fescue
15. *Festuca occidentalis*   Western Fescue
16. *Festuca octoflora*   Six Weeks Fescue
17. *Hordeum leporinum*   Foxtail
18. *Lamarckia aurea*   Goldentop
19. *Lolium multiflorum*   Italian Rye Grass
20. *Melica hartfordii*   Melic Grass
21. *Phalaris minor*   Canary Grass
22. *Poa palustris*   Fowl Bluegrass

23. *Poa pratensis*   Kentucky Bluegrass
24. *Poa scrabella*   Pine Bluegrass
25. *Sitanion jubatum*   Squirrel Tail
26. *Stipa cernua*   Slender Needlegrass
27. *Stipa lemmonii*   Speargrass, Needlegrass

HIPPOCASTANACEAE: Buckeye family
1. *Aesculus californica*   California Buckeye

HYDROPHYLLACEAE: Water Leaf family
1. *Emmenanthe penduliflora*   Whispering Bells
2. *Eriodictyon californicum*   Yerba Santa
3. *Nemophila heterophylla*   Canyon White-eyes
4. *Nemophila menziesii*   Baby Blue-eyes
5. *Nemophila menziesii ssp. atomaria*   Striped White-eyes
6. *Nemophila parviflora*   Small Flowered Nemophila
7. *Phacelia corymbosa*   Serpentine Phacelia
8. *Phacelia distans*   Wild Heliotrope
9. *Phacelia imbricata*   Lazy-flowered Phacelia
10. *Phacelia suavuolens*   Fire-loving Phacelia

HYPERICACEAE: St. John's Wort family
1. *Hypericum anagalloides*   Tinker's Penny
2. *Hypericum concinnum*   Gold Wire
3. *Hypericum perforatum*   Klamath Weed

IRIDACEAE: Iris family
1. *Iris macrosiphon*   Ground Iris
2. *Sisyrinchium bellum*   Blue-eyed Grass

ISOETACEAE: Quillwort family
1. *Isoetes howellii*   Howell's Quillwort

JUGLANDACEAE: Walnut family
1. *Juglans hindsii*   California Black Walnut
2. *Juglans regia*   English Walnut

JUNCACEAE: Rush family
1. *Juncus bolanderi*   Wire Grass
2. *Juncus effusus var. pacificus*   Pacific Rush

222

3. *Luzula subsessilis*   Wood Rush

LABIATAE: Mint family
1. *Lepechinia calycina*   Pitcher Sage
2. *Marrubium vulgare*   Horehound
3. *Melissa officinalis*   Lemon Balm
4. *Monardella villosa*   Coyote Mint
5. *Monardella viridis*   Sweet Coyote Mint
6. *Salvia columbariae*   Chia
7. *Scutellaria californica*   California Skullcap
8. *Stachys rigida ssp. quercetorum*   Hedge Nettle

LAURACEAE: Laurel family
1. *Umbellularia californica*   California Bay, California Laurel

LEGUMINOSAE: Pea family
1. *Astragalus gambelianus*   Gambel's Locoweed
2. *Laburnum alpinum*   Scotch Laburnum
3. *Lathyrus hirsutus*   Rough Pea
4. *Lathyurus latifolius*   Everlasting Pea
5. *Lathyrus vestitus*   Hillside Pea
6. *Lotus humistratus*   Hillside Trefoil
7. *Lotus micranthus*   Small-flowered Trefoil
8. *Lotus purshianus*   Spanish Trefoil
9. *Lotus scoparius*   Deerweed
10. *Lotus stipularis*   Stipitate Trefoil
11. *Lupinus albifrons*   Bush Lupine
12. *Lupinus bicolor ssp. umbellatus*   Coast Range Lupine
13. *Lupinus sericatus*   Cobb Mountain Lupine
14. *Medicago arabica*   Spotted Medick
15. *Medicago lupulina*   Black Medick
16. *Medicago polymorpha*   Bur Clover
17. *Melilotus albus*   Sweet Clover
18. *Pickeringia montana*   Chaparral Pea
19. *Psoralea macrostachya*   Leather Root
20. *Psoralea physodes*   California Tea
21. *Spartium junceum*   Spanish Broom
22. *Trifolium albopurpureum*   Common Indian Clover

23. *Trifolium ciliolatum*   Tree Clover
24. *Trifolium dichotomum*   Branched Indian Clover
25. *Trifolium microcephalum*   Maiden Clover
26. *Trifolium tridentatum*   Tomcat Clover
27. *Vicia americana*   American Vetch
28. *Vicia dasycarpa*   Winter Vetch
29. *Vicia sativa*   Spring Vetch

LILIACEAE: Lily family
1. *Calochortus amabilis*   Diogenes Lantern
2. *Calochortus tolmiei*   Pussy Ears
3. *Chlorogalum pomeridianum*   Soap Plant
4. *Disporum hookeri*   Fairy Bells
5. *Fritillaria lanceolata*   Checker Lily
6. *Lilium pardalinum*   Leopard Lily, Panther Lily
7. *Lilium rubescens*   Chaparral Lily, Chamise Lily
8. *Smilacina racemosa*   False Solomon's Seal
9. *Trillium chloropetalum var. giganteum*   Giant Wake Robin
10. *Zigadenus fremontii*   Star Zygadene

LINACEAE: Flax family
1. *Hesperolinon bicarpellatum*   Two-carpeled Flax
2. *Hesperolinon disjunctum*   Disjunct Dwarf Flax
3. *Hesperolinon spergulinum*   Slender Dwarf Flax

LORANTHACEAE: Mistletoe family
1. *Arceuthobium campylopodum*   Witches Broom, Dwarf Mistletoe
2. *Phoradendron villosum*   Common Mistletoe

MORACEAE: Mulberry family
1. *Ficus carica*   Edible Fig

ONAGRACEAE: Evening Primrose family
1. *Boisduvalia stricta*   Narrow-leaf Summer Primrose
2. *Clarkia concinna*   Red Ribbons, Fringed Clarkia
3. *Clarkia gracilis*   Summer's Darling
4. *Clarkia purpurea ssp. quadrivulnera*   Small Wirecup
5. *Clarkia rhomboidea*   Rhomboid Clarkia
6. *Epilobium ciliatum*   Northern Willow-herb

224

7. *Epilobium brachycarpum*
8. *Epilobium canum*　California Fuchsia
9. *Epilobium minutum*　Dwarf Willow Herb

ORCHIDACEAE: Orchid family
1. *Cephalanthera austinae*　Phantom Orchid
2. *Corallorhiza maculata*　Spotted Coral Root
3. *Corallorhiza striata*　Striped Coral Root
4. *Piperia elegans*　Elegant Rain Orchid
5. *Spiranthes porrifolia*　Western Ladies Tresses

OROBANCHACEAE: Broomrape family
1. *Boschniakia strobilacea*　Ground Cone
2. *Orobanche bulbosa*　Chaparral Broomrape
3. *Orobanche fasciculata var. franciscana*　Franciscan Broomrape
4. *Orobanche uniflora*　Naked Broomrape
5. *Orobanche uniflora var. sedi*　Yellow Naked Broomrape

PAPAVERACEAE: Poppy family
1. *Dendromecon rigida*　Bush Poppy
2. *Eschscholzia californica*　California Poppy

PINACEAE: Pine family
1. *Pinus attenuata*　Knobcone Pine
2. *Pinus lambertiana*　Sugar Pine
3. *Pinus ponderosa*　Ponderosa Pine
4. *Pinus sabiniana*　Gray Pine, Digger Pine
5. *Pseudotsuga menziesii*　Douglas Fir

PLANTAGINACEAE: Plantain family
1. *Plantago erecta*　Dwarf Plantain
2. *Plantago lanceolata*　Ribgrass, English Plantain

POLEMONIACEAE: Phlox family
1. *Allophyllum giliodes*　Struggling False Gilia
2. *Collomia heterophylla*　Mountain Collomia
3. *Gilia capitata*　Globe Gilia
4. *Gilia tricolor*　Bird's Eye
5. *Linanthus parviflorus*　Small-flowered Phlox
6. *Linanthus ciliatus*

7. *Linanthus dichotomus ssp. meridianus*   Diurnal Snow
8. *Microsteris gracilis*   Slender Phlox
9. *Navarretia divaricata ssp. vividior* Mountain Navarretia
10. *Navarretia squarrosa*   Skunk Weed

POLYGALACEAE: Milkwort family
1. *Polygala californica*   California Milkwort

POLYGONACEAE: Buckwheat family
1. *Chorizanthe membranacea*   Pink Spine Flower
2. *Chorizanthe polygonoides*   Knotweed Spine Flower
3. *Eriogonum compositum*   Composit Buckwheat
4. *Eriogonum luteolum*
5. *Eriogonum nudum*   Nude Buckwheat
6. *Eriogonum vimineum*   Wickerstem Buckwheat
7. *Polygonum aviculare* Common Knotweed
8. *Polygonum bolanderi*   Woody Knotweed
9. *Pterostegia drymarioides* Pterostegia
10. *Rumex acetosella*   Sheep sorrel
11. *Rumex crispus* Curly Dock

POLYPODIACEAE: Fern family
1. *Polypodium californicum*   California Polypody

PORTULACACEAE: Purslane family
1. *Calandrinia breweri*   Blue Maids
2. *Calandrinia ciliata*   Red Maids
3. *Claytonia gypsophiloides*   Coast Range Lettuce
4. *Claytonia perfoliata*   Common Miner's Lettuce
5. *Lewisia rediviva*   Bitter Root
6. *Montia perfoliata forma glauca*   Clumping Miner's Lettuce
7. *Montia perfoliata forma parviflora* Small-flowered Miner's
Lettuce
8. *Montia spathulata var. exigua*
9. *Montia spathulata var. tenuifolia*

PRIMULACEAE: Primrose family
1. *Anagallis arvensis*   Pimpernel
2. *Dodecatheon hendersonii*   Shooting Star

226

3. *Trientalis latifolia*   Starflower

PTERICACEAE: Fern family

1. *Adiantum jordanii*   Maidenhair Fern
2. *Adiantum pedatum var. aleuticum*   Five-finger Fern
3. *Aspidotis californica*   California Lace Fern
4. *Cheilanthes covillei*   Lip Fern
5. *Cheilanthes gracillima*   Lace Fern
6. Cheilanthes intertexta   Coastal Lip Fern
7. *Pellaea andromedaefolia*   Coffee Fern
8. *Pellaea mucronata*   Bird's Foot Fern
9. *Pityrogramma triangularis*   Goldenback Fern
10. *Pteridium aquilinum*   Brake, Bracken

PYROLACEAE: Winter Green family

1. *Allotropa virgata*   Sugarstick
2. *Chimaphila menziesii*   Pipsissewa
3. *Chimaphila umbellata*   "
4. *Pyrola picta*   Shinleaf, Leafless Wintergreen

RANUNCULACEAE: Crowfoot family

1. *Aquilegia formosa*   Columbine
2. *Clematis lasiantha*   Clematis, Virgin's Bower
3. *Delphinium nudicaule*   Red Larkspur
4. *Delphinium patens*   Inland Blue Larkspur
5. *Ranunculus muricatus*   Prickle-fruit Buttercup
6. *Rununculus occidentalis* Western Buttercup, Crowfoot

RHAMNACEAE: Buckthorn family

1. *Ceanothus confusus*   Rincon Ridge Buckbrush
2. *Ceanothus cuneatus*   Common Buckbrush
3. *Ceanothus foliosus*   Wavy-leaf Lilac
4. *Ceanothus incanus*   Coastal Whitethorn
5. *Ceanothus parryi*   Lady Bloom
6. *Ceanothus prostratus*   Mahala Mat, Squaw Carpet
7. *Ceanothus velutinus*   Tobacco Brush
8. *Rhamnus californica*   Coffeberry
9. *Rhamnus crocea*   Red Berry

ROSACEAE: Rose family
1. *Adenostoma fasciculatum*   Chamise, Greasewood
2. *Cercocarpus betuloides*   Mountain Mahogany
3. *Cotoneaster pannosa*   Cotoneaster
4. *Crataegus monogyna*   English Hawthorn
5. *Fragaria vesca*   Strawberry
6. *Heteromeles arbutifolia*   Toyon, Christmas Berry
7. *Holodiscus discolor*   Ocean Spray, Cream Bush
8. *Malus sylvestris*   Common Apple
9. *Potentilla glandulosa*   Cinquefoil
10. *Prunus avium*   Sweet Cherry
11. *Prunus emarginata*   Bitter Cherry
12. *Rosa gymnocarpa*   Wood Rose
13. *Rosa spithamea*   Ground Rose
14. *Rubus leucodermis*   Western Raspberry
15. *Rubus parviflora*   Thimble Berry
16. *Rubus procerus*   Himalaya Berry
17. *Rubus ursinus*   California Blackberry

RUBIACEAE: Madder family
1. *Galium andrewsii*   Phlox-leaved Bedstraw
2. *Galium aparine*   Common Cleavers
3. *Galium bolanderi*   Forest Bedstraw
4. *Galium californicum*   California Bedstraw
5. *Galium divaricatum*
6. *Galium murale*
7. *Galium nuttallii*   Climbing Cleavers
8. *Galium parisiense*   Creek-bottom Bedstraw
9. *Galium spurium var. echinospermum*
10. *Galium triflorum*   Sweet Scented Bedstraw

SALICACEAE: Willow family
1. *Populus fremontii*   Fremont Cottonwood
2. *Salix hindsiana*   Sand Bar Willow
3. *Salix laevigata*   Red Willow
4. Salix lasiolepis   Arroyo Willow
5. *Salix scouleriana   Scouler's Willow*

SAXIFRAGACEAE: Saxifrage family
1. *Boykinia elata*   Brook Foam
2. *Heuchera micrantha*   Alum Root
3. *Heuchera pilosissima*
4. *Lithophragma affinis*   Woodland Star
5. *Lithophragma heterophylla*   "
6. *Ribes roezlii var. cruentum*   Coast Range Gooseberry
7. *Saxifraga californica*   Saxifrage
8. *Whipplea modesta*   Yerba de Selva, Modesty

SCROPHULARIACEAE: Figwort family
1. *Antirrhinum breweri*   Lesser Wire Dragon
2. *Antirrhinum vexillo-calyculatum*   Greater Wire Dragon
3. *Castilleja foliolosa*   Wooley Paintbrush
4. *Castilleja roseana*   Wavy-leaf Paintbrush
5. *Collinsia greenei*   Blue Chinese Houses
6. *Collinsia heterophylla*   Chinese Houses
7. *Collinsia sparsiflora*   Blue-eyed Mary
8. *Collinsia tinctoria*   Sticky Chinese Houses
9. *Cordylanthus tenuis*   Hairless Bird's Beak
10. *Keckiella lemmonii*   Bush Beard-tongue
11. *Linaria canadensis*   Lesser Blue Toad Flax
12. *Linaria texana*   Greater Blue Toad Flax
13. *Mimulus aurantiacus*   Sticky Monkey Flower
14. *Mimulus cardinalis*   Scarlet Monkey Flower
15. *Mimulus douglasii*   Chinless Monkey Flower
16. *Mimulus guttatus*   Common Monkey Flower
17. *Mimulus kelloggii*   Monkey Flower
18. *Mimulus layneae*   "
19. *Mimulus moschatus*   Musk Flower
20. *Mimulus nudatus*   Nude Monkey Flower
21. *Orthocarpus attenuatus*   Valley Tassels
22. *Pedicularis densiflora*   Indian Warrior
23. *Penstemon corymbosus*   Redwood Beard Tongue
24. *Penstemon heterophyllus*   Blue Beard Tongue
25. *Penstemon newberryi ssp. sonomensis*   Sonoma's Pride
26. *Scrophularia californica*   Figwort

27. *Verbascum thapsus*   Common Mullein
28. *Verbascum virgatum*   Mullein

SOLANACEAE: Nightshade family
  1. *Solanum xantii var. intermedium*   Chaparral Nightshade

TAXACEAE: Yew family
  1. *Torreya californica*   California Nutmeg

TAXODIACEAE: Taxodium family
  1. *Sequoia sempervirens*   Coast Redwood

UMBELLIFERAE: Carrot family
  1. *Angelica tomentosa*   Common Angelica
  2. *Apiastrum angustifolium*   Wild Celery
  3. *Daucus pusillus*   Rattlesnake Weed
  4. *Heracleum lanatum*   Cow Parsnip
  5. *Lomatium californicum*   California Parsnip
  6. *Lomatium macrocarpum*   Giant-seed Parsnip
  7. *Lomatium marginatum*   Serpentine Parsnip
  8. *Lomatium repostum*   Napa Parsnip
  9. *Lomatium utriculatum*   Bladder, Common Parsnip
  10. *Osmorhiza chilensis*   Sweet Cicely
  11. *Perideridia kelloggii*   Common Yampah
  12. *Sanicula bipinnatifida*   Purple Sanicle
  13. *Sanicula crassicaulis*   Gambel Weed
  14. *Sanicula tuberosa*   Tuberous Sanicle
  15. *Scandix pecten-veneris*   Shepard's Needle
  16. *Torilis arvensis*   Hedge Parsley

VALERIANACEAE: Valerian family
  1. *Plectritis ciliosa*   Long-spurred Plectritis

VERBENACEAE: Vervain family
  1. *Verbena lasiostachys*   Western Vervain

VIOLACEAE: Violet family
  1. *Viola lobata*   Lobed Pine Violet
  2. *Viola odorata*   Sweet Violet, English Violet
  3. *Viola quercetorum*   Oak-loving Violet

VITACEAE: Grape family
  1. *Vitis californica*   Wild Grape

Silk tassel bush.

Fauna of Robert Louis Stevenson State Park*

Mammals

Scapanus latimanus caurinus California Broad-footed Mole
Neurotrichus gibbsii hyacinthinus California Shrew-Mole
Sorex trowbridgii montereyensis Monterey Trowbridge Shrew
Sorex ornatus californicus California Ornate Shrew
Myotis evotis chrysonotus Golden Long-eared Myotis
Myotis thysanodes thysanodes California Fringed Myotis
Myotis californicus caurinus Northwestern Little California Myotis
Pipistrellus hesperus merriami Merriam Pipistrelle
Eptesicus fuscus bernardinus Big Brown Bat
Lasiurus borealis teliotus Western Red Bat
Lasiurus cinereus cinereus Hoary Bat
Corynorhinus rafinesquii townsendii Townsend Long-eared Bat
Antrozous pallidus pacificus Pacific Pallid Bat
Tadarida mexicana Mexican Free-tailed Bat
Ursus americanus altifrontalis Northwestern Black Bear
Procyon lotor psora California Raccoon
Bassariscus astutus raptor California Ring-tailed Cat
Mustela frenata munda Redwoods Long-tailed Weasel
Mustela vison aestuarina California Lowland Mink
Spilogale gracilis phenax California Spotted Skunk
Mephitis mephitis occidentalis Northern California Striped Skunk
Urocyon cinereoargenteus townsendii Townsend Gray Fox
Canis latrans ochropus California Valley Coyote
Felis concolor californica California Mountain Lion
Lynx rufus californicus California Wildcat
Eutamias sonomae Sonoma Chipmunk
Sciurus griseus griseus California Gray Squirrel
Thomomys bottae agricolaris Sacramento Valley Botta Pocket Gopher
Dipodomys heermanni californicus Northern California Kangaroo Rat
Reithrodontomys megalotis longicaudus Long-tailed Western Harvest Mouse
Peromyscus maniculatus gambelii Gambel Deer Mouse

* Compiled by Ranger W.T.Grummer

Peromyscus boylii boylii Boyle Brush Mouse
Peromyscus truei gilberti Gilbert Pinyon Mouse
Neotoma fuscipes fuscipes Dusky-footed Wood Rat
Microtus californicus eximius Sanhedrin California Meadow Mouse
Lepus californicus californicus California Black-tailed Jackrabbit
Sylvilagus bachmani tehamae Tehama Brush Rabbit
Odocoileus hemionus columbianus Columbian Black-tailed Deer
Didelphis virginiana virginiana Virginia Opossum
Myotis yumanensis Yuma Myotis
Myotis volans Long-legged Myotis
Myotis lucifugus Little Brown Myotis
Lasionycteris noctivagens Silver-haired Bat

Reptiles

Sceloporus occidentalis occidentalis Western Fence Lizard
Sceloporus gradiosus gracilia Sagebrush Lizard
Cnemidophorus tigris mundus Western Whiptail
Eumeces skiltonianus Western Skink
Gerrhonotus multicarinatus multicarinatus Foothill Alligator Lizard
Charina bottae bottae Rubber Boa
Diadophis amabilis occidentalis Western Ring-necked Snake
Contia tenuis Sharp-tailed Snake
Coluber constrictor mormon Racer
Masticophis lateralis California Striped Whipsnake
Pituophis catenifer catenifer Gopher Snake
Lampropeltis getulus californiae Common King Snake
Lampropeltis zonata zonata Saint Helena Mountain King Snake
Thamnophis sirtalis fitchi Common Garter Snake
Thamnophis elegans terrestris Western Garter Snake
Thamnophis elegans aquaticus
Hypsiglena torquata nuchulata Spotted Night Snake
Crotalus viridus oreganus Western Rattlesnake

Amphibians

Taricha granulosa Rough-skinned Newt
Dicamptodon ensatus Pacific Giant Salamander

Ensatina aschscholtzii xanthoptica Yellow-eyed Salamander
Batrachoseps attenatus California Slender Salamander
Aneides flavipunctatus flavipunctatus Black Salamander
Aneides lugubris lugubris Arboreal Salamander
Bufo boreas halophilus Western Toad
hyla regilla Pacific Tree-Frog
Rana boylei boylei California Yellow-legged Frog

Fish

Salmo gairdnerii Steelhead Rainbow Trout

Insects

Neophasia menapiatau Pine White
Coenonympha tullia california California Ringlet
Danaus plexippus Monarch
Vanessa cardui Painted Lady
Gunonia coenia Buckeye
Plebejus acmon Acmon Blue
Euphydryas chalcedona Common Checkerspot
Callaphrys dumetorum Bramble Hairstreak
Celastrina echo Echo Blue
Anthocaris sara sara Sara Orange-tip
Euchleo hyantis Creusa Marble
Pieris sisymbrii California White
Colias eurytheme Common Sulphur
Erynnis propertius Propertius Duskywing
Nymphalis californica California Tortoiseshell
Habrodias grunus Canyon Oak Hairstreak
Srtymon auretorum Gold-hunter's Hairstreak
Strymon saepium Hedge-row Hairstreak
Hesperia columbia Columbian Skipper
Erynnis tristis Sad Duskywing
Chalcidoidea Chalcidids
Calliphoridea Blow Flies
Sacrophagidae Flesh Flies
Aeshnidae Darners

Acrididae   Short-horned Grasshoppers
Miridae   Leaf or Plant Bugs
Coreidae   Leaf-footed Bugs
Pentatomidae   Stink Bugs
Cicadidae   Cicadas
Cupedidae   Reticulated Beetles
Dasytidae   Soft-winged Flower Beetles
Buprestidae   Metalic Wood-boring Beetles
Syrphidae   Syrphical Flies
Muscidae   Muscid Flies
Noctuidae   Noctuid Moths
Pteromalidae   Pteromalids
Formicidae   Ants
Vespidae   Vespid Wasps
Sphecidae   Sphecid Wasps
Megachilidae   Leafcutting Bees
Apidae   Digger, Honey, and Carpenter Bees
Tettigoniidae   Long-horned Grasshoppers
Berytidae   Stilt Bugs
Raphidiidae   Snakeflies
Cicadellidae   Leafhoppers
Coccinellidae   Ladybird Beetles
Chrysomelidae   Leaf Beetles
Geometridae   Geometer Moths
Tortricoidae   Tortricid Moths
Tabanidae   Horse and Deer Flies
Bombyliidae   Bee Flies
Asilidae   Robber Flies
Tachinidae   Tachinid Flies
Hippodamia convergens   Convergent Ladybird Beetle
Saxinis saucia   Red-shouldered Leaf Beetle
Adelpha bredowi californica   California Sister
Callophrys augustinus iroides   ? Hairstreak
Cercyonis sp.   Satyr
Callophrys eurtheme   ? Hairstreak

Appendix D

Avifauna of Robert Louis Stevenson State Park*

Vulture, Turkey
Hawk, Sharp-shinned
      Cooper's
      Red-tailed
Eagle, Golden
Hawk, Marsh
Falcon, Peregrine
      Prairie
Kestrel, American
Quail, California
      Mountain
Pigeon, Band-tailed
Dove, Mourning
Owl, Screech
   Great Horned
   Pygmy
Poor-will
Swift, White-throated
Hummingbird, Anna's
      Rufous
      Allen's
Flicker, Common
Woodpecker, Pileated
      Acorn
      Hairy
      Downy
      Nuttall's
Sapsucker, Yellow-bellied
Flycatcher, Ash-throated
      Western
      Olive-sided
Swallow, Violet-green

* Compiled by Ranger W. T. Grummer

Swallow, Cliff
Martin, Purple
Jay, Steller's
    Scrub
Raven, Common
Crow, Common
Nutcracker, Clark's
Chickadee, Chestnut-backed
Titmouse, Plain
Bushtit
Nuthatch, White-breasted
       Red-breasted
       Pygmy
Creeper, Brown
Wrentit
Wren, Winter,
    Bewick's
    Canyon
    Rock
Mockingbird
Thrasher, California
Robin
Thrush, Varied
     Hermit
     Swainson's
Bluebird, Western
Solitaire, Townsend's
Gnatcatcher, Blue-gray
Kinglet, Ruby-crowned
Waxwing, Cedar
Vireo, Hutton's
    Solitary
    Warbling
Warbler, Orange-crowned
     Yellow
     Yellow-rumped

Warbler, Black-throated Gray
      Townsend's
      Hermit
      MacGillivray's
      Wilson's
Oriole, Northern
Blackbird, Brewer's
Tanager, Western
Grosbeak, Black-headed
Bunting, Lazuli
Finch, Purple
      House
Siskin, Pine
Goldfinch, Lesser
Towhee, Rufous-sided
      Brown
Sparrow, Lark
      Golden-crowned
Junco, Dark-eyed

Switchback on the RLS monument trail.

Area Precipitation

	Sonoma	S.Rosa	Mount St. Helena	Calistoga	St.Helena	Oakville	Napa
January	4.94	6.68	14.40	8.81	9.50	11.63	5.26
February	5.21	4.92	12.04	6.16	6.27	4.46	3.88
March	4.51	4.26	10.33	5.47	3.63	5.91	3.34
April	1.79	1.62	3.36	2.35	1.42	1.13	1.72
May	1.15	1.30	2.11	1.18	0.79	0.34	0.85
June	0.20	0.23	0.55	0.33	0.21	0.35	0.19
July	0.02	0.05	0.02	0.04	0.00	0.00	0.01
August	0.01	0.02	0.01	0.02	0.04	0.00	0.02
September	0.47	0.57	1.53	0.48	0.66	0.42	0.52
October	1.87	1.57	2.30	1.95	1.05	0.66	1.11
November	3.75	3.16	6.07	3.61	3.07	2.74	2.38
December	4.71	5.57	7.26	6.28	6.71	5.65	4.18
Annual	28.63	29.95	59.98	36.68	33.35	33.29	23.46

Monthly and annual means

San Francisco 012087   4—1008-1t.

The United States of America,

To all to whom these presents shall come, Greeting.

WHEREAS, a Certificate of the Register of the Land Office at **San Francisco, California,**

has been deposited in the General Land Office, whereby it appears that, pursuant to the Act of Congress of May 20, 1862, "To Secure Homesteads to Actual Settlers on the 'Public Domain,'" and the acts supplemental thereto, the claim of

Claude Leslie Russell

has been established and duly consummated, in conformity to law, for the **Lots one, two, three and four of Section thirty-five in Township ten north of Range seven west of the Mount Diablo Meridian, California, containing one hundred fifty-four acres and thirty-six hundredths of an acre,**

according to the Official Plat of the Survey of the said Land, returned to the GENERAL LAND OFFICE by the Surveyor-General:

NOW KNOW YE, That there is, therefore, granted by the UNITED STATES unto the said claimant   the tract of Land above described; TO HAVE AND TO HOLD the said tract of Land, with the appurtenances thereof, unto the said claimant   and to the heirs and assigns of the said claimant   forever; subject to any vested and accrued water rights for mining, agricultural, manufacturing, or other purposes, and rights to ditches and reservoirs used in connection with such water rights, as may be recognized and acknowledged by the local customs, laws, and decisions of courts; and there is reserved from the lands hereby granted a right of way thereon for ditches or canals constructed by the authority of the United States.

IN TESTIMONY WHEREOF, I,   **Calvin Coolidge,**

President of the United States of America, have caused these letters to be made Patent, and the seal of the General Land Office to be hereunto affixed.

GIVEN under my hand, at the City of Washington, the   **ELEVENTH**

(SEAL.)   day of   NOVEMBER   in the year of our Lord one thousand

nine hundred and   TWENTY-SIX   and of the Independence of the

United States the one hundred and   FIFTY-FIRST

By the President: *Calvin Coolidge*

By   *Viola B. Pugh*   Secretary.

M.P. LeRoy

Recorder of the General Land Office.

RECORD OF PATENTS: Patent Number __989005__

Master Title Plat accorded to Claude Russell on November 11, 1926, for land he homesteaded in Troutdale Canyon. Note U.S. President Calvin Coolidge's signature.
Coutesy of Bureau of Land Management

Road Mileages
Mount Saint Helena

Mile 0 : Downtown Calistoga
Mile 1.9: Junction, Old Lawley Toll Road
Mile 2.0: Start of the modern grade
Mile 5.5: Junction, upper Old Lawley Toll Road
Mile 6.0: Brandon's
Mile 6.3: Hanley's
Mile 7.3: Christmas Tree Farm (Happy Valley)
Mile 7.8: Summit, RLS Park trailhead
Mile 8.1: Fireroad entrance
Mile 9.5: Troutdale Creek
Mile 10.1: Mountain Mill House
Mile 10.4: Rattlesnake Spring
Mile 12.4: Mirabel Mine
Mile 14.3: Western Mine Road
Mile 15.4: Dry Creek Road
Mile 16.0: Middletown

June 25,1993

Dear Ken:

Just a note to let you know how happy I was to finally have an opportunity to sit with you a few minutes and discuss your book. Your book is a lot more encompassing than I thought. I must say that I was somewhat disappointed in that you had deleted some of the paragraphs relating to my grandfather, aka Tom Dye Rock. Disappointed because I thought the real interest should be in the story that has passed down through the family for decades that Tom was convicted on the Flip of a coin. I still believe that should make "The rest of the story" more interesting too.

If you have read the document regarding Tom's pardon from the four jurors you will note in the petition they state that the jury was deceived by the foreman. Even the judge petitioned the governor and stated "I think that I am warranted in saying there was some kind of compromise among the jurors who tried the case and for such compromise the verdict would not have been for a higher crime than manslaughter." I also think that that deceit is why a man in Middletown knew the verdict of the jury before it was even voted on or before the judge was advised. I've done a lot of thinking about this, the fact that there was a hung jury and that a man in Middletown knew what the verdict was going to be and that since the jury was deceived or the vote was rigged, my thoughts have wandered back to the two-headed coins that were in vogue in those days.

One other letter that was rather convincing was the one from Tom's attorney who was now a judge who informed the governor, "I think, speaking dispassionately, he never should have been sentenced to San Quentin at all." Further, "And don't think he should have been convicted". Add to all this, the quote in the jury's petition "Thus betrayed us into a verdict, our conscience did not approve."

Ken, I do think that the "rest of the story" should be told for it's never been told before and I think that our good family name deserves so.

Sincerely,

(signed)

Tom Dye
Long Beach, California

Alt, D.A. , and Hyndman, D.W. , *Roadside Geology of Northern California* , Missoula, Montana: Mountain Press Publising, 1975

Archuleta, Kay. *The Brannan Saga,* Calistoga: Archuleta, 1977

Arnold, Caroline. *Saving The Peregrine Falcon,* Minneapolis: Carol rhoda Books Inc., 1985

Bailey, Edgar H. *Geology of Northern California,* California Div. of Mines and Geology, Bulletin 190. San Francisco, 1966

Bancroft's Tourist Guide. Historical Society Library, 1873

Beard, Yolande S. *The Wappo-A Report.* Banning, California: Malki Museum Press, 1979

Berry, William D. and Berry, Elizabeth. *Mammals of the San Francisco Bay Region* , Berkeley: University of California Press, 1959

Brewer, *William H. Up and Down California-1860 to 1864* . Berkeley: University of California Press, 1974

Cade, Thomas J. *Peregrine Falcon Populations, Their Management and Recovery,* Boise, Idaho: The Peregrine Fund Inc., 1988

Coborn, John. *Snakes and Lizards, Their Care and Breeding in Captivity* , Sanibel Island, Florida: Ralph Curtis Publishing,1987

Dillon, Richard. *Wells, Fargo Detective-A Biography of James B. Hume,* New York: Coward-McCann, 1969

Dutton, Joan Parry. *They Left Their Mark, famous passages through the wine country,* St. Helena, California: Illuminations Press, 1983

Engbeck, Joseph H. *State Parks of California, from 1864 to the present.* Portland, Oregon: Charles H. Belding, Publisher, 1980

Fox, Kenneth F. *Tectonic Setting of Late Miocene, Pliocene, and Pleistocene Rocks in Part of the Coast Ranges North of San Francisco, California.* Washington D.C. : United States Geological Survey Professional Paper 1239, 1983

Fox, Kenneth F. *Potassium-Argon and Fission-Track Ages of the Sonoma Volcanics in an Area North of San Pablo Bay, California.*

Washington D.C. :U. S. Geological Survey, MF 1753, 1985

Goss, Helen Rocca. *The Life and Death of a Quicksilver Mine*, Los Angeles: The Historical Society of Southern California, 1958

Goss, Helen Rocca. *The California White Cap Murders*, Santa Barbara : Goss, 1969

Goss, Helen Rocca. *Gold and Cinnabar, the Life of Andrew Rocca, California Pioneer*, Montgomery, Alabama: unpublished ms. 1950

Gudde, Erwin G. *California Place Names*. Berkeley: University of California Press, 1960

Hanna, Phil Townsend. *Dictionary of California Land Names*, Los Angeles: Automobile Club of Southern California, 1946

Hanson, Harvery J.and Miller, Jeanne Thurlow. *Wild Oats in Eden: Sonoma County in the Nineteenth Century*, Santa Rosa, California : Hanson and Thurlow, 1962

Heizer, Robert F. *Handbook of North American Indians , Volume 8, California*, Washington: Smithsonian Institution, 1978

Heacox, Kim. *California State Parks*. Helena, Montana: Falcon Press, 1987

Hickey, Joseph J. *Peregrine Falcon Populations, Their Biology and Decline*, Madison: University of Wisconsin Press, 1969

Hinds, Norman Ethan Allen. *Evolution of the California Landscape*. San Francisco: Div. of Mines, Bulletin 158, 1952

Hungerford, Edward. *Wells Fargo*. NY: Random House, 1949

Hunt, Marguerite and Harry Lawrence Gunn. *History of Solano and Napa Counties-From Their Earliest Settlement to the Present Time*. Chicago: S.J. Clarke,1926

Ingles, Lloyd G. *Mammals of the Pacific States*, Stanford, California: Stanford University Press, 1965

Issler, Ann Roller. *Happier For His Presence-San Francisco and Robert Louis Stevenson*. Stanford: Stanford University Press, 1949

Issler, Ann Roller. *Our Mountain Hermitage-Silverado and Robert Louis Stevenson*. Stanford: Stanford University Press, 1950

Jenkins, Olaf P. *Geologic Guidebook of the San Francisco Bay Counties*. Division of Mines, Bulletin 154, San Francisco, 1951

Kaiser Engineers. *Task Force Report on Upper Eel River Routing Studies*- Prepared for Lake County Flood Control and Water Conservation District- Report No.68-2-RE. Oakland,CA Februrary, 1968

King, Norton L. *Napa County-An Historical Overview*. Napa: Office of the Napa County Superintendent of Schools, 1967

Klages, Ellen. *Harbin Hot Springs*, Middletown: Harbin Springs Publishing, 1991

Klein, H. Arthur. *Oceans and Continents in Motion*, Philadelphia: J.B. Lippincott and Company, 1972

Kroeber, A.L. *Handbook of the Indians of California* , Berkeley: California Book Company Ltd., 1953

Leet, Don L. and Judson, Sheldon. *Physical Geology* , Englewood Cliffs, New Jersey: Prentice-Hall, Inc., 1965

Lick, Rosemary. *The Generous Miser,* the Story of James Lick of California, The Ward Ritchie Press, 1967

Lipps and Moores. *Geologic Guide to the Northern Coast Ranges, Point Reyes Region, California.* Department of Geology, University of California at Davis,1971

Matthes, Francois E. *Geologic History of the Yosemite Valley,* USGS Professional Paper 160, Washington : 1930

McCarthy, Paul M. *Looking Back.* Napa: Napa Office of Education, 1987

Menefee, Campbell A. *Historical and Descriptive Sketch Book of Napa, Sonoma, Lake, and Mendocino Counties.* Napa: Reporter Publishing House, 1873

Metcalf, Woodbridge. *Introduced Trees of Central California,* Berkeley: University of California Press, 1968

Miller, Howard and Lamb, Samuel. *Oaks of North America,* Happy Camp, California: Naturegraph Publishers Inc., 1985

Miller, Joaquin. *True Bear Stories,* Santa Barbara, California:

Capra Press, 1987

Munz, Philip A. A *California Flora,* Berkeley: University of California Press,1959

Nickerson, Roy. *Robert Louis Stevenson In California.* San Francisco: Chronicle Books, 1982

Norris, R.M. , and Webb, R.W. , *Geology of California* , New York: John Wiley and Sons, Inc., 1976

Osbourne, Katharine D. *Robert Louis Stevenson In California.* Chicago: A.C. McClurg and Company, 1911

Osterbrock, Donald E., Gustafson, John R., Unruh, W.J. Shiloh. *Eye On The Sky, Lick Observatory's First Century,* Berkeley: University of California Press, 1988

Pearson, T. Gilbert. *Birds of America* , Garden City, New York: Garden City Books, 1936

Peattie, Donald Culross. *A Natural History of Western Trees,* New York: Bonanza Books, 1950

Pickwell, Gayle. *Amphibians and Reptiles of the Pacific States* , New York: Dover Publications Inc., 1972

Radin, Paul. *Wappo Texts in California University Publications in American Archaeology and Ethnology, Vol. 19* , New York: Kraus Reprint Corporation, 1965

Schick, Alice. *The Peregrine Falcons,* NY: The Dial Press, 1975

Slocum, Bowen and Co. *History of Lake County,* Ed. Lyman L. Palmer. San Francisco: Slocum and Bowen Publishers, 1881

Smith and Elliot. *Illustrations of Napa County, California with Historical Sketch,* Oakland: Smith and Elliot Publishers,1878

Stebbins, Robert C. Reptiles and Amphibians of the San Francisco Bay Region,Berkeley: University of California Press, 1971

Stevenson, Robert Louis. *Silverado Squatters* , Ashland, Oregon: Lewis Osbourne, 1974

Taylor, Bayard. *Home and Abroad.* NY: G.P. Putnam, 1862

Tuomey, Honoria. *Historic Mount Saint Helena.* California Historical Society Quarterly, Volume III, number 2, July, 1924

Walker, Lewis Wayne. *The Book of Owls* , NY: A.A. Knopf, 1974

Wallace, David Rains. *The Klamath Knot* , San Francisco: Sierra Club Books, 1983

Whitman, Ann H. *The Audubon Society Pocket Guide, Familiar Birds of North America,* Western Region , NY: A.A. Knopf , 1986

Wichels, John. *John Lawley-Pioneer Entrepreneur.* Napa: Napa County Historical Society, Gleanings Volume 3, Number 1, 1982

Wright, Elizabeth Cyrus. *Early Upper Napa Valley.* Society of California Pioneers, 1949

Weaver, C.E. *Geology of the Coast Ranges Immediately North of the San Francisco Bay Region,* Baltimore, MD: Baltimore Press,1949

Hole-in-the-Rock and Hailstone Rock

248

254

Please send:

copies of Mt. St. Helena and R.L. Stevenson State Park,
a history and guide @ $17.95   cost _____

California residents add 7.25% sales tax   tax _____

shipping and and handling U.S. orders@$2.00   ship _____
(foreign orders $5.00)

total _____

please print:

name: _____

address: _____

city/state: _____ zip _____

please make check payable to:
Ken Stanton, P.O. Box 804, St Helena, Ca 94574

CORRECTIONS AND COMMENTS

P. 29 par. 4 - Air miles from Mt. Diablo to the Great Western Divide is 13, not 12 miles farther than from Mt. St. Helena to Mt. Shasta

P. 40 par. 1 - The Weenas cabin in recent years was used by squatters as a temporary home and became a liability for the park. It was sold to a private party and will be reassembled in another location

P. 61 par. 3 - The quote "It is nothing less than a literary calamity..." comes from a masters thesis on Robert Louis Stevenson by George R. Stewart, teacher, historian and author whose book Ordeal by Hunger is the definitive work on the Donner Party

P. 124 par. 3 - The words "Spanish Broom (Spartium junceum)" should be replaced by "Scotch Broom (Cytisus scoparius)"

P. 134 par. 2 - Collecting of the Mt. St. Helena mountain king snake is forbidden *anywhere*

P. 144 par. 2 - The Petrified Forest has since made the correction in their pamphlet to explain why it is volcanic but not a volcano

P. 161 par. 2 - In August 1997 California State Parks bought 590 acres in the Palisades above Calistoga, between Table Rock and the Oat Hill Mine Trail, one of the most important purchases in the history of RLS Park. A new trail will be built along the base of the Palisades with access to the crest at one point. A hiker-only trail, it is not scheduled to be completed until 1998. When finished hikers will be able to walk from Mt. St. Helena to Calistoga, making it the finest trail in the county and one of the best in the Bay Area

P.168 par. 3 - The General Plan for Stevenson Park was not implemented in 1996 nor unfortunately is there any reason to think it will be in the near future

P. 169 par. 1 - The hiking trail to Stevenson monument is closer to a 5% grade

P. 169 par. 5 - No redwoods are found in Troutdale Canyon

P. 171 par. 1 - Since the first printing of this book, hundreds of new acres of forest have been cleared for vineyard on the lower western slopes of Mt. St. Helena. On the north side, clearing for vineyard and housing has marred the once pristine viewshed. There is worse to come. The wine industry is projecting that many thousands of acres of hillside forest in Napa county will be put to the "saw" in the next ten to twenty years

P. 191 par. 1 - The USGS has officially lowered the height of the mountain to 4,339 feet

P. 192 par. 2 - RLS park may soon have a self-pay collection box (iron ranger) installed. The modest fee will be $2

P. 196 par. 3 - In recent years conditions at the Far Side have improved and we haven't seen the litter problem that occurred when it first became popular. Thank you everyone involved

P. 209 par. 3 - At the 4 1/2 mile mark a road leads to one of the middle peaks. Another ghastly microwave tower has been installed, this one 100 feet high

P. 210 par. 2 - For several years the lookout tower was not in use due to lack of funds. In the winter of 1995-96 the tower was dismantled and taken away

P. 213 line 24 - should read "1954 - a U.S. Navy jet crashes on the west ridge just below the north peak, no survivors"

P. 213 line 25 - should read "1956 - a U.S. Air Force jet crashes in Kimball Canyon, no survivors"